Views of the Pearl River Delta
Macau, Canton and Hong Kong

珠 江 風 貌

澳門、廣州及香港

19 November 1996 ― 16 February 1997

一九九六年十一月十九日 ― 一九九七年二月十六日

Hong Kong Museum of Art　香港藝術館

19 June 1997 ― 14 September 1997

一九九七年六月十九日 ― 一九九七年九月十四日

Peabody Essex Museum　皮博迪艾塞克斯博物館

Jointly presented by the Urban Council , Hong Kong and the Peabody Essex Museum , U.S.A.

Jointly organised by the Hong Kong Museum of Art and the Peabody Essex Museum , U.S.A.

香港市政局及美國皮博迪艾塞克斯博物館合辦

香港藝術館及美國皮博迪艾塞克斯博物館聯合籌劃

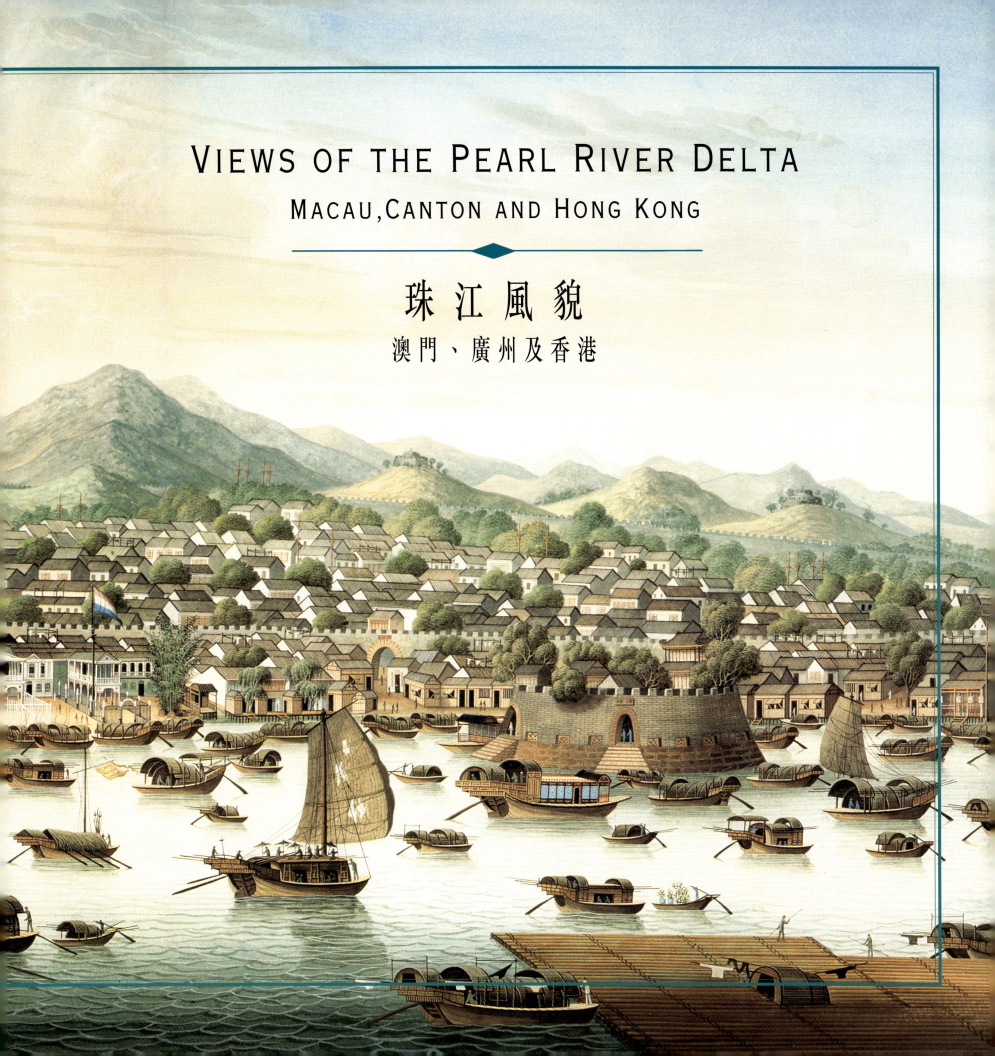

VIEWS OF THE PEARL RIVER DELTA

MACAU, CANTON AND HONG KONG

珠江風貌

澳門、廣州及香港

ISBN 962 - 215 - 147 - 7

UC 10637

本刊物由香港市政局於一九九六年首次編印

香港藝術館製作

版權屬香港市政局所有——一九九六年

版權所有，未經許可不得翻印、節錄或轉載

香港市政局負責為香港約三百萬市區居民提供文康市政服務

First published by the Urban Council of Hong Kong, 1996

Produced by the Hong Kong Museum of Art

Copyright © 1996 Urban Council of Hong Kong

All rights reserved

The Urban Council of Hong Kong is responsible for the provision of municipal services
to some three million people in the urban areas of Hong Kong

PRODUCTION TEAM

Peabody Essex Museum

William R. SARGENT	Curator, Asian Export Art
Margaret PALMER	Collections Manager, Asian Export Art

Hong Kong Museum of Art
Exhibition Management, Translation and Editorial

TSANG Chu-chiu, Gerard	Chief Curator
HO Kam-chuen	Curator (Chinese Antiquities)
YEUNG Lai-chung, Stoney	Assistant Curator I (Historical Pictures)
CHAN Mui-fan, Veronica	Assistant Curator II (Historical Pictures)

Graphics and Exhibition Design

KWAN Wai-kan, Winnie	Senior Technical Officer
CHOI Lai-wah, Candy	Technical Officer I
SUNG Wai-bing, Olivia	Technical Officer II
CHAN Fook-wai, Jessica	Technical Officer II
KWAN Tse-wan, Iris	Design Assistant
CHAU So-kuen, Caren	Design Assistant

Catalogue Design

CHOI Lai-wah, Candy	Technical Officer I

Photography

WONG Yin-yiu, Angela	Technical Officer II
CHOW Kam-lan	Senior Photographer
WONG Kwok-leung, Arthur	Photographer I

Photo Credit

Photographs of objects from the Peabody Essex Museum, by Jeffrey Dykes and Mark Sexton

CONTENTS

目 錄

FOREWORD

"Thousand foreign vessels sailed across the sea" and *"Blocking the moon, Western liners crowded along the shore"* depicted the splendid busy port of the Pearl River Delta a hundred years ago.

The Pearl River, also known as the Canton River, is the largest river at the south coast of China. The name 'Pearl' comes from a round, pearl-like island amidst the river. The delta is formed with the triangular location of Canton, Macau and Hong Kong at the estuary, linked by the tributaries of the Pearl River at its outflow to the sea. All through history, the Pearl River Delta with Canton as the gateway of trade, and the subsequent rise of Macau and Hong Kong as the thresholds, had been the most significant hub of communication with the West.

The maritime trade of China took shape as early as the Han dynasty (206BC–220AD). In the Tang dynasty (618–907) an open trade policy was launched and commercial exchange between China and neighbouring countries prospered. The prosperity continued in the Song (960–1279) and Yuan dynasties (1279–1368). With the establishment of the Commissioner of Customs in Canton , the customs system of China thus commenced in the tenth century. Trade partners extended to cover Arabia, Europe and America, the newly found continent. It was so documented by a Qing scholar: "Since the Tang dynasty, trade ambassadors were established at Canton, and merchants from all directions came and settled henceforth". The Ming Empire (1368–1644) relied even heavier on Canton trade revenue to off-set the enormous national expenditure. Unfortunately, when it came to late Ming and Qing (1644–1911) period, a new policy of isolation was imposed and the external world was entirely shut out.

The policy, however, forced dramatic concentration and development of trade at the south door of China. Trade along the River Delta reached its prime when all other ports were banned since 1756 except Canton which remained open to the world. The Delta thus became a focal point of interaction between the East and the West. All kinds of merchandise landed here – import and export, gathered and dispersed. Along with the roaring trade, scientific invention, new technology, religion and Western culture were all shipped into this ancient kingdom. Canton then acted as an entrepot for these inputs into the other parts of China. Apart from literary description, historical scenes were also widely captured in visual records. European artists who had come to visit this oriental country had left a rich artistic legacy. They had initiated some native artists and craftsmen into a new form of expression. Art studios sprang up when an export market for East-and-West blended art objects was created.

The Hong Kong Museum of Art was founded in 1962, taking custodianship of Government's collection of historical pictures. The museum has focused collection efforts on the Pearl River Delta area since then. The museum is in a strategic position to net this wealth of export art items and information at the gateway of their origin, while our counter-part, the Peabody Essex Museum of Salem occupies a collection point at the other end of the export journey. The tie that links the two museums together is an exchange programme sponsored by the American Association of Museums, through which museums exchanged staff to study the collection of each other. The current joint exhibition attempts to review the context, the East-West interaction and the end-products of China trade, is proposed as a result of the study which started two years ago.

This unique exhibition features a wide spectrum of export arts, including works by both renowned artists and anonymous ones. Trade wares range from daily utensils to pure decorative articles; from pictorial items: paintings, drawings, prints and maps, to 3-dimensional objects: lacquer wares, silver wares, ivory products, porcelain and wood furniture. Centuries ago, exported 'curiosities', 'luxuries' or 'delicacies' travelled a long way to the other side of the globe. They now take this opportunity to return to their provenance for a dream-like reunion. Whilst pictorial items accompany the real objects in their home journey, a full testimony of the cultural exchange between the East and the West is given. Their assembly will illustrate the patron needs and aesthetic tastes in the heydays of the China trade.

Alike the rock in mid-stream, the Pearl River Delta had been marked with an intricate legend during the past centuries. Glory and shame together coated it; prosperity and corruption came hand in hand; it grasped something and lost others; it was an epoch to be proud of, whilst on the other hand an era to be regretted. No matter how, there they were yesterday, and hence what we are today. The web of history interweaves man and incidents, time and space, altogether. At the turn of the century, it is hoped that "The Pearl River Delta: Macau, Canton and Hong Kong" exhibition will offer a true reflection of the Delta history, a history of our own.

The actualization of the exhibition owes much to some. Our gratitude goes to Dr. Patrick Conner who contributes an enlightening essay to the catalogue. A special vote of thanks is due to Mr. William Sargent, Curator of the Peabody Essex Museum, who has taken up the responsibility of writing up the catalogue entries as well the article that gives us a vision of the Asian art collection history in Salem. Our deep appreciation goes to the Asian Cultural Council as well for their generous sponsorship of the Hong Kong catalogue. We are grateful to the Royal Asiatic Society (Hong Kong Branch) for jointly organizing thematic lectures with the museum during the exhibition period. Lastly, we are honoured to share the joy of presenting this unique exhibition with the Peabody Essex Museum and I look forward to such partnership again in future.

Gerard C C Tsang
Chief Curator, Hong Kong Museum of Art

序　言

上述詩文刻劃出百年前珠江三角洲盛極一時的貿易繁榮景象。

珠江是南中國沿岸最大的河流，因河中有一圓珠狀石島而得名。珠江三角洲指位處河口三個鼎足而立的城市 — 廣州、澳門及香港所形成的三角地帶，上游支流於此滙聚成江，奔流出海。歷代以還，珠江三角洲都是中國對外最重要的交通樞紐，先有廣州作其門戶，及後澳門及香港亦成為了貿易門檻。

中國海上貿易在漢代（公元前206年至公元220年）已具雛形。唐代（618-907）實行開放政策，中國與毗鄰國家貿易往還，發展迅速。宋（960-1279）、元（1279-1368）兩代基本上繼承此開放風氣，貿易發展更趨蓬勃。北宋時首設市舶司於廣州，中國的海關制度由是建立，對外貿易更擴展至亞拉伯、歐洲及當時新發現的美洲。晚明顧炎武《天下郡國利病書》有此記述：「自唐設結好使於廣州，自是商人立戶，迄宋不絕」。明（1368-1644）國祚支出龐大，須倚仗廣州貿易稅項以增加收入。至明末及清室（1644-1911）實行海禁，對所有外來事物皆閉門不納。

閉關政策不單沒有使廣州的貿易從此衰落，相反地更利於她的發展。乾隆二十一年（1756）下令全面海禁，獨留廣州一口通商，珠江三角洲地區遂成為中國與西方接觸的要衝，各式各樣的進出口貨品於此吞吐集散。隨着貿易的興旺頻繁，歐洲科技發明、宗教及西方文化亦紛湧而至，以廣州作為跳板，傳送至中國內地。將當日這等歷史風光記錄下來的，除通過文字以外，又有藉藝術素材者。來華的歐洲畫家遊歷之餘，引進了西方寫實繪畫，為本土畫師匠人揭示了一種嶄新的表達媒介。適值外銷市場又對此類融合了中西風味的畫作大為渴求，於是畫室作坊一時如雨後春筍般湧現。

香港藝術館於1962年創立，當時接管了一批政府藏畫，並開始收藏有關珠江三角洲歷史的畫作。藝術館僥倖處於這些藝術品發源地出口之有利位置，故藏量尚豐；賽倫市皮博迪艾塞克斯博物館則為當日外銷藝術旅程提供了終站，所藏外銷品無論質量俱佳。兩年前，藉賴美國博物館協會舉辦之交流計劃，兩館得以派員互相交流觀摩，並為這次展覽訂下初階。

是次展出的藏品種類繁多，有著名畫家的作品，亦有佚名之作；有實用器物，亦有純觀賞玩藝。畫作方面包括油畫、素描、版畫及地圖，而器物則包括漆器、銀器、象牙製品、陶瓷及家具。數個世紀前遠越重洋的外銷品如今重返故地，與伴隨着他們踏上歸程的畫作，一起見證昔日東西方文化滙聚的氣象，亦反映出中國古代貿易黃金時期，外銷市場的需求及顧客品味。

仿如飽經磨鍊的中流砥柱，珠江三角洲過去數百年的歷史，釜鑿着錯綜複雜的痕跡：榮耀與恥辱、興盛與腐敗、得與失……同時湧現。回想既與有榮焉，又不無遺憾。撫今追昔，一切人與事、時與空、編織成一張歷史網絡。當此世紀轉移之際，盼望藉「珠江風貌：澳門、廣州及香港」展覽與大家作一次憶苦思甜的回顧。

是次展覽得以順利進行，全賴以下人士的支持及幫助。感謝帕特里克‧康納博士惠賜鴻文，令展覽目錄生色不少。特別感謝皮博迪艾塞克斯博物館長威廉‧沙進先生，負起撰寫展品解說之責，又為文闡述賽倫市博物館亞洲藝術藏品之由來。並對贊助香港目錄出版的亞洲文化協會致以萬分謝忱。我們亦非常感激皇家亞洲學會（香港分會）於展覽期間協辦一系列講座。最後，有幸與皮博迪艾塞克斯博物館合作籌劃是項展覽，本人深感欣慰，並冀盼日後再有此攜手共事的機會。

曾柱昭
香港藝術館總館長

PREFACE

"Views of the Pearl River Delta" celebrates more than two centuries of artistic and commercial exchange between China and the West. From the fifteenth century to the present, the ports of Macau, Canton, and Hong Kong have been a focus of global maritime trade. In the eighteenth and nineteenth centuries, the Pearl River Delta was a meeting place for the world's leading venture capitalists. Ships from the young United States as well as from England, India, and several European countries anchored side by side.

New England merchants were among the first Americans to travel to China, the ship *Grand Turk* from Salem, Massachusetts, reaching Canton in 1786. A dozen years later, the East India Marine Society was formed by Salem captains and supercargoes who had sailed beyond the capes of Horn and Good Hope. Members of the new society donated articles collected during their travels to a museum which continues today as the Peabody Essex Museum.

Before the age of photography, paintings, drawings, and prints were the means of depicting for the West the "exotic" locales of the China trade. Views of unusual landscapes and remarkable architecture, especially pagodas and temples, were much in demand. In the fulfillment of this need, a unique artistic style was created, a blending of Chinese and Western artistic traditions and techniques that is now known as Asian Export Art.

Many Western fortunes were made in the trading of Chinese silk, porcelain, and tea. The American and European traders who made these fortunes were enamored of the luxury goods available in China and frequently commissioned works that reflected their own romantic views of the country, thus helping to shape other Westerners' perceptions of China. These works were rendered both by visiting Western painters and by Chinese artists, many of whom established workshops specifically to create a variety of wares for the export trade.

The artworks in this exhibition may be enjoyed on several levels. They do constitute an accurate record of long-ago ways of life. Views of busy ports and crowded streets provide a window into the past. Conversely, some landmarks both natural and man-made, can still be recorded by the cameras of today's tourists.

The exhibition can also be enjoyed for such aesthetic treasures as Thomas Daniell's striking depiction of *The Lianhua Pagoda*, George Chinnery's romantically melancholy *View of the Praya Grande from a Doorway*, and an unknown Chinese artist's masterful portrayal of *The China Tea Trade*. Paintings of the great Canton fire of 1882 not only depict an historical event, they evoke a universal human emotion in the face of advancing flames.

The exhibition's examples of such luxury goods as furniture, silver, and porcelain display the artistry of Chinese craftsmen who were famed for their skills long before Portuguese seafarers discovered maritime trade routes to China. These works were collected not for their value as trade items but for their owners' personal appreciation of their beauty and, perhaps, as reminders of the land which most had found fascinating.

It is perhaps too often forgotten that the human race has a long history of cultural and mercantile exchange: the global marketplace was not invented yesterday. Bearing impressive witness to this fact are the collections of Asian Export Art at the Peabody Essex Museum and the Hong Kong Museum of Art. With this exhibition we celebrate these collections and all those who participated in their creation.

Dan L. Monroe
Executive Director
Peabody Essex Museum

前　言

　　「珠江風貌」展覽賀揚二百年來中西貿易與藝術的交流。由十五世紀迄今，澳門、廣州及香港一直是全球海上貿易的中心點。十八、十九世紀的珠江三角洲，更是世界冒險資本家滙聚之地。英、美、印度及歐洲各國來華船舶如過江之鯽，皆寄碇於此。

　　新英格蘭商人是首批美國訪華船旅之一，他們乘“大土耳其”號從麻省賽倫市出發，於1786年抵達廣州。十數年後，曾遠航合恩角及好望角的一些賽倫船長和營運主管們，一起成立了東印度海事學會。學會得到成員們捐獻出歷年於旅途上搜集的珍奇，並逐漸發展成為今天的皮博迪艾塞克斯博物館。

　　在攝影技術發明以前，只有藉賴油彩、素描及版畫等繪畫媒介，才能把來華西方商人在「異域」的所見所聞記錄下來。新奇的風景與建築，特別是古塔廟宇等題材，大受歡迎。為滿足當日的藝術市場需要，遂衍生了一種獨特的、中西方混合的風格，就是現今所謂亞洲外銷藝術。

　　中國絲綢、陶瓷與茶葉貿易造就了大量西方財富。致富的美國及歐洲商賈又極之戀慕各樣中國奇珍，並經常購訂一些能夠反映他們個人浪漫情懷的中國風景畫，這些作品亦順帶締造了其他西方人對中國的印象。受委託的有來華畫家，亦有中國本地藝術家。他們當中許多都開設了專門店舖，從事各類外銷貿易品的創作。

是次展覽中的藝術品，可從不同的層面去欣賞。首先，它們準確地記錄了舊日的生活面貌、繁忙的海港與擁擠的街道。然而，一些天然的或人造的陸標，卻仍遺留下來，供今日的遊客拍攝留念。此外，展品的美學價值亦不容忽視，如托瑪斯‧丹尼爾＂蓮花山城及蓮花塔＂憾人的描繪，喬治‧錢納利浪漫憂鬱的＂西望洋山的石門外遠眺南灣景色＂，以及佚名中國畫家冼鍊筆觸下的＂中國茶葉貿易＂，都深具欣賞價值。而一系列關於1822年廣州大火的油畫，描繪的不單是一項歷史事件，在捕捉紅紅烈焰撲面而來的一刻，更觸動了普世的人類感情。

展品中的貴重物器如家具、銀器及陶瓷等，顯示了中國工匠超人的技藝，這等天賦在葡萄牙航海家發現中國貿易路綫前已享盛譽。購藏者訂購這些作品，不一定是為着它們的貿易價值，而是出於個人對美之鑑賞；又或者，是作為對這塊使人着迷的土地的一點緬懷。

我們很容易遺忘人類文化與商品交流已有久遠的歷史 —— 環球貿易並非始自昨日。皮博迪艾塞克斯博物館的亞洲外銷藏品，及香港藝術館的歷史繪畫珍藏，都可為此作出明證。藉着是次展覽，我們同慶這些珍貴的收藏，同時特向它們的創造者致意。

丹‧門羅
皮博迪艾塞克斯博物館行政總監

ACKNOWLEDGEMENTS

The Friends' Committee of the Asian Cultural Council in Hong Kong is very pleased to help support the printing of the Hong Kong catalogue of this wonderful exhibition, "Views of the Pearl River Delta: Macau, Canton and Hong Kong" which is a joint presentation of the Hong Kong Museum of Art and the Peabody Essex Museum in Salem, Massachusetts.

The Asian Cultural Council is an American foundation which promotes cultural exchange in the visual and performing arts between Asia and the United States. Headquartered in New York, the Council has field offices in Hong Kong, Tokyo, and Taipei. This fall, the ACC observes the tenth anniversary of its Hong Kong Arts Programme, and we are delighted to have been given the opportunity to commemorate the occasion with a benefit gala at the Hong Kong Museum of Art on November 22, 1996, featuring a special viewing of this remarkable show.

Funds raised at this event will support fellowship grants for arts specialists from Hong Kong and China to visit the United States on programmes arranged by the Asian Cultural Council in New York. In the course of the past decade, 125 individuals and ten organizations have received assistance from the ACC's Hong Kong office, and all of us associated with the Council are most grateful to our donors, patrons, sponsors, and friends for contributing so generously to the continuing development of Hong Kong's exciting cultural community.

On behalf of the Friends' Committee, I would especially like to express our sincere appreciation to the Urban Council and its Hong Kong Museum of Art, as well as the Peabody Essex Museum for making it possible for the ACC to celebrate its tenth birthday in Hong Kong in such a beautiful setting. I would also like to thank our Chairpersons of this gala evening, Desiree Jebsen and Ann Hotung Walkovik, for their hard work and dedication in organizing this event.

Kenneth H. C. Fung, Jr.
Chairman, Friends' Committee
Asian Cultural Council, Hong Kong

鳴　謝

香港藝術館及美國麻省皮博迪艾塞克斯博物館合辦了一個精彩的展覽 ─ 「珠江風貌：澳門、廣州及香港」。亞洲文化協會香港分會深感榮幸，能成為是次展覽香港目錄的贊助機構。

亞洲文化協會是美國的一個基金會，向以促進亞洲與美國視覺藝術及表演藝術的相互交流為目標。本會的總部設於紐約，而在香港、東京及台北均有辦事處。今年秋天，適值該會的香港藝術計劃成立十週年，我們很高興能夠在一九九六年十一月二十二日，假座香港藝術館舉行籌款晚會，並以是次展覽的特備觀賞酒會揭開序幕。

此項活動籌集所得之款項，將用作頒予香港及本地藝術專才的獎助金，以資助他們前赴美國，參與亞洲文化協會紐約辦事處所安排的活動。在過去十年間，亞洲文化協會香港分會曾資助過一百二十五名本地人士及十個機構赴美交流，本會全人衷心感謝各位捐助者、贊助者及各界朋友慷慨襄助，促使香港生氣盎然的文化界不斷地向前發展。

亞洲文化協會得以在如此優美的環境中慶祝在港成立十週年，本人在此謹代表本會對市政局及其轄下香港藝術館，和美國皮博迪艾塞克斯博物館，致以懇切謝意。同時也得感謝此項活動的籌委會主席謝普誠夫人及華國榮夫人，辛勤努力籌辦此項盛會。

馮慶鏘
亞洲文化協會香港分會
會友委員會主席

VIEWS OF THE PEARL RIVER: A DEVELOPING ART

Early export scenes

'The people in these parts are very Ingenious, Laborious, and Nimble, and can imitate any thing which they see made before them: And whatsoever the *Portuguesses* bring thither out of Europe woven of Gold, Silver, or the like, which is strange unto them, they will immediately endeavour to work the same, and in a short time will accomplish what they undertake...'[1]

Such were the observations of Johan Nieuhof, Steward to the Dutch Embassy to China, who arrived at 'the Famous and chief City of Canton' in 1655. By this time the skill and versatility of Cantonese craftsmen were already celebrated. These qualities had been recognised a century before by the Portuguese pioneers of the sea route to China; moreover, an Arab trading colony had been established in Canton as early as the 8th century, and the Cantonese had been adapting their exported porcelain and other wares to suit foreign tastes long before any Westerners appeared on the China coast.

In the 18th century the Cantonese repertoire of art and artefacts for export was extended to painting. By the end of that century a Western visitor could buy or commission a variety of painted subjects, executed in a recognisably Western idiom while retaining certain Chinese aspects. Indeed, it seems that by 1750 certain Cantonese painters had already begun to adapt their pictures in line with Western expectations. The evidence for this comes not so much from

surviving works as from the long-overlooked testimony of Peter Osbeck, who visited Canton in 1751 as chaplain aboard the Swedish East India Company's ship *Prince Charles.*. A pupil of Linnaeus and Member of the Academy of Stockholm, Osbeck proved a keen observer, and not only of botanical specimens. In a footnote he stated:

'Some years ago the *Chinese* were very defective in their drawings: but of late, since they have had the opportunities of seeing the performances of *European* artists, they are much improved, and particularly in perspective, with which they were before perfectly unacquainted.'[2]

It appears from this remark that some forms of export painting were already being practised. Moreover clay models of Europeans, with details of dress carefully observed, were being produced by south Chinese artists some thirty years before. It seems that Osbeck was describing such a modeller when he observed in Canton 'the famous *Face-maker*...who makes men's figures, mostly in miniature. *Europeans* often go to this man to be represented in their usual dress; and sometimes he hits them exceedingly well'.[3]

Osbeck does not speak specifically, however, of topographical scenes by Cantonese artists. Well before his voyage, it was possible for visitors to acquire views of Canton executed in the Chinese style, either on paper or in the form of

[1]   Johan Nieuhof, *An Embassy from the East-India Company of the United Provinces to the Grand Tartar Cham Emperour of China*, tr. J. Ogilby, 1669, p.34.

[2]   Peter Osbeck, *A Voyage to China and the East Indies*, trans. J.R. Forster, 1771, vol.1, pp.242-243n.

[3]   ibid., p.221. For examples of Chinese portrait figures of Europeans dating from the second decade of the eighteenth century see Craig Clunas, 'Mounding a physiognomy-a Chinese portrait figure', Victoria & Albert Museum Album 3, 1984, pp.47-51.

decorated lacquer; for example, a gilt-on-red lacquered chest lid produced for the Portuguese market in the late seventeenth century clearly represents the city of Canton, with Flowery Pagoda, Huai Sheng Mosque and river fort[4] — all conspicuous also in Nieuhof's view (no. 41). Less stylised, but still executed in a wholly Chinese manner, is a painted view of Canton contained in an album of Pearl River scenes painted in the first half of the eighteenth century, which was brought later in that century to the Chinese Pavilion at Drottningholm in Sweden.[5] Here we see also a group of Chinese buildings which flanked the river just to the west of the city: it was here that the Western traders first established their trading bases or Factories; Osbeck defined 'Factory' simply as 'a general denomination of the houses built towards the river, or over it upon piles, and which are let by the *Chinese* merchants to the *European* ships during their stay'.[6]

After a severe fire in 1748 — the first of several which were to affect the visiting merchants — the Western trading companies began to rebuild their accommodation in a partly Western manner. In 1769, when William Hickey visited the place, he found much to admire in the Factories — 'handsome' sets of rooms with 'every sort of convenience', and, outside each, 'the flag of its nation on a lofty ensign staff before it'.[7] By this time a number of the Factory buildings had been remodelled with Westernised façades, including balustrades and pilasters, and (in the case of the Dutch and English Factories) classical pediments above columned porticos. The new 'Westernised' Factories feature prominently on a lacquer screen decorated with a view of Canton, which was probably installed in the first Chinese Pavilion at Drottningholm in 1753.[8] As this distinctive and flag-bedecked waterfront developed, so did it present an appearance with which, in pictorial form, a China merchant might proudly return to his homeland; indeed, 'the Canton Factories' became the essential and symbolic Western image of the China Trade.

It can be no accident that the earliest Chinese export views of the Canton River (that is, views painted in a partly Western idiom) seem to have appeared soon after this rebuilding. Although painted to some extent according to Western notions of perspective, they continued to employ traditional Chinese materials: the British Library's earliest view of Canton (c.1760) is in the form of a scroll-painting 26 feet in length, in gouache on silk.[9] The Western 'Factories' or 'Hongs' occupy the westernmost two feet of this scroll. The remainder of the scroll depicts in continuous detail the Chinese city of Canton with its suburbs, followed by open country and low-lying islands to the east, culminating in the long island and deep-water anchorage of Whampoa (Huangpu), where the East Indiamen from the Western trading nations lay at anchor.

Landmarks appear at frequent intervals along the route — forts, pagodas, temples, custom-posts, distant hills. It is clear that such a scroll had an eminently practical value to an incoming Westerner. For a sea-captain making his way along an uncertainly-charted route, there was an obvious value in drawings of the coastline which showed variations, landmarks and distances as accurately as possible. Once it had been brought home its decorative potential could be realised: other strip-paintings of this kind have survived, no longer as scrolls but divided into sets of twelve scenes, each separately framed. The view of the foreign Factories fitted neatly into a single frame, and the view of the anchorage at Whampoa fitted into another.

Whampoa and the Canton River

For the ships' officers and especially for the crew, Whampoa was a place of no less significance than Canton. It was at Whampoa that the ships were repaired and maintained, Chinese customs officials formally received and entertained, and duties assessed. While a ship remained from three to six months at Whampoa, its crew would be allowed no more than a few (perhaps only one) 'liberty days' at Canton.[10] From a pictorial point of view, moreover, Whampoa could rival Canton: against a backdrop of islands and pagodas were the splendid East Indiamen themselves. 'No finer sight of the kind could be seen in any part of the world than the Company's fleet collected at Whampoa',

[4] Via Orientalis', Fundaçaõ Oriente / Europalia Portugal, Galerie de la CGER, Brussels, 1991, no.156 (col. ill.; in the catalogue the location is described as Peking). The Mosque and the Flowery Pagoda - known as the 'unadorned' and the 'adorned' pagodas – had been long regarded as symbols of the city: 'The geomancers say, the whole city is like a great junk; the two pagodas are her masts, the five storey house (which rises the hill close by the northern wall) her stern sheets' (see Anders Ljungstedt, *An Historical Sketch of the Portuguese Settlements in China...*, Boston, 1836, p.215).

[5] Album FE 274, page size 385 x 325 mm; see Bo Gyllensvärd, 'Catalogue of Far Eastern Objets d'art' in *The Chinese Pavilion of Drottningholm*, by Ake Setterwall et al., Malmö, 1974, pp.200, 322, illd. p.206

[6] Osbeck, op. cit., p.204.

[7] *Memoirs of William Hickey*, ed. Peter Quennell, 1975, p.125. Hickey's recollections of Canton are however unreliable in several respects.

[8] The screen had certainly been installed in the Chinese Pavilion before 1777: see *The Chinese Pavilion at Drottningholm*, op. cit., pp.279-280, illd. pp.132-133.

[9] See P. Conner, 'The China Trade 1600-1860', Brighton Museums, 1986, no.23 and frontispiece; see also no.22 (illd.). The sale at Christie's (15 Feb. 1799) of A.E. Van Braam's Chinese artefacts included 'a tinted drawing of the whole city of Canton and its suburbs, on a roll, 16 feet' (lot no.55).

[10] See for example the MS log of the *Essex* covering her voyage of 1785-1786, entry for 6 Jan. 1786: 'Fine weather throughout. Sent 10 Men to Canton on liberty for 3 Days.' However W.C. Hunter recalled that 'it was customary to give the crew liberty day at Canton. This *one* and only day of liberty would be talked about and looked forward to during the whole passage out...' (*Bits of Old China*, 1911, p.3).

claimed the American China trader William Hunter.[11] And along the shore of Whampoa Island were ranged the 'bankshalls' (narrow buildings used by the visiting traders for storage), which were often shown beneath the vivid national flags of the Western nations.

Whampoa is the subject of some of the earliest identifiable Chinese export views of the China coast. These are painted not on silk or paper, however, but on porcelain. In 1743 Commodore Anson put in at Canton in the course of his voyage around the world, and a service was made for him which included on the rim of each plate views of both Plymouth and Whampoa, the latter with hills, pagodas and Indiamen at anchor. It is possible that the designs were supplied initially by one of Anson's officers, Lieutenant Piercy Brett.[12] These scenes were repeated — sometimes in debased form — in some twenty services in the next ten years (see no.29); all of them predate any recorded export images of Whampoa in other media.

Nor are these the first of such scenes. An armorial service made in c.1733 for the family of Lee of Coton (see no.42) carries around its rim two identical views of the Canton River, alternating with two views of the London skyline with its forest of rebuilt City churches.[13] The Canton River scene shows the Chinese buildings fronting the river and the crenellated city walls , but its principal feature is the river fort to the south of the city: later this was to be known as the Dutch Folly Fort, but Nieuhof himself regarded this and the companion fort by the eastern suburbs as 'strong water castles... which render this City invincible.'[14] At this early date these forts were the most conspicuous and readily identifiable objects on the river.

Angles of vision

Early Chinese export pictures of the Canton Factories were generally head-on views, seen from a point directly across the river. This ran counter to current Western notions of 'the Picturesque'; to a Western artist at this time, the conventional view was from an angle. This was the approach employed by Thomas and William Daniell, who came to Canton in August 1785 on their way out to India, and again in September 1793 on their way home. No.49 presents an angled view of the Factories from the south-east, and the shipping too is

martialled according to Western pictorial ideals; whereas the export scenes show the river crowded with craft in a seemingly haphazard (and perhaps naturalistic) manner, Daniell gathers his junks and sampans into twin masses at left and right, to direct the eye along the gently curving channel which the artist has cleared in the centre.

Angled views were adopted sometimes by Cantonese artists,[15] particularly after the arrival of Chinnery. But the history of China coast port scenes is not simply a case of Western influence upon Chinese artists; one may also see the reverse process at work. Half a dozen oil paintings of Canton by both Thomas and William Daniell have now come to light, most of them painted more than a decade after the artists' return to England. In a number of instances their depictions of junks and sampans appear to have been inspired at least partly by Chinese export pictures - and indeed the Daniells would have been able to supplement their own sketches with reference to such paintings, which were not difficult to find in London. This seems all the more likely as one inspects the Chinese subjects reproduced in the Daniells' volume *A Picturesque Voyage to India by the way of China* (1810), in which not only the shipping but also figures, terraces and pavilions are evidently derived from Chinese export scenes.

Unconventional views

Among the most intriguing of all export pictures of Canton are the two large views (nos. 54 and 59) taken from the roofs of the Factories themselves. Both incorporate dramatic contrasts, between the starkly ordered angularity of walls, roofs and fences in the foreground and the seemingly random scattering of small craft in the river beyond. Neither painting pays much regard to Western conventions of Picturesque composition, which would have interrupted the balustrade in no. 54 with a figure or two, and would have ensured that the trees in no. 59 intersected the skyline in a more decided fashion. The follower of Picturesque convention would moreover have arranged the composition so that the street-vendors and other detailed human activity appeared in the foreground; in no. 59, however, the animated quayside is seen at some distance from the spectator, and in no. 54 the Factory district yields no signs of life at all. We catch a glimpse of the open frameworks which

[11] *The 'Fan Kwae' at Canton before Treaty Days 1825-1844*, 1882, p.104.

[12] See David S. Howard, *Chinese Armorial Porcelain*, 1974, pp.46-48 and 128-129; also David Howard and John Ayers, *China for the West*, 1978, vol.1, pp.202-203.

[13] See David S. Howard, *Chinese Armorial Porcelain*, 1974, p.329; also David Howard and John Ayers, *China for the West*, 1978, vol.1, pp.204-205.

[14] Nieuhof, op. cit., p.36.

[15] See for example Chinese artist c.1807, "A Section of the Foreign Factories" in the collection of the Hong Kong Museum of Art (AH 64.28), with versions in the National Maritime Museum, London, and the Henry Francis du Pont Museum, Winterthur.

stood on top of the stalls in Hog Lane, which ran along the western side of the British Factory – but the elevated viewpoint prevents us from seeing anything of the crowds which normally thronged this narrow and busy shopping street.

In no. 59 there is no direct evidence of a Western presence; however, the animals in the the fenced area in the centre foreground – chickens, sheep, goats and a cow – were no doubt kept for the benefit of the Western community, with its occidental taste for dairy products. The theme of domestic animals in the foreground is not uncommon in European country-house views; here, instead of the country house itself, the Red (or West) Fort on the Honam shore provides a distant focal point. For both Chinese and Western eyes, the circular, crenellated river fortresses presented distinctive points of reference.

These pictures are also revealing in their use of perspective . Both scenes rely heavily on Western-style linear perspective, but in neither is it used consistently; in no.59, for example, the horizontals of the white balcony do not converge sufficiently, and in no. 54 the angled part of the balustrade does not converge at all. In neither case are the rooflines consistent in their angles. Of course, errors of perspective are to be found often enough in Western paintings also (George Chinnery, the leading Western artist to visit China, being a frequent offender); but in the context of such carefully-constructed compositions as these Cantonese paintings, errors of this kind are all the more conspicuous. The inference is that Western linear perspective was so fundamentally alien to the Chinese pictorial tradition that it escaped the notice of artists who in other respects were highly skilled and flexible in their ability to adapt to Western preconceptions.

Of all export pictures of Canton, no. 54 is perhaps the least conventional. The foreground of roofs and empty balcony occupies over half the pictorial area; most of the rest is sky, so that the topographical elements, including forts, harbour and the Honam shoreline, is restricted to a distant strip comprising perhaps ten percent of the image. For what purpose, or what client, could such a picture has been painted ?

A possible answer can be found in a small pamphlet of 1838, entitled 'Description of a View of Canton, the River Tigress; and the surrounding country, now exhibiting at the Panorama, Leicester Square'.[16] This descriptive text, together with an outline diagram (see fig. A) and key, were printed to accompany a mural panorama which was painted by Robert Burford for his Panorama off Leicester Square in London. The painting would have extended around the walls of his purpose-built rotunda, in which visitors might (in exchange for a shilling) imagine themselves transported to Canton – specifically, to 'a terrace on the summit of the British Factory', as the text makes clear. The text also states that the original work on which Burford's mural based was by 'Toonequa, a native artist of Canton'.[17] Comparing no. 54 with the engraved outline of the panorama (Burford's mural painting no doubt disappeared long ago), we can see that the appropriate portion of the former corresponds very closely with the latter.

Burford's version has a good deal more foreground incident; with both education and 'human interest' in mind, Burford peopled the terrace with picturesque groups of figures: smoking, gambling, serving tea, making music and preparing a puppet-show. But the coincidence of viewpoints is so striking that it forcibly suggests a purpose and a context for No. 54: accompanied by (perhaps) three other paintings taken from the same point, it would have comprised a full 360° view, taking in the Canton River from Whampoa to the Macau Passage Fort, sweeping across the rooftops of the Chinese city with its temples, towers and mosque, and thus round again to the distant Whampoa pagoda.

It is hardly surprising that Burford's panorama should have been based on a Chinese export painting. Ever since Robert Barker set up the first panorama in 1788 (and coined the term in 1791), a premium had been placed on 'truth' and 'accuracy' of representation. Burford's panoramas of Jerusalem and Thebes, for example, both exhibited in 1835-1836, were based on drawings by the archaeological draughtsman Frederick Catherwood. No Western artist of this kind, however, had visited the China coast — with the exception of William Alexander and the Daniells in 1793, when the concept of the panorama was still in its infancy. Who better then to supply the preliminary pictures than one of the Cantonese export studios, with their topographical expertise and skill in the presentation of detail?

[16]   British Library 010057 i 11, no.1.

[17]   Two artists, named 'Toonqua' (or 'Tonqua') and 'Toonqua Jr.' (or 'Tonqua Jr.)', are listed as 'Painter' and 'Miniature painter' respectively at Canton in 1820: see Carl Crossman, *The Decorative Arts of the China Trade*, 1991, pp.54, 60. In the absence of any recorded works which are signed by the elder Tonqua or definitely attributable to him, one may tentatively suggest that 'Toonqua' was responsible for no. 54.

No less appropriate was the timing of the Canton panorama. In 1837 and 1838 public attention had been focused increasingly upon Canton and the China trade, as relations deteriorated between the Chinese Government and the British merchants; this hostility was to erupt into war in the following year. Indeed, the Canton display was succeeded by panoramas of both Macau (1840) and Hong Kong (1843). As *The Times* observed in its obituary notice of Robert Burford, 'an event of public interest seemed scarcely to have received its due acknowledgement until the spot where it had occurred had formed the subject of one of his beautiful panoramas.'[18]

Macau

In most early views of Macau it is plain that the artist has either failed to see the place at first hand, or has seen it only distantly and fleetingly. The buildings in De Bry's engraving of 1598 have a European appearance, but this has as much to do with the artist's ignorance in Chinese architecture as with the actual aspect of the developing Portuguese outpost at that time. Johan Nieuhof, Steward (and amateur artist) to the Dutch Embassy to China of 1655, passed by Macau on his voyage to Canton on 15 July 1655, but as he admitted in his account of the entreprise, 'we came not near her.'[19] Not surprisingly, his view of Macau from the sea (no. 6) is a fanciful concoction of generalised turrets and battlements, which could as well represent Malta, Madras or Mozambique.

From Penha Hill, at the extremity of the peninsula, a panoramic view of Macau could be obtained, encompassing both the Inner Harbour and the Praya Grande, and looking ahead in the distance to the isthmus which led to the Chinese mainland. A number of versions of this view survive (no.11), in various formats, from the late eighteenth century and the first quarter of the nineteenth. Then this view seems to have lost favour in the middle years of the nineteenth century, before being adopted again in the 1870s (no. 27). By now the urban area had increased considerably, especially on the eastern side, and moreover the camera had become a powerful aid to the topographical artists. As a result the entire balance of landscape with townscape has altered: in place of the earlier image of a somewhat arid strip of hilly land, sprinkled at its narrowest point with individual buildings, the later panoramic views give an appearance of almost unbroken roofs and façades, punctuated by a few wooded and fortified outcrops.

For the greater part of the nineteenth century, the most familiar view of Macau was that of the Praya Grande (nos. 7, 11). Whether observed from the north-eastern or the south-western end of the sweeping bay, the scene had much to offer the artist — the grandly classical structures in the centre of the bay, the forts and hilltop churches at either end, and the fishermen and small craft at the water's edge. It can hardly have been an accident that this was the view of Macau which proved most popular with a Western clientèle; while most export views of the Canton Factories and the Whampoa anchorage (and of Macau from Penha Hill) remain essentially non-Western in composition, views of the Praya Grande were generally in accord with the conventions of Western pictorial composition.

These conventions called for a clearly demarcated foreground, preferably animated with figures; vertical features *(repoussoirs)* near the left or right margins (or both); and some distant focal objects not quite at the centre of the picture. Chinnery's oil painting of the Praya (no. 10) is a prime example, with its Tanka boats crossing the breakers in the foreground, verticals in the form of a sail to the left and a flagstaff to the right, and the Convent on Penha Hill as the distant object of attention. Chinese paintings of the same location, whether or not influenced by Chinnery, often appear so 'Western' in concept that they have often been mistaken at first glance for views of the Bay of Naples, souvenirs acquired by successive generations of cultural tourists in Europe.

Western paintings of Macau are dominated by the work of the two professionals-in-residence, George Chinnery (who lived in Macau for most of the period 1825–1852) and Auguste Borget (who spent nearly a year here in 1838–1839). Their contribution lay not in competing with the Chinese export artists in detailed topography, but rather in marrying topography to human life. The Ma Kok Temple and the Jesuit churches, near-contemporary monuments of different cultures, are portrayed by Chinnery and Borget not only for the sake of their remarkable architecture, but also as a backdrop to the activity which customarily surrounded them.

For it is the everyday activities of the local people, rather than those of the colonists or visitors, with whom Chinnery and Borget were principally concerned — street vendors with their customers, itinerant barbers plying their trade, gamblers and porters in the street, agricultural workers, boat-people and

[18] *The Times,* 2 March 1863.

[19] Nieuhof, p.31.

fishermen. In contrast, the figures who populate De Bry's early print (no. 5) seem to consist largely of Portuguese merchants, who stride about with brimmed hats, swords, and servants to follow them with raised sunshades. And the dominant figures in the eighteenth-century engraving by Lowry (no. 7) are not the local inhabitants but Portuguese priests — one of whom appears to be ushering a Chinese man towards the Franciscan monastery at the north-east end of the Praya.

Hong Kong

As the fortunes of Macau waned in the middle years of the nineteenth century, so did those of Hong Kong prosper. Yet early paintings of Hong Kong, taken as a group, are disappointing. Whereas export views of Canton and Macau continued to be produced for a period of more than a century, comparable scenes of Hong Kong began to appear only in the 1840s, when the genre as a whole was already in decline. The view of Hong Kong Island from Kowloon, with the crowded harbour in between, quickly became a standard formula, with generalised architecture creeping up the slopes. Architectural landmarks — churches, government buildings, godowns — were picked out, but seldom with the finesse and sharpness of observation which is characteristic of the preceding generation of Canton and Macau views.

It may be worth observing that the young colony of Hong Kong was not usually regarded with the misty nostalgia which was evoked by Macau at least in its heyday. William Hunter, Kentucky-born partner of Russell & Co. who spent fifteen years on the China coast, wrote (after his return to North America) of Macau's 'calm quiet life, its brilliant atmosphere, and lovely climate... They may say with truth that the 'dolce far niente' here exists in perfection'.[20] But Hong Kong seemed to many of its Western residents a good deal less appealing — a place of discomfort and pestilence, and a trading place about which the Government at home showed little enthusiasm. The first Colonial Treasurer of Hong Kong wrote disparagingly of its 'straggling town' and 'abrupt precipices', beneath hills of 'rotten granite' which were coloured 'a greenish hue, like a decayed Stilton cheese'.[21]

Whether for this reason or by chance, Western artists devoted little time to Hong Kong during the colony's early years. Borget made some sketches of the Chinese settlements on Hong Kong Island and Kowloon in August 1838, two and a half years before the Union Flag was raised at Possession Point. Chinnery spent six months there, in 1846, when the 72-year old artist was (as he wrote) 'so very unwell, not to say ill, that I had the power of doing but little.'[22] By 1857 Marciano Baptista had moved from Macau to Hong Kong, where he advertised views (see no. 81) 'after the late Mr. Chinnery' as well as original views of his own. But the majority of Western depictions of Hong Kong were amateur drawings by young officers, surgeons and engineers, many of them competent and informative but artistically unambitious.

Perhaps the most remarkable nineteenth-century pictures of Hong Kong are views by Chinese artists of particular buildings. A fine example is 'The Hong Kong Mint' (no. 78), in which the shrubs and flowers in the formal gardens are depicted with as much vivid and detailed precision as the cast iron double-and triple-verandahs which faced the harbour at East Point. At the entrance porch of the building a Chinese and a Western figure appear to be greeting each other — an apt metaphor for the enduring phenomenon of Chinese export art.

Patrick Connor

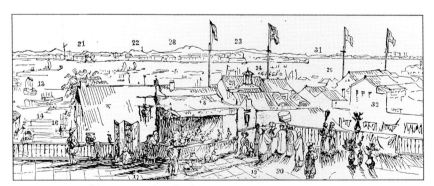

Fig. A Panorama of Canton, an outline sketch

[20]   William C. Hunter, *Bits of old China*, 1911 ed., p.147.

[21]   Robert Montgomery Martin, quoted in Frank Welsh, *A History of Hongkong*, 1993, p.158.

[22]   Letter from Chinnery to Captain D'Aguilar, 20 February 1848, in the collection of the Hongkong and Shanghai Banking Corporation.

珠江風貌：藝術的進程

早期外銷景況

「此間人民生性靈巧、刻苦且聰敏，對任何手藝製作一看即能學效。葡萄牙人從歐洲帶來式樣嶄新的金銀器物，他們都能勉力在短時間內仿製出來....」。[1]

以上是畫家紐荷芙1655年隨荷蘭使節團抵廣州時，對這個城市的觀感。當時中國工匠的才藝教這些訪客大為歎服。但其實在此前一個世紀，這種天賦已為葡萄牙東來的航海先驅發現；此外，早在第八世紀，亞拉伯商旅已於廣州聚居，中國巧匠為迎合他們的品味，製作外銷陶瓷及其他器物。由此可見在這批西方來客踏足中國之前，是類創製已有先例。

到了十八世紀，中國外銷工藝品增闢了繪畫一項。西方來客除購買現成畫作外，更可託請畫師繪製特定題材、中西風格趣味兼備的作品。事實上，經觀察家彼得·奧斯伯克長時間研究所得，中國畫師在1750年代已開始按西方顧客要求作畫。奧斯伯克師承林尼厄斯，亦是斯德哥爾摩（瑞典首都）學會會員，於1751年以傳教士身份隨瑞典東印度公司輪船"查理斯皇子"號抵達廣州。他嘗在書中記道：「若干年前中國人繪畫的技藝不高，但近年來因得以見識歐洲藝術家的造詣，他們在這方面已大為進步 — 尤其在透視學上，從前他們對此是一無所知的。」[2]

由這段註述看來，當時類似外銷畫的作品已開始盛行。而在此更早前三十年，已有從事陶塑製作的華南藝術家替歐洲人造像，塑工細緻，衣履摺紋纖毫畢現。「有名的肖像藝術家....專門從事小巧的肖像創作。歐洲人常登門造訪，多穿戴常服造像；時有佳作。」[3] 奧斯伯克在此論述的大抵便是這類造像師了。

可惜，奧斯伯克的記述並無提及廣州畫家所作的地方風貌繪畫。在奧斯伯克來華之前，造訪者可購得純中國藝術風格的廣州風景畫，繪畫在紙張或漆器上。例如一款十七世紀晚期製造的外銷葡萄牙鎏金剔紅漆盒蓋，上面清晰地繪畫了廣州城內古塔河堡等建築物，[4] 與紐荷芙所繪作品（展品圖號41）同等令人注目。另一件作品同樣繪畫了廣州景色，雖無此典型風格，卻饒富中國色彩，被收藏於一本以珠江風貌為題的畫冊

[1] 約翰·紐荷芙：《東印度公司使節團訪華紀實》，奧格爾比譯（英譯本），1669，頁34。

[2] 彼德·奧斯伯克《中國及東印度航旅》，福斯特譯（英譯本），1771，第一冊，頁242-243。

[3] 同前註，頁221，有關十八世紀二十年代以後中國的歐洲人肖像造型其他例子，參看貝克格雷·克盧拿思《容貌造型 — 中國人之肖像》，維多利亞與艾伯特博物館，圖冊(三)，1984，頁47-51。

[4] 《東方之路》，歐洲葡萄牙東方基金會，CGER藝術館，布魯塞爾，1991，156號（彩色插圖；圖錄內該處被指為北京）。稱為「光」的回塔及「彩」的花塔一直被視為此城的象徵：「據堪輿師說，整個城就像一隻大帆船，兩座寺塔是船桅，五層樓（聳立於靠近城牆北之山坡）是船尾的帆腳索」（見安德斯·揚施泰特：《葡萄牙人居華簡史》，波士頓1836，頁215）

內。此畫冊繪於十八世紀前半期，及後存放於瑞典德羅廷格爾摩的中國庭館。[5] 畫中城西河岸上的一列中式建築，正是西方商人最早建立的商行或貿易基地。奧斯伯克只將「商行」簡單定義為「泛指一些臨河或建於水面木椿上、由中國商人租予歐洲船員居停的樓房」。[6]

外商洋行區先後發生過幾次影響深遠的大火。1748年第一次嚴重火災後，外國商人開始建造半西式的居所。威廉·希基1769年過訪此地時，對那些「房間漂亮」、「設施方便」、「門前國家旗幟高揚」的商行甚表欣賞。[7] 當時部份外商洋行的門樓外觀 — 包括陽台欄杆、壁柱、柱廊上的雅典三角頂（見於荷蘭及英國商館）等，均已按西方形式建造。1753年，德羅廷格爾摩的中國庭館內擺設了一扇漆面屏風，屏風上所繪的廣州風景，便將這等新型「西化」的商行突顯出來。[8] 這片綴以旗幟的海旁地帶就此發展起來，呈現如畫風光，教歸故里的僑商也引以為榮，而商館區亦成為西方在華貿上的重要象徵。

最早期描繪珠江風貌的外銷畫（就是那些以半西方筆觸繪畫的作品），在商館重建之後迅速興起，看來是無可置疑的事實。儘管這些作品在某程度上參照了西方透視原理，卻繼續採用傳統中國繪畫素材：大英博物館藏的一幅早期（約1760年）廣州風景畫，是長廿六呎的水粉絹本卷軸，正好作為典型例子。[9] 畫卷上所繪的「商館」，或稱為「行」的部份，佔畫面兩呎之譜，其餘部分繪畫了廣州城及連綿的市郊、鄉野景貌，極目處是水深島窄的黃埔，以及寄碇的西方貿易船艦。

沿河航標眾多：碉堡、古塔、寺廟、稅關桅桿、遠處岡巒等，都逐一在畫面上展現。這種畫卷明顯對西方來客有著實際用途 — 對未曾熟習路線的領航者來說，它準確地記錄了沿岸變化、航標和距離，可補充資料的不足，極具參考價值；付運回國之後，這些作品本身的裝飾性用

途亦得以發揮，只是不再以畫卷形式呈現。現存例子中，類似的作品被分割為十二幅獨立裝裱的畫作，化成洋行區一景，黃埔船泊一景等等。

黃埔與珠江

黃埔對於航海將領，特別是船員而言，其重要性並不遜於廣州。她是船隻修理補給、評核課稅、甚而是招待中國關員的地方。船隻可以在黃埔停留三至六個月之久，船員卻只能在「自由日」逗留廣州三數天（甚或一天）。[10] 景色方面，黃埔亦堪與廣州媲美：一列島嶼及寺塔，配襯著如鯽的東印度輪船，本身已是奇景一幅。美國貿易商威廉·亨特曾如此形容：「公司船隊蝟集在黃埔江上的景象，世界別處難以復見」。[11] 黃埔島沿岸有一列列插著國旗的「岸棚」，專租賃予外國商人作貨倉用途。

黃埔風光是最早期描繪中國沿岸的外銷題材之一，但初時只是繪於瓷器上，而非紙絹上。海軍上將安森的環球航艦在1734年抵達廣州時，特別訂製了一批碟子，碟沿飾有英國普里茅斯及黃埔兩個地方的風景繪畫，黃埔景物主要是山丘、寺塔及寄碇的東印度公司輪船。碟上的紋樣設計相信是由安森的屬下軍官皮爾西·布雷特提供。[12] 隨後十年這些圖象被反覆使用於約廿套餐具上，部份成品質素亦下降（參看展品圖號29），但無論如何，它們是現存最早記錄黃埔風光的其他製品。

除此以外，科頓李氏家族約於1733年訂製了一套飾以族徽的餐具，碟沿繪有兩幅相同的珠江景貌，與另外兩幅描繪倫敦市教堂重建後的畫象相間出現（參看展品圖號42）。[13] 在珠江畫面上，可見臨江的中式樓房

5 圖冊FE274，冊頁385 x 325厘米見方；見博·蓋倫斯瓦德：《遠東藝術品圖錄》，德羅廷格爾摩之中國亭館藏，埃克·塞特沃爾著；瑪珥摩，1974，頁200，322，附圖，頁206。
6 奧斯伯克，如前，頁204。
7 《威廉·希基回憶錄》，彼得·昆內爾編著，1975，頁125。但希基對某些事物的記憶卻未必那麼真切可信。
8 可確定該屏風在1777年之前已裝置於中國庭館內：參看《德羅廷格爾摩的中國庭館》，如前，頁279-280，附圖，頁132-133。
9 參看帕特里克·康納：《中國貿易1600-1860》，布萊頓博物館，1986，圖號23及卷首插畫；另圖號22（附圖）。佳士得拍賣（1799年2月15日）范·布拉姆收藏的中國工藝品之中，包括「一幅長十六呎淡彩畫卷，描繪廣州全城及其市郊景色」，拍賣品第55項。

10 例如艾色斯克皇家號1785-1786年航海日誌上，1786年1月6日那天記述說：「天氣持續良好。十人准往廣州享用三天自由日」。但據威廉·亨特的回憶：「按慣例船員可獲准在自由日逗留廣州。這僅有的一天自由日將在整個航程上被反覆談論著...」，《舊中國雜記，1911，頁3》
11 《1825-1844年條約簽署前的廣東番鬼錄》，1822，頁104。
12 參看大衛·霍沃德：《中國瓷器製造》，1974，頁46-48及頁128-129；另大衛·霍沃德及約翰·艾爾斯：《西方中國瓷》，1978，第一冊，頁202-203。
13 參看大衛·霍沃德：《中國瓷器製造》，1974，頁329；另大衛·霍沃德及約翰·艾爾斯《西方中國瓷》，1978，第一冊，頁204-205。

及護城牆；而作為主景的，是後來稱為海珠砲台的城南碉堡。紐荷芙認為此砲台及市郊東面的碉堡，乃「捍衛此城不被攻克的堅固堡壘」。[14] 這些防衛建築，確是早期珠江上最顯眼的標記。

觀景角度

早期描繪廣州商館區的中國外銷畫，大多是從對岸正面取景，這跟西方繪畫觀念截然不同。對當時的西方藝術家而言，傳統方式是從側面角度取景。托瑪斯及威廉‧丹尼爾叔姪，便慣常採用這種繪畫方式。他們曾於1785年8月往印度途中經訪廣州，又於1793年9月經廣州返回英國。展品49號描繪從東南方眺望廣州商館的景貌，而畫中的船艇位置亦是根據西方美學原則處理。一般外銷畫家喜將河道上的船艍畫得密密麻麻，丹尼爾則細意將帆船艕舨分佈左右，以便將觀眾的視線集中在畫面中央蜿蜒的水道上。

錢納利來華後，廣州畫家亦有以側面取景方法作畫。[15] 但在中國沿海商埠繪畫史上，這種影響並非只是單向地發生，亦有倒過來西方畫家受東方影響的例子，這在托瑪斯及威廉‧丹尼爾回英十多年後所創作的六幀廣州風景油畫中可見一斑。畫中多處出現的帆船艕舨，都有著中國外銷畫的影子。而當時此類外銷畫在倫敦比比皆是，正好作為丹尼爾叔姪作畫的參考。在丹尼爾氏1810年出版《經中國往印度繽紛之旅》一書內，有部份關於中國題材的插畫，畫面上的船舶、人物、亭樓，皆明顯參照中國外銷作品，由此更可印證上述推論。

非傳統角度

廣東外銷畫最饒有趣味的作品之中，有兩幅是描繪從商館樓頂向外眺望的巨作（展品圖號54、59）。兩者皆以排列整齊的屋脊、牆垣及欄杆作近景，遠處是河面上星羅棋佈的小舟。前後景緻形成強烈的對比，且都摒棄了傳統西畫構圖，致令圖54的陽台風景沒有被安插的人物遮擋；

而圖59中的大樹得以在景物輪廓線上突顯出來。傳統畫家處理構圖時，慣常將街頭販賣等活動置於前方，但圖59中熙攘的碼頭卻與觀眾相隔了一段距離；圖54的商館區更是處於靜態。畫中可瞥見英國館西邊的新荳欄街沿途店舖的棚頂，但因從高處取景關係，這條本應熱鬧擁擠的狹街此刻卻隱藏在視線範圍以外。

圖59的畫面上雖無明顯西方人居住的表徵，但前景中央欄柵內的牛羊家禽，毫無疑問是為滿足外國人社群對乳品的需求而飼養的。以家飼禽畜作前景，在歐洲農莊風景畫中其實相當普遍，只不過此間河南岸邊的紅砲台取代了歐洲農舍，成為此畫的景深焦點。不論在華人洋人眼中，這座圓形的防禦河堡都是至具特色的標記。

此外，可以看得出兩件畫作都採用了透視法 — 兩者同樣倚重西方的線構透視原理，但使用得並不貫徹。例如圖59中描畫白色陽台的橫線並不完全滙聚，而圖54陽台欄杆的斜角部份根本不能靠攏，兩幅畫屋頂線條的角度亦不連貫。當然，許多時就是西畫裏頭也有透視上的錯誤（以具代表性的訪華畫家喬治‧錢納利為例，他便經常在透視方面破格），但這種謬誤出現在結構嚴謹的廣東繪畫作品上，難免格外引人注目。歸根究底，西方透視法則相對中國繪畫傳統而言，基本上是陌生的概念，中國畫師雖擅於掌握各種西方繪畫技巧，對透視學卻未予重視。

眾多廣州外銷畫之中，圖54許是最脫離傳統的一幅。前景的屋頂及空蕩的陽台竟佔畫面過半的空間，餘下面積大半是天空，而地平線上的砲台、碼頭及河南沿岸景物局囿於遙遙一線，只佔畫面約百份之十。究竟是基於什麼原因，又或是哪一位主顧，促令這樣特殊的畫幅誕生？

1838年出版的一本展覽小冊子，也許可以為這個問題提供答案，這份小冊子的標題為「描繪廣州、珠江及其鄰近地景貌的一幀作品，現正於萊斯特廣場的‘全景畫廊’展出」。[16] 這篇附有輪廓簡圖（圖A）的敘述文字，是為羅伯特‧百福德繪製的全景壁畫，在倫敦萊斯特廣場展出而刊印的。壁畫圍環著為百福德特別建造的圓頂建築物之弧形牆壁。觀眾付以一先令，便可換取飛越廣州的幻想旅程，置身於文章所提及的「英國商館樓頂平台」。文字亦說明百福德的壁畫是根據「一位名‘通呱’的廣

[14] 紐荷芙，如前，頁36。

[15] 約1807年中國畫師作品的例子，可參看香港藝術館藏（藏品編號A H 64.28）"外商洋行區一隅"。
是畫另一版本藏於倫敦國家航海博物館及溫特圖爾的亨利‧弗西斯‧都朋博物館。

[16] 大英圖書館 010057 i 11，編號1。

州本地畫師」[17] 的原作製成。如果將圖54與上述畫作的輪廓圖（不消説百福德時代的壁畫早已不存）作一比較，不難看出兩者吻合之處。

百福德的畫本有較多前景活動：為顧及教育與趣味性，他在平台上加插了人群 — 抽煙的、聚賭的、奉茶的、奏樂的、弄木偶戲的....各適其式。但由於取景角度與 圖54 驚人地雷同，無形中為它的成畫背景提供楔機：試將圖54與另外三張相類角度的繪畫並排，即形成一個三百六十度全景觀，涵蓋了由黃埔至澳門水道砲台的珠江河段，將這個城市的廟宇、塔樓等建築都盡收眼底。

百福德的全景圖若真的以中國外銷畫為藍本，其實毫不令人感到意外。自1788年羅伯特·貝克創作第一幅全景畫（並於1791年創用這名稱）開始，講求「真實感」與「準確性」的繪畫方式便受到推崇。例如百福德於1835至1836年展出的作品‘‘耶路撒冷’’及‘‘底比斯古城’’全景，便是源自考古學繪圖員費德里克·卡瑟伍德的素描畫。然而在全景圖意念的萌芽階段，除威廉·亞歷山大及丹尼爾叔侄以外，並無此類畫家踏足中國沿岸。 既然如此，還有甚麼比採用熟知地貌、兼精於細描的中國畫師作品作為全景圖藍本，更為理想呢？

而實際上，繪製廣州全圖是有其歷史背景的。在1837、1838年間中國朝廷與英商關係趨惡化，翌年交惡更演變為戰爭，外界對廣州的中國貿易地位更為關注。繼廣州全景圖後，澳門全圖(1840年)及香港全圖(1843年)亦陸續完成。但正如《時報》刊登的羅伯特·百福德訃聞所論：「要待至事發地點成為畫家筆下美景後，這件引起公眾注目的事件才廣為人知」。[18]

澳　　門

大部份澳門風景畫明顯地並非實地繪畫，頂多是畫家從遠處一瞥的作品。德·布里1598年的鑴刻版畫中所繪畫建築物，雖有歐式外形，卻無視中國建築特色，亦忽略了這個葡萄牙遠方殖民地發展中的面貌。1655年約翰·紐荷芙以隨員（兼業餘畫家） 身份隨荷蘭使節團來華，是年7月15日乘船往廣州時途經澳門，他在紀事上也承認：「我們並沒有怎麼靠近。」[19] 紐荷芙的澳門風景畫，無非是從海上遠觀，將角樓小塔、城垛鋸壁等一鱗半爪，加上想象而成的虛構作品。若被誤解為描繪馬爾他、馬德拉斯、或是莫三比克的風景畫，也不足為奇。

從西端的西望洋山可以俯瞰全澳門景色，包括內港及南灣，以及極目遠處通向中國大陸的隲地。由十八世紀末至十九世紀初，好些以不同素材捕捉這一角度的風景畫保存了下來（展品圖號11）。到十九世紀中葉，此處風景的受歡迎程度下降，至1870年代又山河重拾（展品圖號27）。現下〔澳門〕市區範圍，特別是東面部份，已大大擴展，攝影機亦已成為風景畫家倚重的輔助工具。由於市區面貌的蜕變，整個地方的景觀平衡亦受到影響。早期荒蕪崎嶇的赤貧地，今在其最狹窄部份都遍佈建築物。鱗次櫛比的樓房連成一條長帶子，間中點綴了幾處山林及護土坡。

十九世紀澳門最為人熟悉的當是南灣風景（展品圖號7、11）。無論從東北或西端眺望，都可以飽覽南灣中部宏偉典雅的建築物、砲台、遙遙相對的山頂教堂，以及岸邊的漁舟漁民。南灣為畫家提供俯拾即是的題材，是以描畫此地景緻的作品深受西方主顧歡迎，實非偶然。再者，南灣風貌的畫作大致上都是以西方傳統畫構圖，不同於以廣州商館和黃埔船舶（及從西望洋山俯瞰澳門）為題的外銷畫，基本上仍是採用非西式圖畫結構。

傳統西畫要求界限分明的前景，通常輔以人物活動，襯景靠邊（或左右兩旁），側中是遠景；錢納利的一幅南灣風景畫（展品圖號10）便是此中最典型例子：近景是正在渡越防波堤的蜑家艇，左方是直豎的帆桅，右方是旗杆，西望洋山上的修道院成為遠景焦點所在。而繪畫同一景觀的中國外銷畫，不管有沒有受錢納利的影響，看起來總是那麼刻意地「西式」，以致第一眼常被錯認是歐洲拿玻里的風景畫，專門賣給絡繹的文化遊客作紀念品。

[17] 通呱及小通呱，1820年名列廣州「畫家」及「袖珍畫像師」，參看卡爾·克羅斯曼《中國貿易的裝飾藝術品》，1991，頁54、60。現存雖沒有老通呱署名或傳屬他的畫作，但大致上可推算展品圖號54應是他的作品。

[18] 《時報》，1863年3月2日

[19] 紐荷芙，如前，頁31。

描繪澳門的西洋風景畫，以喬治‧錢納利（1825-1852年間主要居於澳門）及奧古斯特‧波塞爾（1838-1839在此差不多逗留一年）兩位駐留當地的專業畫家作品為主流。他們的成就不在於與中國外銷畫家在描繪細節方面互分高下，更重要的是他們將地方景物與民情生活結連起來。媽閣廟、耶穌堂這些不同文化下產生的名勝古蹟，在他們筆下不單是耀目的建築，也是周遭人群活動的天幕。

錢納利與波塞爾關心當地人的生活 ─ 街頭小販和顧客、忙著生意招徠的流動理髮匠、街上的賭徒與苦力、農工、艇戶及漁民 ─ 遠多於殖民統治者及遊客的活動。相反，德‧布賴的早期版畫（展品圖號5）捕捉的多是頭戴邊帽、身掛配劍、由侍從擎傘、昂視闊步的葡國商賈。同樣，十八世紀畫家勞里的鐫刻版畫（展品圖號7）中的主角亦非本土居民，而是葡萄牙教士 ─ 其中一位似正引領著一名中國人，步向南灣東北角的聖方濟各修院。

未知是否基於這個因素，抑或純屬巧合，西方畫家對早期香港傾注的不多。1838年8月英國旗在佔領角升起之前兩年半，波塞爾在港九多處繪有一些中國居民速寫。錢納利於1846年也曾逗留在港六個月，但其時這位七十二歲的藝術家已經（據他自己形容）：「嚴重不適，少能作事」。[22] 至1857年，馬西安諾‧巴普蒂斯塔從澳門移居香港，發表過一批（參見展品圖號81）「仿已故錢納利先生」的作品，亦有部份是他自己的原創畫。其他大多數的香港繪畫都是年輕軍官、醫生、工程師等業餘之作，當中有些水準不差，頗具參考價值，但藝術水平則普遍不高。

最矚目的十九世紀香港歷史畫，許是中國畫師所繪的個別建築物。"香港造幣廠"（展品圖號78）是其中佳例：井然有序的花園內的樹籬及花床，跟面向東角海港的多層鑄鐵陽台，都以生動細膩的筆觸描繪出來；建築物遊廊入口處，一中國人及一西洋人正互相握手問好.....中國外銷畫熱潮歷久不衰，此情此景，正好為這個中西文化相會的歷史時空，提供了最貼切的象徵比喻。

帕特里克‧康納

香　港

十九世紀中葉澳門經濟衰落，香港則乘時崛起；但總體而言，早期的香港風景畫卻令人失望。以廣州及澳門為題材的外銷畫已有過百年歷史，香港的類似作品要到1840年代才起步，斯時此類畫種已開始沒落。從九龍隔岸眺望港島，及沿山而上籠統的建築物，不久便成為公式構圖。主要的教堂、政府大樓和貨倉等雖勉強可辨，卻欠缺先前廣澳風景畫特有的細緻。

有一點值得注意的是，全盛時期的澳門特有一種令人懷緬的氣氛，是開埠初期的香港未可比擬的。肯塔基出生、拉塞爾公司的合伙人威廉‧亨特，曾在中國沿海地區居留十五年之久，他（在歸回北美後）這樣記述澳門：「寧靜安謐的生活、煥發的氣氛、宜人的氣候....說實話，這裏十足是個樂園」。[20] 相比之下，香港對她的西方居民來說，吸引力就弱少得多：她只是一個毫不舒適、令人懊惱、又不受本家政府重視的貿易站。就連香港第一任財政官，也對這個只得「落後市鎮」、「陡峭崖壁」、「山腳下是色澤如發霉的斯提爾頓乾酪的花崗岩層」[21] 的殖民地小島不予好評。

圖A　廣州全景輪廓簡圖

[20] 威廉‧亨特：《舊中國雜記》，1911編，頁147。
[21] 羅伯特‧蒙歌馬利‧馬丁所言，引述於佛蘭克‧偉爾什：《香港史》，1993，頁158。

[22] 1848年2月20日錢納利寫給德已立上尉的信件，香港上海匯豐銀行藏品。

SALEM AND THE PEARL RIVER DELTA

With the ending of the American Revolution and the signing of the Treaty of Paris on September 3, 1783, many world ports were for the first time directly accessible to American traders. One of the first destinations was Canton, China, for which the New York ship *Empress of China* set sail in February of 1784. Within the year, the third vessel to arrive in Canton from America, the ship *Grand Turk*, left the small seaport of Salem and returned in 1787, setting the stage for Salem's leading role in the China trade.

Salem prospered during the next several decades because of its quick and decisive involvement in trade with China. The town's leading ship captains and supercargoes, who travelled beyond the South American and African continents, determined to organize themselves for the benefit of trade and for the betterment of the town's citizens. Toward that end, they established the East India Marine Society.

On October 22, 1799, the Rev. William Bentley, Salem's Federal-era diarist, recorded: "It is proposed by the New Marine Society to make a Cabinet". The merchants of Salem had long been interested in the world beyond the city's harbours and many had their own cabinets of curiosities, the concept of which was soon to be fully developed in the Marine Society's efforts "to form a Museum of natural and artificial curiosities, particularly such as are to be found beyond the Cape of Good Hope and Cape Horn".

Immediately, members of the new organization gave items which they had collected on their previous world travels. One object which later came to the Museum — a nodding-head clay figure from China — is known through documentation to have been acquired by the Rev. Bentley in 1790 and is representative of the "curiosities" of the time. This figure, a standing Chinese monk with painted and gilded robes, was proudly displayed in Bentley's personal cabinet of artifacts, which included objects donated to him by friends who were sea captains, and which he subsequently donated to the Society. That Marine Society's collection, established in 1799, was the forerunner of the Peabody Essex Museum, now the oldest continuously operating museum in the United States.

Described as "artificial curiosities" in the founding papers of the institution, examples of the material culture of many nations were to be exhibited in the halls of the Society. Among the artificial curiosities from China given to the Museum in its early years, were those listed in its first published catalogue of 1821: official papers, razors, battle axes, spears, swords, opium pipes, ornaments of stone, alabaster figures of gods, nodding-head clay figures, and a "model of the foot of a Chinese lady of fashion $3\frac{3}{4}$ inches long". Chinese clothing was admired and examples collected while captains waited in Canton for the trading season to conclude. Some donations to the collection included such articles of clothing and adornment: Chinese hats, robes, shoes and slippers worn by men and women, fans, and a string of beads "made of Nuts with the head of Jos, carved on each". Other additions were cultural artifacts: a "Chinese Swanpan, or Abacus, used by most Asiatic nations in making Arithmetical calculations", a Chinese ink-pallet and letter, candles, coins, "Two elegant Bowls, (from Canton) made for, and presented by Benjamin Hodges", compasses, calendars, locks, chopsticks, and a "Dotchin or Ballance, for weighing gold in China". During the nineteenth century, members of the Museum would parade annually through the streets of the town dressed in the luxurious and, to the landbound Salemite, curious textiles of China, Japan and India, carrying swords, spears and other paraphernalia of distant countries.

Natural curiosities from China which entered the collection in the first two decades of its existence included "a Green Viper, (*Coluber Mycterizans,*) from

Fig. 1
Punch Bowl, c. 1785
China
Porcelain, 14 x 40.5 cm (5 ½ x 15 ⅞ in.)
Peabody Essex Museum, Gift of Elias Hasket Derby, Jr., *E62,499,*
1800-1801

Fig. 2
Pair of Tureens, c. 1800
China
Porcelain, 52 x 62 cm (20 ½ x 24 ⅜ in.) each
Peabody Essex Museum, Gift of Captain Ward Blackler, *E56,985AB,*
1801

Cochin-China, the bite of this Snake is said to be mortal", as well as "Insects from China, in the Pupa state". Interest in Chinese medical practices is seen in the donation of *The Chinese Art of Curing Diseases,* by assuming and maintaining for a length of time certain attitudes of the body and limbs — illustrated by 24 figures and descriptions by a Chinese Author, with a Latin translation by a Jesuit Priest, [donated by] E. H. Derby.

In 1801, this same Captain Elias Hasket Derby, Jr., son of the owner of the *Grand Turk,* gave the Museum a punch bowl (Figure 1). This bowl had been presented by Pinqua, a Hong merchant, as a souvenir to the officers of the ship. It is decorated in the well with a ship, above and below which are banners declaring "SHIP GRAND TURK/ AT CANTON 1786". When given to the Society, the design was described as a true picture of the *Grand Turk;* in fact, the design was taken from the frontispiece of William Hutchinson's *A Treatise on Practical Seamanship* (London, 1777), and depicts the British ship *Hall.* Nearly a dozen examples of these punch bowls are now known, each individualized to suit the occasion of the gift; a second example in the Museum's collection was made for the Boston captain, James Magee.

Captain Ward Blackler made another important gift of Chinese export porcelain to the Society in 1801. The pair of oversized, undecorated goose tureens (Figure 2) appear to be unique to this day. These tureens were first identified as swans because of their large size and white colour; more common examples exist in a smaller, more natural size and decorated in polychrome enamels. Among the other elegant decorative objects given within the first several years of the Museum's existence were the "beautiful model of a Chinese Pagoda" displayed in this exhibition (no. 34) and "A Painting of the Emperor of China, surrounded by his Family, done by a Chinese artist, [gift of] Nathaniel Page".

A year later, Captain Benjamin Hodges gave a life-size figure of the Canton Hong merchant Yamqua (Figure 3). The figure wears the actual clothing of Yamqua, and it is assumed that the face is a life portrait. At some point in time, the original portrait head and hands of unfired clay, crafted by a Chinese artisan, were nearly destroyed and the surviving pieces were copied in wood by the Salem architect and carver, Samuel McIntire (1757-1811). Another life-size "carved statue of a Chinese Mandarin, in his proper costume" was donated at about the same time by W. Ward.

Throughout the 18th century and into the 19th century, Cantonese modelers produced unfired clay figures as decorative curiosities, a number of which have nodding heads. The earliest documented clay figure of a Westerner, an English merchant, dated 1717, is now in the Peabody Essex Museum. Additionally, a pair of nodding-head figures (Figure 4) listed in the 1821 catalogue of the Museum as "Copied from the life and brought from Canton" were donated in 1803 by Captain Richard Wheatland, first president of the East India Marine Society. Wheatland also donated a painted clay figure of a Chinese labourer carrying boxes of tea, which was recently exhibited at the Hong Kong Museum of Tea Ware. Captain Wheatland had his portrait painted in Canton, by Spoilum or a follower, and also commissioned his wife's portrait, probably copied by the artist from a miniature (Figures 5a and 5b).

Fig. 3
Portrait Figure of Yamqua, c. 1801
China and Salem
Wood and fabric, 156.2 cm (61 ½ in.)
Peabody Essex Museum, Gift of Captain Benjamin Hodges, *E7,161,*
1801

Fig. 4
Pair of Nodding-head Figures, c. 1800
China
Unfired clay, 65 cm (15 ½ in.) each
Peabody Essex Museum, Gift of Captain Richard Wheatland, *E7097;*
E7,098, 1803

It was common practice for Western merchants such as Captain Wheatland to have their portraits painted by Chinese artists and the Museum's collection has many examples. It was also customary for Chinese merchants to give portraits of themselves to Western colleagues as souvenirs and many of these are in the Museum's collection as well. One such portrait is that of the well-known Cantonese silk merchant, Eshing (Figure 6), painted by Spoilum and given by Captain Thomas W. Ward in 1806 when it was listed as "A Portrait of Eshing, a Silk Merchant in Canton, by a Native artist".

Ships' portraits were also common commissions in many ports, and the artists of China were not to be outdone. Numerous portraits of Salem ships set in the port cities of Whampoa, Canton, Hong Kong, and later, Shanghai, have been added to the collections of the Peabody Essex Museum. The *Henry Tuke*, a Salem ship of 366 tons, was depicted at anchor at Whampoa Reach, flying the American flag, with the Whampoa Pagoda to the left and the so-called "lesser pagoda" to the right (Figure 7). Whampoa continued to be a popular setting for ship portraits well into the third quarter of the 19th century, even after Hong Kong became the main location for executing these paintings. Some of the views of Whampoa include Dane's Island where today one can find grave markers for sailors from Salem and the adjacent town of Beverly. The same is true in the Protestant cemetery of Macau, where many native New Englanders found their final resting places.

Among the most intriguing items relating to the Pearl River Delta in the Peabody Essex Museum is a fireboard (Figure 8) painted by the French artist Michele Felice Corne (1752–1845) for the East India Marine Society. Corne, who arrived in Salem from Italy in 1800, never visited Canton and would have copied his view directly from a China trade painting of about 1790–1795 that had been brought to Salem. The fireboard, a large decorative panel used to cover an open fireplace during the warmer months, was one of three he was commissioned to paint in 1804 with scenes pertinent to the Society's maritime interests.

Today, portraits of its first members and the ships they sailed line two walls of the 1824 Great Hall of the Peabody Essex Museum. Many of these paintings are by Chinese artists, and many of the ships are depicted in the Chinese ports of Whampoa and Hong Kong. There are now over 300 oil paintings on canvas by Chinese artists, including portraits, ship portraits and port views in the Museum's collections. Since its founding, the collections have grown and encompassed two-dimensional works relating to Asian trade by the leading artists, printmakers and draftsmen of the 18th and 19th century Europe. Among these are paintings (8), watercolours (30) and sketches (200) by George Chinnery, some of which once belonged to the China trade merchant Augustine Heard of Ipswich, Massachusetts.

Today, four centuries of decorative art objects from the Asian trade are displayed in eleven galleries, and the Peabody Essex Museum, began almost 200 years ago, continues an active programme of acquisition, care, exhibition, interpretation and publication of its collections of Asian export arts. With this exhibition, we renew and strengthen the ties between Salem, Massachusetts and the Pearl River Delta.

William R. Sargent

Figs. 5a and 5b
Portraits of Captain Richard and Elizabeth Wheatland, 1800-1805
China, Spoilum
Oil on canvas, 59.7 x 45 cm (23 ½ x 17 ¾ in.) each
Peabody Essex Museum, Gift of Mr. Richard Wheatland, *M22,878; M22,879, 1990*

Fig. 6
Portrait of Eshing, 1800-1805
China, Spoilum
Oil on canvas, 67.4 x 51.5 cm (26 ⅝ x 20 ⅝ in.)
Peabody Essex Museum, Gift of Thomas W. Ward, *M364, 1809*

 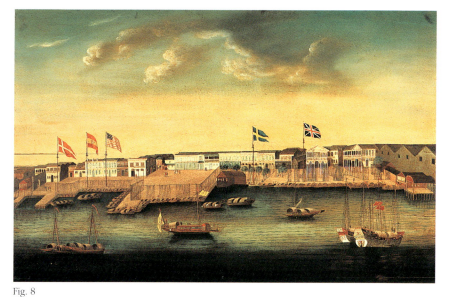

Fig. 8
The Foreign Factories of Canton, 1804
United States, unsigned, Michele Felice Corne (1752-1845)
Oil on board, 85.1 x 135.3 cm (33 ½ x 53 ¼ in.)
Peabody Essex Museum, Commissioned by the East India Marine Society, *M292, 1804*

Fig. 7
Henry Tuke, **American Ship at Anchor in Whampoa**, c. 1835
China, unknown artist
Oil on canvas, 43.8 x 58.4 cm (17 ¼ x 23 in.)
Peabody Essex Museum, Gift of Mr. George W. Williams, *M160, 1891*

Acknowledgements

This exhibition is, in part, a result of a project funded by the United States Information Agency (USIA), administered by the American Association of Museums (AAM) as part of the International Partnership Among Museums (IPAM). For me, a five-week study of the collections of the Hong Kong Museum of Art and the surviving historic sites in Hong Kong, Macau, Whampoa and Canton was made possible by the generosity of IPAM. A four-week study of the Peabody Essex Museum's collection and related private and public collections in the Boston area was subsequently supported for the then Assistant Curator of Historical Pictures at the Hong Kong Museum of Art, Ms. Lesley F. H. Lau. I am greatly indebted to Lesley Lau and her colleagues for their very generous support of my visit and for their friendship; these included Ho Ching-hin, Dr. Joseph S. P. Ting, Chau Hing-wah, Ms. Siu Lai-kuen, Ms. Wong Yin-fong and, especially, Lee Man-chiu, then Assistant Curator of Historical Pictures who so patiently showed me every painting, drawing and print in the collection and who now, as education coordinator, together with Ms. Mimi Cho will organize programmes around this exhibition. Mrs. Margaret Lee, Manager Archives, The Hongkong and Shanghai Banking Corporation, extended the courtesy of showing me that collection. Also, Patrick J. Corcoran, Director of USIF, American Consulate General, Nigel Cameron, Anthony J. Hardy and Robert Brothers shared their knowledge and friendship with me.

Mr. Gerard Tsang, Chief Curator of the Hong Kong Museum of Art expressed enthusiasm for the IPAM project and this exhibition and I am indebted to his commitment to both the exhibition and the catalogue. I thank the Urban Council of Hong Kong for their support of the exhibition in Hong Kong, and the Asian Cultural Council for their support of the Hong Kong catalogue. I thank Mr. Ho Kam-chuen, Curator and Ms. Stoney L. C. Yeung, current Assistant Curator of Historical Pictures, who have been instrumental in seeing this exhibition to its conclusion.

I was fortunate to accompany my colleagues from Hong Kong for a visit to Canton (Guangzhou) and was treated to special tours of the landmarks of the China trade era illustrated by the works of art in this exhibition. I would especially like to thank: Prof. Mai Yinghao, for his gracious hospitality and tours of Whampoa and surrounding areas; Mr. Deng Bing-quan, then Curator of the Guangzhou Museum; and Haji Nur Muhammad Ma Feng-da, Vice-President, Guangzhou Islamic Association. In Macau I must give very special thanks to my friend and colleague Dr. Maria Margarida L. G. Marques Matias, who's hospitality knows no bounds. Also in Macau, I thank as well Dr. César Guillén-Nuñez, and Dr. Luis Manuel do Carmo Trindade for their help.

Here, in Salem, I wish to thank Dr. H. A. Crosby Forbes, Margaret Palmer, Lucy Butler, Jane Key, Jeffrey Dykes, Mark Sexton and the staff of the Phillips Library at the Peabody Essex Museum for all their work in seeing this complex project to completion. I especially want to thank Peter Fetchko, Director of Curatorial Operations for his support of this project and Merrily Glosband for her dedicated research and painstaking editing of the manuscript.

Dr. Patrick Conner's essay on the traditions of China trade paintings is of utmost importance to this study and I appreciate his eagerness in agreeing to participate. I wish to thank him also for his many helpful comments on the contents of the catalogue.

Finally, I would like to thank all those scholars who have paved the way to our appreciation of these views of the Pearl River Delta, and whose works I have leaned heavily on for the entries in this catalogue: these include, Geoffrey W. Bonsall, Dr. Christina K. L. Chu, Dr. Patrick Conner, Carl L. Crossman, Dr. H. A. Crosby Forbes, Martyn Gregory, David Sanctuary Howard, Robin Hutcheon, G. H. R. Tillotson, Dr. Joseph S. P. Ting, and James Orange.

William R. Sargent
Salem, Massachusetts

CATALOGUE

◆

圖版目錄

by William Sargent

威廉·沙進撰寫

THE PEARL RIVER DELTA REGION

珠江三角洲流域

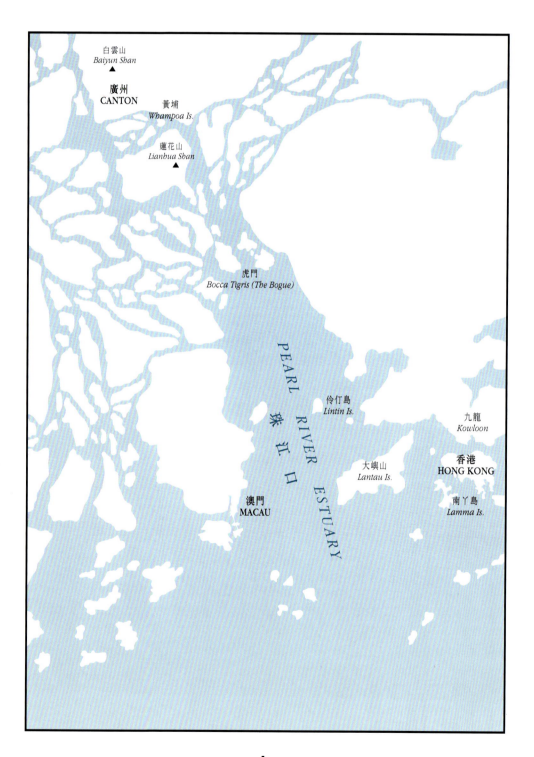

NOTES TO THE READER

凡　例

Entries are listed in the following manner:

展品項目依據下列格式闡述：

Catalogue Number

展品編號

Title, Date

標題、時期

Country of Artist's Origin; Artist (Dates)

藝術家原籍、生卒年份

Material

物料媒介

Size

尺碼大小

Sizes are listed first in centimetres, then in inches; height precedes, width/diameter, precedes depth; sight size is listed, then frame size when the frame is an original Chinese frame; height may only be given for some three dimensional objects.

先列公制厘米，後列英制呎吋；順序列出高度，闊度／圓周，深度，畫心大小，若畫框是中國原裝，則畫框大小亦一併示列。部分立體作品只標明高度。

Museum, Donor and Accession Number

所屬博物館、捐贈者、藏品編號

ENTRY

Provenance

Published

This listing includes only references in which this specific object has been published, but does not include auction references which are listed under 'Provenance'.

Exhibited

Includes all references to exhibitions where objects are known to have been displayed; these are in chronological order. For works which have been exhibited in the Hong Kong Museum of Art before are listed under 'Published'.

Related Works

References includes objects that have been published in scholarly works.

展品説明

收藏歷史

刊載書目

只包括曾刊載該作品的出版書籍，但在拍賣目錄內刊出者則歸「收藏歷史」類，不在此列。

展覽

包括在已知範圍內，該作品曾參與展出的所有展覽資料，按日期先後臚列。凡在香港藝術館展出過的香港藏品，不在此列，可參考「刊載書目」內的展覽目錄。

相關作品

包括與作品有關之出版文獻。

NB: All place names in text are given in versions and spellings contemporaneous with the old China trade, such as Canton (Guangzhou), Dane's Island (Chang Zhou), Honam Island (Henan Dao), Pearl River (Zhu Jiang) and Whampoa (Huangpu Dao). Pinyin system of spelling is used. With Portuguese names, the most commonly used English spelling is followed, ie, St. Paul (São Paolo) and St. Lawrence (São Lourenço).

Fo-chew

Nan-kang

King

Naw-king

KIna lucying b

Zhan-chew

Kyew

Yen-chew

Kwulin

Kyu-chew

Tay-chew

CHE-KIAN

Cheng-cha

Shwy-chew

Quang-fin

Kyang

Schu-chew

le Kyang

Lin-kyang

Fu-chew

Wen-chew

Yuen-chew

Shau-u

S I

Kyen-chang

Fun-ching

Ki-ugau

Kyen-phing

Hang

Ueng-chew

K I A N G

O K

Yen-pin

Tong-chew

FO

FU-CHEW

Wae-y'eng

Ning-win

Hay-tan-ching

Yau

Chin

Kam-chew

Nan-yang

FU-KW

Ting-chew

Nu-wigan

Luen

Nan-ying

Shan-chew

G

Swen-chew

TAY-WAN or FORMOSA I.

Ching-chew

U

Amoy

Chau-Chew

U

I. Pong-hu
or Pescadore

I

Chau-king

N

I-chew

CANTON

Tchin-chau-ching

Te-kin

M-

St-shan

W-chew

Hey-men

Tay-wan

chew

Hu-men

Macao

Shang-chwen-Shan
or Isle of Sancian

Hay-lin
Chin

Remarks.
Capitals of Provinces are in
Capitals, other City of the 1st
Rank in Roman & those of the
2d in Italic.

INTRODUCTION

引言

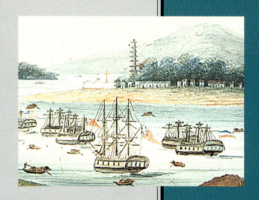

I. INTRODUCTION

The artist Auguste Borget, who visited the China coast from 1838 to 1839, wrote, "...the country is really unlike every other, I found in the landscape an air of strangeness which charmed me".[1]   It is this attraction which fascinated so many who came before Borget and would follow in his footsteps, to this day. While many sought riches through commerce along the shores of the Pearl River, most were not immune to the beauties of the land in which they pursued their fortunes. It is the love of the landscape of China, the Pearl River Delta specifically, that we celebrate with this exhibition.

Many of the views in this display, especially those by Chinese artists, are not unique. European artists, in particular George Chinnery, would sketch or paint the same scenes over and over, or would later produce multiple print images. A nearly insatiable market for views of the Pearl River was fueled by the entrepreneurs who conducted business there, their business partners and family members, and many who never travelled there but heard marvellous tales of the land and culture of China.

The works in this exhibition, which date from 1598 to 1860, were selected not only on artistic merit but also to display the widest degree of variation in views. All the paintings and objects are from the two most important repositories of works of art related to the China Coast; half are from the Hong Kong Museum of Art and half are from the Peabody Essex Museum of Salem, Massachusetts. This is as much a celebration of these two great collections as it is of the art inspired by the Pearl River Delta itself.

While the views in this exhibition are displayed as individual works of art, many were produced as part of an ensemble; Chinese artists frequently created sets of four port views in oil or watercolour, or entire albums of up to twenty-four or more related scenes, while some scrolls have since been cut into individual views. European artists frequently produced drawings with the idea of transferring them through the print medium into books of travel and sets of prints on China. A few examples have been selected here to illustrate this facet of the export arts, while many of the individual paintings in this exhibition are, or once were, only part of larger sets.

[1]   Hutcheon 1979, p. 42.

I. 引言

畫家波塞爾在 1838 至 1839 年間訪遊中國時記道:「這個國家充滿著異彩,她的奇麗景色深深地吸引著我。」[1] 這塊迷人的國土其實在波塞爾來華前已有無數人踏足,至今仍有不少人跟隨他的步伐漫遊中國。昔日在珠江一帶營商致富的外國人,大都為這幅美麗的土地着迷。是次展覽,便是為了賀揚這份對中國風土景物 ── 尤其是珠江三角洲一帶 ── 的熱愛。

是次展品中出現了不少相類的風景題材,特別見於中國畫家的作品。而歐洲畫家如錢納利,亦喜將同一景物描繪多次。有些更將畫作刻印成版畫,發行無數。這些作品不斷地為一個龐大的市場所吸納:一班在華貿易的企業家便對描繪珠江風貌的作品十分渴求,其他的顧客,包括了這羣商人的合夥人和家眷,他們很多都未曾親往中國遊覽,但卻聽聞了不少有關中國的各樣美麗的傳說及其深厚的文化。

是次展覽選取的展品,涵蓋自 1598 年至 1860 年兩百多年的創作,揀選的著眼點並非只側重其藝術價值,亦須考慮題材的多樣化。所有畫作及器物都是香港藝術館及麻省賽倫市皮博迪艾塞克斯博物館的珍藏,兩館均以庋藏與中國沿海歷史有關的藝術品著名。

這次的展品雖是個別獨立展出,但很多原本是來自一套組件的。中國畫家喜繪一套四幀的油畫或水彩畫,以海港景色為題;或繪製一套套以相關景物為題的畫冊,內有廿四幀或更多的冊頁;另外一些則喜作長卷畫,後來再分切成個別的畫作。而歐洲畫家的習慣,則喜將素描作品刻製成版畫,用以刊印旅遊書籍或成冊的中國景物版畫。以下數件作品就是這些以套件形式製作的外銷藝術品例子,而其他的畫作,很多都是原畫套件的一部分。

1　哈其森,1979,頁 42。

◄ 1 ►

Fan mid-19th century
China, unknown artist
Gouache on paper, ivory sticks and feathers
27.5 x 52 cm (10 ¾ x 20 ½ in.)
Hong Kong Museum of Art, *AH91.2*

彩繪摺扇 19世紀中葉
中國，畫家佚名
水粉紙本，象牙扇骨及羽毛
27.5 x 52 厘米 （10 ¾ x 20 ½ 吋）
香港藝術館 *AH91.2*

Created for the export market, this brisé (folding stick and paper) fan edged with feathers, is decorated with three views of, from left to right, Canton between 1846 and 1856, the Praya Grande in Macau, and Hong Kong from Causeway Bay. The end sticks are intricately carved; the fifteen centre sticks are pierced. Because such specially made fans were much admired for their beauty when they were first acquired and were generally not used, they survive in relatively good condition.

此摺扇以羽毛圍飾，扇面由左至右繪有1846至1856年的廣州商館外貌、澳門南灣景緻及香港銅鑼灣一帶景色，專為外銷市場而製。首尾扇骨雕鏤精巧，其餘十五小骨通雕圖案。此類摺扇多作觀賞用途，傳世作品狀況頗佳。

Another fan, with a view of Whampoa, is thought to depict the American ship *Empress of China,* the first ship to sail directly from the United States to China. The fan is said to have been presented by a Chinese merchant to the vessel's Captain, John Green.[2] The Peabody Essex Museum's large collection of fans includes examples which depict individual scenes of Whampoa, Hong Kong, and Canton, as well as those with multiple scenes.

另外一扇描繪黃埔江景色，江中船隻可能就是從美國駛往中國的第一艘商船"中國皇后"號，據稱一中國商人將此扇贈與該船船長約翰·格林。[2] 皮博迪艾塞克斯博物館藏有大量摺扇，其中有選用黃埔、香港及廣州一地或多地景色為題。

相關作品：參閱克羅斯曼1991，頁323－328，當中繪有澳門、黃埔、廣州和一古塔的彩扇。

Related works: Crossman 1991, pp. 323-328, fans with views of Macau, Whampoa, Canton, and a pagoda.

[2] Crossman 1991, p. 328, no. 118.

[2] 克羅斯曼 1991，頁328，編號118。

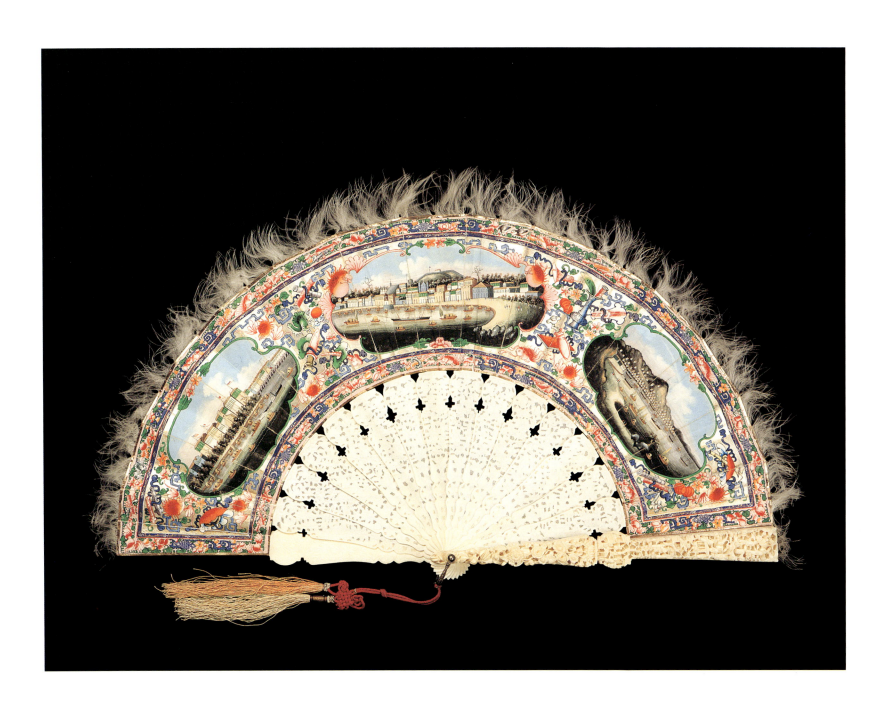

Four Port Views   c. 1810

China, unknown artist

Oil on copper

Sight: 11.7 x 15.4 cm (4 $\frac{5}{8}$ x 6 in.) each

Framed: 20.1 x 23.9cm (7 $\frac{7}{8}$ x 9 $\frac{3}{8}$ in.) each

Peabody Essex Museum, Gift of Mr. Harry T. Peters, Jr. *M20,530-533*

海港景色四幀   約 1810

中國，畫家佚名

銅板油畫

各 11.7 x 15.4 厘米 (4 $\frac{5}{8}$ x 6 吋)

原框：各 20.1 x 23.9 厘米 (7 $\frac{7}{8}$ x 9 $\frac{3}{8}$ 吋)

皮博迪艾塞克斯博物館，小哈里・彼得斯先生捐贈   *M20,530 − 533*

This small set of oil paintings is typical of groups of port views; depicted here are Macau, Bocca Tigris, Whampoa and Canton. Small sets were frequently painted on copper, while later sets of this size were sometimes painted on pith paper. In this set, the view of Whampoa contains twenty-one ships, eight of which are American. Two Western ships can be seen departing through Bocca Tigris; one is British and the other possibly American. Later sets would subsitute a view of Hong Kong for Bocca Tigris.

Provenance: Harry T. Peters, Jr.

此四幀小幅油畫描繪了澳門、虎門、黃埔及廣州的海港景貌，是十分常見的組合。這類小型作品大多繪畫在銅板上，後期有些則繪在通草紙本上。黃埔一景中，可清晰見到廿一艘商船停泊在港海內，其中八艘屬美國公司。另外一幀作品內繪有兩艘商船，經虎門河道徐徐離去，其一為英國船，遠方的應是美國船。後來描繪海港景色的套裝作品，多以香港代替了虎門。

收藏歷史：小哈里・彼得斯

3

Two Nesting Tables   1830 – 1840

China

Lacquer over wood

(.1) 70.7 x 50.2 x 30.6 cm (27 3/4 x 19 3/4 x 12 in.)

(.2) 68.8 x 43.8 x 29.2 cm (27 x 17 3/16 x 11 1/2 in.)

Peabody Essex Museum, Museum Purchase with Funds Donated

Anonymously, *E80,758.1,.2*

套几兩件   1830 – 1840

中國

木胎漆面

(1) 70.7 x 50.2 x 30.6 厘米 (27 3/4 x 19 3/4 x 12 吋)

(2) 68.8 x 43.8 x 29.2 厘米 (27 x 17 3/16 x 11 1/2 吋)

皮博迪艾塞克斯博物館，以無名氏基金購藏。   *E80,758.1,.2*

"Quartetto" tables, made in graduated sizes to fit one below another in sets of four, were introduced in England at the beginning of the 19th century. Cantonese lacquer cabinetmakers produced this rare set with views of Canton and Macau. A third table depicts Bocca Tigris while a fourth is missing. The view of Canton shows the harbour in the foreground, with various ships, junks and boats with the Hongs centreing on a courtyard with an American flag. The view of Macau shows the harbour with hills in the foreground, many Chinese boats and one Western ship. Both tables have lyre-shaped legs with gilt floral designs at top and bottom, and claw feet.

One of the earliest views of Canton on lacquer is found on the interior of a lacquered trunk, dated to the 17th century; it is decorated with a view of Canton with the Mohammedan Tower and Flowery Pagoda prominently mislaid.[3] Such lacquered views are extremely rare. For another example, see the lacquered sewing table (no. 13) with a view of Macau also in this exhibition.

十九世紀初期，英國首先出現了一款以四件組合而成的套几家具，它們的體積由大至小，可以重疊起來。廣州的漆器工匠據此製成了這套以廣州及澳門景色作裝飾的珍品。第三件几案以虎門為題，而第四件作品現已失落。廣州一景中，前方為珠江，各類船艦雲集，圖中央可見在美國花園內的商館。澳門的港口內則停泊了多艘中國船艇，只有一艘是外國商船，海港前方山巒起伏。案足皆以古豎琴為造型，上下鍍有花紋，腿足類狀獸爪。

最早出現在漆器上的廣州畫象，其中一幀在一個十七世紀的漆器衣箱內發現。畫面上描繪有光塔和花塔，但位置不確。[3] 此類作品十分罕見，是次展品中另有一張女紅桌（展品編號13），上有澳門景象。

收藏歷史：紐約蘇富比，1978 年 3 月 3 日，編號 1241

Provenance: Sotheby Parke Bernet, Inc., New York, March 3, 1978, lot 1241

[3] Lisbon 1983, p. 247, no. 229, there identified incorrectly as Macau.

[3] 里斯本,1983，頁 247，編號 229，此處誤作澳門。

Macau

◆

澳門

   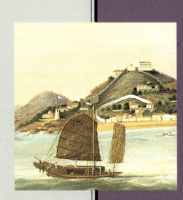

II. Macau

The Portuguese first set foot on Chinese soil in 1513 at the mouth of the Pearl River on the peninsula which came to be known as Macau (Macao), later acquired by them in 1557. There, a European community with luxurious houses and baroque churches was established by the Portuguese and the Macanese (mixed-blood descendants of the Europeans and native population). From its founding as a European community and through the 17th century, Macau enjoyed prosperity, primarily as an important link in Portugal's early trade with Japan. A second period of prosperity began with the lifting of restrictions against non-Portuguese in 1757, after which all Europeans trading in Canton were allowed to reside in the colony.

Macau was a natural location to supply Canton-bound vessels because of its two harbours: the inner harbour on the West River, and the outer harbour facing the Pearl River. It was also a pleasant refuge for Western merchants after the Canton tea season. Macau's small landmass with three prominent hills served well for the construction of protective forts. The peninsula was not formally ceded to the Portuguese until an 1887 treaty which recognized Portugal's sovereignty, but which also allowed for the return of the territory to the control of China in 1999.

Macau is still a remarkable city of important landmarks, many of which were chosen as subjects by both Chinese and Western artists. Perhaps the most famous of the great landmarks are the remains of the old Church of Our Lady of the Assumption of the Jesuit College of Mother of God, known as **St. Paul** (São Paolo). Situated at the foot of Monte Fort, the Church was built in 1602 by the Portuguese and their Japanese Christian students and followers. In the 1630s Father de Rhodes said that the Portuguese built "such a beautiful church, that I have not seen anything that can equal it, even in all the beautiful churches of Italy, except St. Peter's". In 1835 both the Church, built entirely of carved and gilded wood, and its college, caught fire and were burnt to the ground, leaving only the façade, constructed between 1620 and 1627, and the dramatic 130 granite steps.

St. Lawrence (São Lourenço) was built during the earliest days of settlement; the church was rebuilt in 1758, and again in 1844; the façade was built of stone from 1801 to 1803 and the twin square towers were added in 1846. A cemetery once existed where the gardens now lie and there is still a stone cross dated 1811 on the grounds. **St. Dominic** (São Domingos), one of Chinnery's favourite subjects, was built in the 17th century and is considered to be the most beautiful of Macau's baroque churches. Nearby are the **Senate Square** (Largo do Senado), the **Santa Casa da Misericordia** (established in 1569, and the oldest charitable organization in Macau, constructed during the late 18th century, with the surviving façade added in the next century), and **Leal Senado** (Loyal Senate, the main administrative body for municipal affairs). Other religious structures include **The Cathedral**, a basilica with two towers designed by J. T. Aquino and built between 1844 and 1850, and **Peñha Hill and Church**. The third highest hill at the southern end of the Praya Grande, and formerly the site of a fort, Peñha Hill became the location for the church built in 1622 which was rebuilt once in 1837; the present church dates to 1935.

Monte Fort was built on the hill above St. Paul's by the Jesuits in the early 17th century. It was connected by a concealed passage to both the college and the church, and was later taken over as the official residence of the governors until 1746. The original **Franciscan Fort** was built in 1629 on the coastline at the northern end of the Praya Grande. British soldiers were stationed there in 1806; it was rebuilt in 1864 when the nearby Convent of St. Francis, to which the fort was attached, was replaced by barracks and the fortress demolished. **Guia Fort** was built between 1637 and 1638 on the highest point of the peninsula, Guia Hill, where in 1865 a lighthouse (now the oldest surviving example on the China coast) was built.

The **Praya Grande**, or main street, swept along in a great crescent, "in obedience to the graceful and regular bend of the bay", as Thomas Allom and the Rev. G. N. Wright said in their 1843 book on China. A stone wall, broken occasionally for access to the sea, followed the embankment, behind which a line of grand houses and businesses stood. The view of this dramatic topographical element was long a favourite of artists; today it is a narrow, busy street and the bay is being filled in for the construction of casinos.

Legend identifies the **Camões Grotto** (also, Camoens) as the site where the great Portuguese poet Luis Vas de Camões wrote his epic poem, *Os Lusiadas.* The poem, published in Lisbon in 1572, recounts Vasco da Gama's voyage to India. Tradition states that Camões was exiled in 1557 to Goa as a result of his political writings and from there he was sent to Macau. But the earliest reference to his presence in Macau is in the Jesuit seminary register of 1635 when the monolithic boulders at the north end of the inner harbour were referred to as the Rocks of Camões. The site was developed for tourism in 1840 and remains today as a garden, with a bronze bust of the poet as a memorial.

The **Protestant Cemetery** was established on land which had been a garden incorporating the Camões Grotto. Ecclesiastical law forbade the burial of Protestants on Catholic soil, while the Chinese refused Western burials on their land. In 1814 a cemetery committee was established and in 1821 the governor allowed a local merchant to sell some land to the British East India Company. Many important residents were buried there, including George Chinnery, and several Salem and Beverly natives.

The **Ma Kok Temple** (Mage, Ma-kok or Ma Cho Kau Temple) is situated at the foot of the Barra Hill on the edge of the sea. The temple was erected in the Ming dynasty, during the reign of Wanli (1573-1620) by Fukienese fisherman and dedicated to the goddess Tin Hau (Heavenly Queen), the Ancestral Grandmother and patroness of seafarers, in gratitude for their having survived a typhoon. The Portuguese knew the goddess as A-Ma-Gao, from which they derived the name of the colony. Staunton related that "Of the two pagan temples at Macao, belonging to the Chinese, one is curiously situated among a confused heap of immense masses of granite. This temple is comprised of three separate buildings, one over the other; the only approach to which is by a winding flight of steps hewn out of the solid rock".[4] Auguste Borget (1808-1877) described the temple as "the greatest marvel I have yet seen ... almost daily I visit this temple either in the morning when all is shadow or in the evening when every stone and tree and roof reflects the sun, or at midday when the extreme heat obliges me to seek its grateful shade". Other artists, such as Webber, Baptista and Chinnery, were as fascinated by the rock formations at the edge of the sea as by the temple gateway itself.

[4] Staunton 1797, p. 432.

II. 澳門

1513年，葡萄牙人初次踏足中國，並於珠江口的澳門半島登陸，到了1557年，他們更進佔了這個地方。葡人及澳門人（當地人與歐洲人的混血後裔）在這裡建立了歐洲人的社羣，並興建了一座座豪華的樓房以及巴羅克式的教堂。從此時開始至十七世紀，可算是澳門的第一個黃金時期，它成為了葡萄牙與日本兩地貿易的主要橋樑。其後，中國在1757年解除了多項對非葡萄牙人的禁令，自此，所有在廣州經商的歐洲人，都獲准在這片殖民地居住，形成了澳門的第二次繁盛期。

當遠航船隻進入廣州之先，澳門是必經之道。它擁有兩個天然港口：位於西江的內港及連接珠江的外港。每年當廣州的貿易季節完結，它就成為外國商人舒適的收容所。澳門面積不大，但島上有三座主要的山丘，山上建有炮台以防禦敵人。1887年，澳門正式割讓予葡萄牙，但到1999年，這塊土地又會重新交回中國政府管轄。

如今，澳門仍是一美麗的城市，古跡遺痕，而且大多是昔日中外畫家筆下常見的題材。最負盛名的可算是位於大炮台山麓的**聖保祿教堂**遺址（大三巴），這座教堂是由葡萄牙人和日本的基督教徒及學生於1602年合力興建。在1630年代，羅德斯神父稱讚葡萄牙人建築了「前所未見的一座如此宏偉壯麗的教堂，除了聖彼得大教堂外，其他在意大利所有具美譽的教堂都不能與之相比。」整座教堂以雕木及鑲木築建，但可惜

在1835年的一場大火中，教堂及書院燒成灰燼，只剩下在1620年至1627年建成的前壁，及一百三十塊以花崗岩舖砌成的階梯。

聖老楞佐堂（風順堂）是最早期的建築之一，建於1758年，並於1844年重建，前壁是於1801至1803年以石材建成，方形的雙連塔則於1846年加建。昔日的墳場現已成為一座座花園，遺留下來的是一尊刻有1811年的十字架形碑石，供後人憑吊。**玫瑰堂**（板樟堂）是錢納利鍾愛的繪畫題材，它被公認為濠江最華麗的巴羅克式教堂，建於十七世紀。鄰近有**議事廳廣場、仁慈堂**和**市政廳**（管理市政事務的行政機關）。仁慈堂是澳門最古老的慈善團體，於1569年成立，會堂建於十八世紀晚期，前壁則於十九世紀加建，至今仍在。其他宗教建築物包括有建於1844年至1850年的**大堂**（主教座堂），兩座鐘樓由阿奎諾設計。而西望洋山上有**西望洋聖母堂**，最早於1622年興建，1837年重建。現今所見的是1935年改建後的面貌。西望洋山是澳門高度居第三位的山丘，位於南灣南端，山上從前曾築有炮台。

大炮台位於大三巴遺址上的山峯，是十七世紀早期耶穌會教士築建的。一條秘密通道把大炮台與聖保祿教堂及其書院連結起來。這座炮台曾作澳督官邸之用。原本的**嘉思欄炮台**於1629年興建在南灣北端的海濱。1806年，英軍駐紮於此，1864年再加以改建。與此同時，連接嘉

思欄炮台的**聖方濟各修院**被拆卸，改為軍營，炮台亦被除去。**松山炮台**在1637至1638年間興建，矗立在全島最高的松山（東望洋山）上，山上有一座中國沿岸現存最古老的燈塔，建於 1865 年。

南灣的地形就如一彎新月，「馴服地倚傍在這個優雅而擁有漂亮弧形的海灣上」，艾林及賴特在他們於1843年的中國遊記中有以上描述。一列石牆依著海堤而建，間有缺口以便通往海灘。石牆後排列著高大的樓房及商用房舍。這一帶景物曾是藝術家鍾愛不捨的題材。如今，南灣已成為一繁盛地區，狹窄的街道充滿了賭博及娛樂場所。

傳說中，偉大的葡國詩人賈梅士，曾於**賈梅士洞**完成他的史詩《葡國魂》，此詩於1572年在里斯本出版，內容是有關瓦斯科·達·伽馬往印度之旅程。相傳賈梅士因其作品中帶有政治意味，於1557年流放到果阿，其後再放逐到澳門。1635年的耶穌會文獻，最早提及賈梅士曾踏足澳門，他們將矗立在內港北端的巨石稱為賈梅士石。在1840年，這裡發展成旅遊區，並加置了一座這位詩人的半身紀念銅像，現時位於白鴿巢公園內。

基督教墳場的所在地，原本是一個與賈梅士洞相連的花園。根據過往的教會規條，基督徒不能安葬於天主教的屬土上，而中國人亦不容許外國人在其地方築建塋墓。 1814 年，墓地委員會成立，其後澳督於1821年批准一位本地商人賣地予英國東印度公司興建墳場。此後很多重要人物如錢納利及從賽倫市和比華利鎮來澳的外國人都安葬於此。

媽閣廟位於巴勒山麓的海濱，是福建漁民為奉祀天后而在萬曆年間（1573-1620）建成的，漁民在一次風暴中順利歸航，並相信此乃託天后之庇佑所致。斯湯頓曾記道：「澳門有兩座中國人的廟宇。其一座落於一堆花崗岩亂石之上，十分奇特。此廟由三座獨立的建築相連而成，唯一的入口須行經一串蜿蜒曲折的石梯級。」[4]波塞爾（1808-1877）描述此廟為「我所曾遇見的最美妙的景物…幾乎每天都到此一遊，或是清早，整個廟宇都被陰影籠罩；或是黃昏，石、樹和屋脊都沐浴在餘輝中；或是中午，灼熱的陽光逼使我在廟宇內納涼…在這壯觀的廟宇內，一切都是那麼令人欣喜：它的布局、它在樹石襯托下如詩如畫的美態以及四周華麗的雕飾。」其他畫家如韋伯、巴普蒂斯塔和錢納利，都受這海濱一帶的石羣及媽閣廟景色所吸引。

⁴ 斯湯頓，1797，頁432。

4

A Plan of the City and Harbour of Macau   1796

England, B. Baker

Engraving

Sight: 69 x 52 cm (27 ¹/₈ x 20 ¹/₂ in.)

Hong Kong Museum of Art, *AH64.431.11*

澳門市及海港圖   1796

英國，貝加

鐫刻版畫

69 x 52 厘米 (27 ¹/₈ x 20 ¹/₂ 吋)

香港藝術館　*AH64.431.11*

This map was published by Sir George Staunton in 1796 and appeared in the Folio Volume accompanying his account of Macartney's embassy to China. He described the map as:

> A plan of the city and harbour of Macao, a colony of the Portugueze, situated at the southern extremity of the Chinese empire; containing references to all the forts, colleges, convents, and other public buildings and places of note; and also the depth of the water, and nature of the ground in every part of the inner harbour, as well as the space between the peninsula and the northern entrance into the Typa; taken from an accurate survey made by a gentleman long resident on the spot.[5]

此地圖是喬治‧斯湯頓爵士於1796年印製，並在他的馬戛爾尼出使中國記的對開本裏出現。他對這圖有如下描述：

> 此乃澳門城市及海港地圖。澳門地處中國版圖的最南端，其時屬葡萄牙殖民地。圖中載錄了所有城堡、書院、修道院、公共場所和其他重要設施的位置。又記載有內港的水深、河面的土質地形以及從半島到氹仔北面入口的距離。以上資料是從一位長居此地的人士實地勘察得來的。[5]

[5] Staunton 1797, pg. XVIII.

[5] 斯湯頓，1797，頁 XVIII。

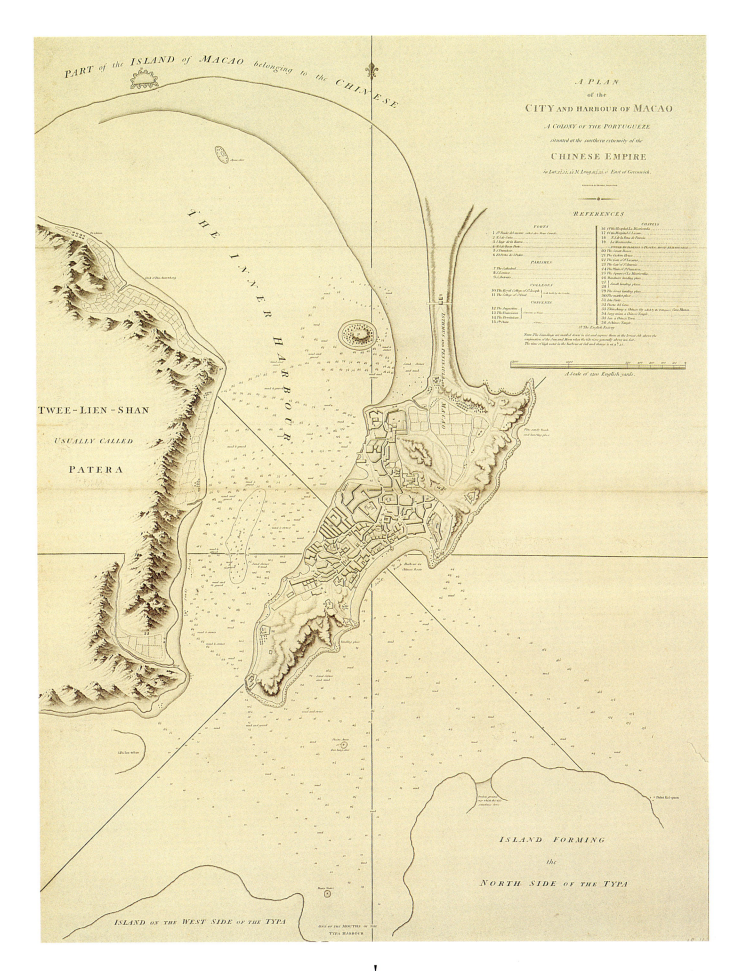

PART of the ISLAND of MACAO belonging to the CHINESE

A PLAN
of the
CITY AND HARBOUR OF MACAO
A COLONY OF THE PORTUGUEZE
situated at the southern extremity of the
CHINESE EMPIRE
in Lat.22.12.11 N. Long.113.35.0 East of Greenwich.

REFERENCES

THE INNER HARBOUR

TWEE-LIEN-SHAN

USUALLY CALLED

PATERA

A Scale of 1500 English yards.

ISLAND FORMING

the

NORTH SIDE OF THE TYPA

ISLAND ON THE WEST SIDE OF THE TYPA

ONE OF THE MOUTHS OF THE
TYPA HARBOUR

5

Amacao   c. 1598
The Netherlands, Theodore de Bry (1528 – 1598)
Copper plate engraving
Sight: 25.8 x 33.3 cm (10 $^1/_8$ x 13 $^1/_8$ in.)
Hong Kong Museum of Art, *AH81.21*

早期澳門全圖   約 1598
荷蘭，狄奧多・德・布里 (1528 － 1598)
銅版鎸刻版畫
25.8 x 33.3 厘米 (10 $^1/_8$ x 13 $^1/_8$ 吋)
香港藝術館   *AH81.21*

Macau is shown with the Fort of St. Francis in the upper left, the Praya Grande along the top, and Peñha Hill on the right. To the far right and bottom of the view, the inner harbour is filled with Western ships, while the connecting isthmus is at the middle left. Church towers are prominent and Westerners fill the town, being carried about in palanquins or followed by servants carrying umbrellas, the latter a motif which would symbolize Asia for the next two centuries. By the start of the seventeenth century there were about a thousand Portuguese residing here with several thousand Chinese Christian converts, mixed-race Christians, Japanese Christians and others.

Published: Hong Kong Museum of Art 1991, p. 52.
Related works: Cuthbertson 1986, p. 57, an example in the Derwent Collection.

此幅描繪澳門早期的面貌，左上方是嘉思欄炮台，隨著是南灣由左至右沿著海岸線伸展，直達西望洋山。下方的水域是內港，外國商船多泊於此。左邊中央位置是一狹地。圖中分佈著象徵教堂的鐘樓，也見到西洋人在城中四處蹓躂，並有僕人打傘，另外一些則坐在轎子內。其後的兩個世紀，打傘往往使人聯想起亞洲。根據記載，於十七世紀初期居住在澳門的居民，包括有約一千名的葡萄牙人、數以千計的中國、日本和其他種族的基督教徒等。

刊載書目：香港藝術館，1991，頁 52。
相關作品：卡斯伯森，1986，頁 57，參見德溫特藏品一例子。

AMACAO.

6

View of Macau with Dutch Ships   c. 1665

Holland, Johan Nieuhof (1618 – 1672)

Engraving

Sight: 18.9 x 29.1 cm (7 3/8 x 11 1/2 in.)

Hong Kong Museum of Art, *AH67.27*

澳門遠眺及海港上的荷蘭船隻   約 1665

荷蘭，約翰·紐荷芙 (1618 － 1672)

鐫刻版畫

18.9 x 29.1 厘米 (7 3/8 x 11 1/2 吋)

香港藝術館 *AH67.27*

The image, titled within the print "Makou", is a view depicting two Dutch ships in the harbour, one of which is firing a salute. The Praya is immediately behind, with details of the Franciscan Fort to the far right, Peñha Hill to the far left and other stylized Western buildings making up the town. The print is from the Dutch edition of Nieuhof's account of the embassy of the Dutch East India Co. to China from 1655 to 1657, published in 1665. Another image in this exhibition from Nieuhof's account is the view of Canton (no. 41).

Related works: Peabody Essex Museum, Nieuhof 1669, London edition, Phillips Library.

此件版畫刻有澳門的名稱。海面可見兩艘荷蘭商船，其一正鳴炮致敬。沿岸是南灣一帶景色，右方的嘉思欄炮台及左邊的西望洋山皆清晰可辨。城裏已建設了很多西式洋房。1655至1657年間，荷蘭派遣使節及東印度公司成員到中國洽商，紐荷芙將沿途所見事物記載下來，輯錄成書，於1665年出版。此圖是荷蘭文版的插圖。是次展覽另有一件紐荷芙描繪廣州的作品(編號41)，亦出自此書。

相關作品：皮博迪艾塞克斯博物館，紐荷芙，1669，倫敦出版，菲利普斯圖書館。

MAKOU.

7

View of Macau in China   c. 1800

England, engraved by Wilson Lowry (1762 – 1824) after the work of Duché de Vancy,
inscribed in the plate, lower right, "Lowry sculp."
Engraving
Sight: 17.1 x 22.5 cm (6 ³/₄ x 8 ⁷/₈ in.)
Hong Kong Museum of Art, Donated by Sir Catchick Paul Chater, *AH64.120*

澳門南灣景色   約 1800

英國，威爾遜‧勞里 (1762 － 1824) 依照范西公爵作品刻印。下方附有題識。
鎸刻版畫
17.1 x 22.5 厘米 (6 ³/₄ x 8 ⁷/₈ 吋)
香港藝術館，遮打爵士捐贈   *AH64.120*

The silhouette of St. Dominic's church and of the façade of St. Joseph's church are visible in this view of the outer harbour and the Praya Grande from the terrace of the Convent of St. Francis.

Provenance: Sir Catchick Paul Chater
Published: Orange 1924, discussed p. 288, no. 3, illustrated p. 302; Hong Kong Museum of Art 1991, p. 53.
Related works: Hong Kong Museum of Art has another nearly identical engraving (AH64.417) as this one. It is inscribed in the plate lower left "Dessiné par Duché de Vancy", lower right "Gravé par Masquelier", title "VUE DE MACAO EN CHINE", border "Atlas du Voyage de la Perouse H.O. 40" & "L. Aubert scripsit".

此處是由聖方濟各修道院的台階上眺望南灣景緻。遠方可看見板樟堂側貌及聖若瑟教堂，對開海岸是澳門的外港。

收藏歷史：遮打爵士
刊載書目：奧林奇，1924，內容詳見頁 288，圖版見頁 302 編號 3；香港藝術館，1991，頁 53。
相關作品：香港藝術館另有一幀雷同的版畫作品 (AH64.417)，刻記有標題、畫家及刻印者名稱。

8

Camões Grotto   late 18th century
England, Thomas (1749 – 1840) and William (1769 – 1837) Daniell
Aquatint, hand-coloured
Sight: 12.3 x 19.7 cm (4 ⁷⁄₈ x 7 ³⁄₄ in.)
Hong Kong Museum of Art, *AH64.420.10*

賈梅士洞   18世紀晚期
英國‧托瑪斯‧丹尼爾 (1749 － 1840) 及威廉‧丹尼爾 (1769 － 1837)
著色飛塵蝕刻版畫
12.3 x 19.7 厘米 (4 ⁷⁄₈ x 7 ³⁄₄ 吋)
香港藝術館   *AH64.420.10*

The print was produced by the Daniells after a drawing completed during one of their visits to the China coast in August 1785 or in the winter of 1793, and published as an unnumbered plate in *A Picturesque Voyage to India, by way of China* (London, 1810). The rock formation was first identified with the Portuguese poet Luis Vas de Camões in 1635 in documents in the Jesuit seminary, but there is no evidence that he actually visited Macau or wrote his epic poem *Os Lusiadas* there. Harriet Low, the young woman from Salem who lived in Macau between 1829 and 1833, described it as "a wild and delightful spot."[6]

Staunton illustrates the site and relates, "The Cave of Camoen, situated above the loftiest eminence in the town was constructed, probably, in the same manner as the temple above described [ie, the Makok temple], by bringing together a vast number of rocks."[7]   While the lookout platform visible in this and other views of the grotto existed in the 18th century, it was not until 1840 that the site was developed for tourism. Allom's illustration of this site placed it overlooking the ocean, and described it as "a rudely-constructed temple, standing on the brink of a precipice, and commanding a most glorious prospect over the peninsula, and the sea that embraces it...."[8]

Published: Hong Kong Museum of Art 1991, p. 55, no. 4.
Related works: Christman 1984, p. 98, an 1844 watercolour by George R. West (active 1844-1857), Caleb Cushing Papers, Library of Congress; Tillotson 1987, p. 115, no. 130, "The Camoens Grotto in the Garden of Mr. Drummond", engraving by W. G. Tilesius von Tilenau; Allom and Wright 1843, p. 42, an engraving; Conner 1993, p. 186, colour plate 65, an oil by Chinnery in a private collection.

[6] Hillard 1900, p. 34.
[7] Staunton 1797a, unpaginated.
[8] Allom and Wright 1843, p. 42.

畫家托瑪斯‧丹尼爾及威廉‧丹尼爾於1785年秋天和1793年冬天到訪中國，此版畫是依照他們在澳門所作的素描而刻製的，後來刊印在1810年倫敦出版的《經中國往印度繽紛之旅》一書中。根據1635年的一些教會紀錄，葡萄牙最享盛名的詩人賈梅士曾在該洞穴內完成《葡國魂》一詩，但究竟賈梅士曾否踏足澳門，至今仍是一個謎。從美國賽倫市來華的哈里雅特‧洛女士，曾於1829至1833年於澳門居住，她形容此洞穴為「一個荒涼但令人心曠神怡的地方」。[6]

斯湯頓亦有如下記載：「賈梅士洞建於城中高聳的山丘上，又如上述廟宇(指媽閣廟)般，是由大量的石料建造而成。」[7] 除了這幀畫作外，還有很多描繪賈梅士洞不同角度的其他作品，都是在十八世紀時期創作的。到了1840年，這處才發展成旅遊區。艾林亦曾以此洞穴為題作畫，並以汪洋大海為背景。他形容賈梅士洞是一簡陋的祠廟，然而地處懸崖之上，又四面環海，是俯瞰澳門半島景色的上佳位置…[8]

刊載書目：香港藝術館，1991，頁55，編號4。
相關作品：克里斯曼，1984，頁98，參見佐治‧韋斯特 (活躍於1844－1857) 於1844年的水彩畫作，顧盛的紀錄，國會圖書館；蒂洛森，1987，頁115，見編號130泰利西斯‧泰利流的鑴刻版畫「拉蒙德花園內的賈梅士洞」；艾林及賴特，1843，見頁42的一幅鑴刻版畫；康納，1993，頁186，彩色圖版65，私人藏品中的錢納利油畫。

[6] 希拉德，1900，頁34。
[7] 斯湯頓，1797a，無頁碼。
[8] 艾林及賴特，1843，頁42。

9

View of the Praya Grande from the North   1824

England, Captain Robert Elliot, R.N.

Pencil on paper

Sight: 40.5 x 88.5 cm (16 x 34 7/8 in.)

Hong Kong Museum of Art, Donated by Sir Catchick Paul Chater, *AH64.124*

南眺澳門南灣景色   1824

英國，羅伯特‧埃利奧特

鉛筆紙本

40.5 x 88.5 厘米 （16 x 34 7/8 吋）

香港藝術館，遮打爵士捐贈   *AH64.124*

Inscribed in the margin by a son of Sir J. B. Urmston: "Macau October 1824. Drawn by Capt. Elliot, R.N., my father's house with balcony", this view was taken from the north end showing the sweep of the bay and is a pair with another view from the south, also formerly in the Chater collection (p. 292).

At the south end of the peninsula (to the left) are the islands behind which is the Typa anchorage and just to the right, at the base of Peñha Hill, is Fort Bomparto.   The house with the balcony is the residence of Sir Urmston, President of the Select Committee of the East India Company at Canton. The large block, two houses to the right of Urmston's residence, is the Palaccio, followed by the East India Company's House, then the governor's residence with Fort St. Peter in front of it on the sea-shore. Continuing to the right is the Chinese customs office (demolished in 1849), which is signified by the flag post, and the Spanish Factory. The house to the far right is probably the residence of Sir Anders Ljungstedt, the last chief of the Swedish Company's Factory at Canton, who died at Macau in 1835; his portrait by Chinnery is at the Peabody Essex Museum.

Provenance: a son of Sir J. B. Urmston; Sir Catchick Paul Chater

Published: Orange 1924, discussed p. 292, illustrated p. 306, no. 17; Hong Kong Museum of Art 1983, p. 50, and 1991, p. 57.

畫的下方附有艾姆士敦爵士兒子的題識：「1824年10月，埃利奧特上校繪畫。(畫中可見)家父設有陽台的居所。」艾姆士敦爵士是廣州的東印度公司特別委員會的主席。此幅素描繪畫的地點是在南灣的北端，另外一幅繪畫於南灣的南方，是為一組，同屬遮打爵士藏品(頁292)。

畫的左方，是半島南端的島嶼，背後便是氹仔港。南環炮台位於其右的西望洋山的山麓。至於艾姆士敦爵士的居所，便是圖中有陽台的那一間。在它右方的第三間宏偉的建築是澳督府，然後是東印度公司大宅、澳督私邸及前方海濱的聖彼德小炮台。中國海關設立的稅館前方有一旗杆矗立，兩者皆於1849年撤去。接著是西班牙商館。最右方的應是廣州瑞典洋行總裁安德斯‧揚士達爵士的住所，他於1835年在澳門逝世，錢納利曾替他繪畫肖像，現藏皮博迪艾塞克斯博物館。

收藏歷史：艾姆士敦爵士之子；遮打爵士。

刊載書目：奧林奇，1924，內容詳見頁292，圖版見頁306，編號17；香港藝術館，1983，頁50 及 1991，頁57。

10

The Praya Grande 1825 – 1852
England, George Chinnery (1774 – 1852)
Oil on canvas
Sight: 26.7 x 45.7 cm (10 3/8 x 18 in.)
Hong Kong Museum of Art, Donated by Sir Robert Ho Tung, *AH64.10*

濠江漁歌 1825 － 1852 年間
英國‧喬治‧錢納利 (1774 － 1852)
油彩布本
26.7 x 45.7 厘米 (10 3/8 x 18 吋)
香港藝術館‧何東爵士捐贈 *AH64.10*

The vantage point taken here was chosen by many artists to make the best use of the dramatic sweep of the Praya Grande. The view from the north looks south-west from near the San Pedro Fort, with European-style buildings along the shore and Peñha Hill as backdrop. The harbour, the rhythm of turbulent waves and the activities of the Tanka fisherman as they set out across the bay, had long captivated Chinnery. He would return to this scene again and again as a subject. In this example, high winds are indicated by the flurried flag and the fishermen struggling against the waves. The dramatic effect of the dark boats in the foreground, which Chinnery utilized so well here, has been popular since the sixteenth century by Dutch artists in Macau.

Published: Hong Kong Museum of Art 1983, p. 58, 1987, pp. 68-69, and 1991, p. 60.
Related works: Tillotson 1987, pl. 30 and Cameron 1990, no. 18, for a similar oil in the Hong Kong and Shanghai Banking Corp.; Christie's Swire, Hong Kong, Fine China Trade Paintings, September 26, 1989, lot 979, a sepia pen and ink and pencil drawing of the Praya by Mary Dalrymple (fl. 1830s) after Chinnery; Gregory 1994 (64), p. 13, no. 21, a pen, ink and watercolour; Conner 1993, pp. 182-183, colour plates 61-63.

從這個角度描畫的南灣，構圖異常優美，是眾多畫家喜愛取景的地方。此圖是從聖彼德小炮台附近向西南方遠眺，堤岸上歐式建築整齊地排列，背景是西望洋山。灣港上律動的波浪，辛勤作業的漁民，都是錢納利鍾愛不厭的題材。是畫生動地刻劃出風高浪急及漁民在海浪上奮力前進的情景。錢氏並巧妙地以深沉的色調塗畫前方的小艇，與發亮的捲浪形成強烈的對比。自十六世紀開始，駐居於澳門的荷蘭畫家已廣泛採用這種技法。

刊載書目：香港藝術館，1983，頁 58，1987，頁 68 － 69 及 1991，頁 60。
相關作品：參見蒂洛森，1987，圖版 30 及金馬倫，1990，編號 18，香港上海匯豐銀行藏有一幅風格相近的油畫；太古佳士得 (香港)《中國貿易畫》，1989 年 9 月 26 日，編號 979，一幅由瑪俐‧達琳甫 (活躍於 1830 年代) 依照錢納利畫作而繪的淡墨、鋼筆及鉛筆素描；格雷戈里，1994 (64)，頁 13，編號 21，一幅鋼筆淡墨水彩；康納，1993，頁 182 － 183，彩圖 61 － 63。

11

View of the Praya Grande   c. 1830

China, unknown artist

Oil on canvas

Sight: 50.2 x 71.1 cm (19 $^{3}/_{4}$ x 28 in.)

Framed: 64.8 x 86.5 cm (25 $^{1}/_{2}$ x 34 in.)

Peabody Essex Museum, Gift of Mr. Russell Sturgis Paine, *M9,751.1*

南灣景色   約 1830

中國，畫家佚名

油彩布本

50.2 x 71.1 厘米 (19 $^{3}/_{4}$ x 28 吋)

原框：64.8 x 86.5 厘米 (25 $^{1}/_{2}$ x 34 吋)

皮博迪艾塞克斯博物館，拉塞爾‧斯特吉斯‧佩因先生捐贈   *M9,751.1*

This view shows Peṅha Hill in the foreground, Monte Fort right of centre and Guia Fort to the far right. Below Guia is the church and convent of St. Francis, part of which is visible in the drawing by Chinnery also in this exhibition (no. 18). This is one of the most dramatic and "Westernized" realizations of landscape painting by a Chinese artist.

Provenance: Russell Sturgis Paine

Published: Brewington 1968, p. 85, no. 374.

這是一幅中國畫家繪製的作品，風格十分西化，並有濃厚的戲劇效果。此圖前方是西望洋山，中央偏右是大炮台，最右端便是松山炮台。松山炮台下方有聖方濟各教堂及修道院，是次展覽亦包括一幅錢納利繪畫該處角落的素描(編號18)。

收藏歷史：拉塞爾‧斯特吉斯‧佩因

刊載書目：布魯因頓，1968，頁 85，編號 374。

12

View of the Praya Grande from a Porch   1840s

China, unknown artist

Gouache on paper

Sight: 35.8 x 47.3 cm (14 ¹/₈ x 18 ⁵/₈ in.)

Framed: 46.5 x 58.2 cm (18 ¹/₄ x 22 ⁷/₈ in.)

Peabody Essex Museum, Gift of Mr. Stephen Wheatland, *E82,717*

從遊廊上遠眺南灣   1840 年代

中國，畫家佚名

水粉紙本

35.8 x 47.3 厘米 (14 ¹/₈ x 18 ⁵/₈ 吋)

原框：46.5 x 58.2 厘米 18 ¹/₄ x 22 ⁷/₈ 吋)

皮博迪艾塞克斯博物館，斯蒂芬‧惠特蘭先生捐贈 *E82,717*

The view from the south of the Praya Grande was taken from the vantage point of a porch overlooking the harbour. This highly unusual perspective relates to the equally unusual vista of Canton taken from the roof deck of the British East India Company Hong, also in this exhibition (no. 59). All the architectural landmarks of Macau visible from this location are depicted in fine detailing.

Provenance: Stephen Wheatland

Published: Smith 1979, p. 10, no. 1999.

這是從一間住宅的遊廊上南眺南灣的景緻，圖中建築皆以細膩的筆法描繪而成，大部份澳門重要的建築都可辨認。此種取景方法，十分特別。是次展覽編號59的另一作品，是從廣州英國東印度公司的商館屋頂上俯覽珠江河南景色，其手法與此畫有異曲同工之妙。

收藏歷史：斯蒂芬‧惠特蘭

刊載書目：史密斯，1979，頁 10，編號 1999。

Sewing Table   c. 1835

China

Lacquer on wood, ivory, silk

73.5 x 61.1 x 41.8 cm (28 $^7/_8$ x 24 x 16 $^3/_8$ in.)

Peabody Essex Museum, Gift of Mr. and Mrs. Francis B. Lothrop, *E82,997*

女紅桌   約1835

中國

黑漆描金木桌，象牙及絲線配件

73.5 x 61.1 x 41.8厘米 (28 $^7/_8$ x 24 x 16 $^3/_8$吋)

皮博迪艾塞克斯博物館，佛朗西斯‧洛斯羅普先生夫人捐贈

E82,997

Ladies' work tables fitted with ivory accessories were highly desirable exports in the 19th century. The top of this example is decorated with a script monogram W for a member of the Wetmore family of New York and Newport, Rhode Island. The inside of the lid displays a view of Macau and the Praya Grande taken from the south-eastern point, high upon Peñha Hill. The church façades are easily visible. This table is from a suite of lacquered furniture made for the William Shepard Wetmore family, which was engaged in the China trade. In addition, the suite consisted of a bonheur-du-jour, three nests of small end tables of four tables each, and a large round centre table. Miscellaneous lacquered boxes for varied purposes also matched the suite; all were decorated with intricate scenes in lacquer and each has a script W in a circle in gold on the front or top.[9] Wetmore was first employed as a supercargo for his uncles Samuel and Willard Wright of Carrington & Co., Providence, Rhode Island. In 1833 he went to Canton where he further increased his business until 1847 when he withdrew from trade there, returned to Newport and built "Chateau sur Mer", one of the great houses of that city.

十九世紀時期，附有象牙針線工具的女紅桌是甚受歡迎的外銷品。此件珍品蓋面上刻記有一英文字母‘W’，是居於紐約和羅德島紐波特的偉特莫爾家族的標記。蓋子裏層以金漆描繪澳門南灣景貌，前方是其東南面的西望洋山高處。此桌子原屬一套漆器家俬組件，由從事中國貿易的威廉‧偉特莫爾家族訂製。其他組件包括一張迭櫥式寫字檯、三張小套几(每一小套几有四件桌子)和一張大圓桌，並配有各類漆盒，以因應不同用途。每個漆盒上都繪有繁密的景物，並在前方或上方記有‘W’字母，圍以金圈。[9]

偉特莫爾最初受其叔父塞繆爾及威拉德‧賴特聘用為營運主管，他們的卡林頓公司位於羅德島的普洛維頓斯港。1833年，他前往廣州拓展業務，直至1847年才撤回紐波特，並在當地建了一座大宅，名為「海上城堡」。

收藏歷史：羅德島紐波特的偉特莫爾家族；帕克‧伯尼特畫廊公司 (1969年9月16 – 17日)；佛朗西斯‧洛斯羅普先生夫人

刊載書目：克羅斯曼1972，頁175，編號145及1991，頁269，彩圖100。

相關作品：佳士得 (紐約)，1984年2月23日，編號76，是一件十九世紀早期的大漆器屏風，上有澳門城景色；吉默，1992，頁156 – 157，編號70，一件漆器衣箱內繪有澳門圖，並記有「澳門1776」等字樣；另外一件十七世紀描繪廣州的漆蓋，是巴塔吉尼亞‧賴斯藏品，見里斯本杰羅尼姆斯II，頁247，編號229。

Provenance: Wetmore family, Newport, Rhode Island; Parke-Bernet Galleries, Inc., September 16-17, 1969; Mr. and Mrs. Francis B. Lothrop

Published: Crossman 1972, p. 175, no. 145 and 1991, p. 269, colour plate 100.

Related works: Christie's New York, February 23, 1984, lot 76, a large lacquered panel; Guimet 1992, pp. 156-157, no. 70, the interior of a lacquered trunk decorated with a view of Macau and inscribed, "Macao 1776 Anno", and a related lacquer cover, collection of Bataglia Reis, dated to the 17th century and illustrating Canton, in Lisbon 1983, Jerónimos II, p. 247, no. 229.

[9] Crossman 1972, p. 175.

[9]   克羅斯曼，1972，頁175。

View of the Inner Harbour and Ma Kok Temple   1788

England, John Webber (c.1750 – 1793), inscribed in the plate lower left,

"J. Webber Fecit, 1788"

Soft-ground etching with sepia and grey washes

Sight: 28 x 40.6cm (11 x 16 in.)

Peabody Essex Museum, Gift of Mr. Stephen Phillips, *M10,471*

媽閣廟及內港景色   1788

英國，約翰·韋伯 (約 1750 － 1793) ，圖版左下方附有作者題識及年款

軟防蝕劑蝕刻版畫，棕色及灰色墨水

28 x 40.6厘米 (11 x 16吋)

皮博迪艾塞克斯博物館，斯蒂芬·菲利普斯捐贈   *M10,471*

The topographical aspects of this view, taken from the south, were of more interest to the artist than the activities of the Chinese figures who gather before the Ma Kok temple, or of the temple itself. Other artists were to draw similar scenes from the same vantage point, among them George Chinnery with his rendering of 1839.[12] Harriet Low wrote of this scene on October 18, 1829: "We saw a Joss house at a distance which formed a very pretty scene.... It stands among immense rocks and trees on the seashore." [13] Allom and Wright described the location saying that: "... the situation on the water-side, amidst forest-trees and natural rock, is inconceivably beautiful..." [14] Captain James Cook's party was anchored off Macau in December 1779 and again in January 1780; the pencil sketch for this scene, dated December 1779, is in the Hong Kong Museum of Art.[15]   The view, one of the first of what became a much-painted scene, was engraved by Webber in 1788 and published as a coloured aquatint by Boydell, London, 1809, in vol. 3, Chapter XI, of Captain Cook's Last Voyage. Webber was the official artist on the third Cook voyage and this view, along with one other, "The Residence of Camões where he wrote his *Lusiad* [sic]", were the only views of Macau published as a supplement, in the whole folio, in Webber's own, *Views in The South Seas*.[16]

Related works: Lothrop 1967, pp. 3-4, plate II, an oil by Chinnery; Gregory 1985 (40), p. 47, no. 54, a drawing by Dr. Thomas B. Watson; Hong Kong Museum of Art 1985, pp. 90-91, no. 39; Crossman 1991, p. 412, no. 5, a Lam Qua in the Peabody Essex Museum.

[12] Christie's Swire, (H. K.) September 26, 1989, lot 960, a pencil drawing.

[13] Low 1829, November 14, 1829, p. 86.

[14] Allom and Wright 1843, p. 66.

[15] Hong Kong Museum of Art 1987, p. 60, no. 15 (AH87.1).

[16] Webber 1808, Plate XII is the view including the supposed residence of Camões, and Plate XIII is the view of the Ma Kok Temple.

畫家對此地的山石地形甚感興趣，往北面遙望可隱約見到媽閣廟一角及岸邊的漁民。其他畫家如錢納利亦在1839年繪畫同一景色。[12] 哈里雅特·洛對此地景況有如下描述：「我們見到在遠處有一所廟宇，景色十分優美…它兀立在岸邊濃密的樹石叢中。」[13] 艾林及賴特亦有記載：「這地臨近海濱，給山石樹木圍繞著，漂亮之處，無與倫比…」[14]

詹姆斯·庫克船長及其船隊於1779年12月離開澳門，並於1780年1月重臨；香港藝術館藏有一幀繪畫此景的鉛筆素描，題有1779年12月的年款。[15] 韋伯於1788年將他的此幀素描刻印。1809年博伊德爾將其印製為設色飛塵蝕刻版畫，刊登於《庫克艦長的最後航程》第三冊第XI章裡(倫敦出版)。韋伯是庫克的第三次旅程中的隨團畫家，他另著有《南海風貌》，全書只有兩幅澳門景象收錄在補編中，其一是此地景貌，另一幅是「賈梅士的居所，他在此寫成《葡國魂》史詩」。[16]

相關作品：參見洛斯羅普，1967，頁3－4，圖版II，錢納利的布本油畫；格雷戈里，1985 (40) ，頁47，編號54，托馬斯·屈臣的一幅淡彩鉛筆畫；香港藝術館，1985，頁90－91，編號39；克羅斯曼，1991，頁412，編號5，皮博迪艾塞克斯博物館所藏一幀啉呱作品。

[12] 太古佳士得 (香港) ，1989 年 9 月 26 日，編號 960 鉛筆素描。

[13] 洛，1829，1829 年 11 月 14 日，頁 86 。

[14] 艾林及賴特，1843，頁 66 。

[15] 香港藝術館，1987，頁 60，編號 15 （AH87-1）。

[16] 韋伯，1808，圖版 XII 是描繪相傳是賈梅士的住所，圖版 XIII 是媽閣廟。

Protestant Cemetery at Macau 1843

England, John Prendergast (dates unknown)

Pencil on paper

Sight: 18 x 26 cm (7 ¹⁄₈ x 10 ¹⁄₄ in.)

Signed and dated on the reverse, "English Burying ground at Macao/By J. Prendergast Oct 1843"

Hong Kong Museum of Art, *AH88.37*

澳門基督教墳場 1843

英國‧約翰‧普倫德加斯特 （生平不詳）

鉛筆紙本

18 x 26 厘米 （7 ¹⁄₈ x 10 ¹⁄₄ 吋）

畫背附有畫家題識

香港藝術館 *AH88.37*

This view could be a cemetery in the English countryside as the technique, composition and subject matter are wholly European in concept. In 1814 a cemetry committee was founded and by 1821 the governor allowed a local merchant to sell some land to the British East India Company for a Protestant cemetry. The cemetery was established in 1821 for the Protestants of Macau as Ecclesiastical law forbade the burial of Protestants on Catholic soil, while the Chinese refused Western burials on their land.

The obelisk depicted here is for Captain Sir Humphrey Le Fleming Senhouse RN CB & KCH. According to the inscription on the monument, he died on board *H.M.S. Blenheim* at Hong Kong on the 13th of June 1841. The memorial stone was erected by the Officers of the Army & Navy early in 1842, and stands nearly four metres high. On the east front, Senhouse's coat of arms has been carved in low relief, and is visible in Prendergast's illustration. To the left, in the illustration, is the unusual monument for George Cruttenden (1768-1822), a cylindrical column surmounted by closed urn. To the right is a smaller stone surmounted by an urn, probably the one for Captain Daniel Duff (1802-1841). [See, Lindsay and May Ride, *An East India Company Cemetery*. Hong Kong 1996, pp.220-222, 225-226,245.]

Published: Hong Kong Museum of Art 1985, pp. 118-119, no. 53.

此景象與英國鄉間的墓園十分相似。而此圖無論在技巧、構圖及取材方面都具備了典型的歐洲風格。澳門的這個基督教墳場於1821年建成，原來教會的規條禁止基督徒死後埋葬於天主教的屬土上，而中國人亦不容許外國人安葬於其土地上。1814年墳場委員會成立後，澳督於1821年批准了一位本地商人賣地予英國東印度公司，並興建了此座基督教墳場。

圖中的方尖柱是漢佛萊‧森豪斯的墓碑。根據碑上的銘文，他是於1841年6月13日去世，這塊紀念石碑是海軍及陸軍軍官於1842年初建成，約四呎高。在向東的碑面上以淺浮雕刻有森豪斯的盾徽，並見於普倫德加斯特的繪圖。在它的左後方是佐治‧克拉登頓(1768－1822)的墓碑，形狀頗為特別，骨灰盒矗立在一樁圓柱體上。右方的石基面積較小，骨灰盒建於其上，應是丹尼爾‧達夫(1802－1841)的碑石。（以上資料詳見林賽及梅‧拉爾夫一書《東印度公司墳場》，香港，1996，頁220－222，225－226及245。）

刊載書目：香港藝術館，1985，頁 118－119，編號 53。

Chinese Figures and Boat Dwellings   1838

French, Auguste Borget (1808 – 1877)

Signed "Aug. Borget", and inscribed in French, "Inner Harbour, Macau"

Pencil on paper

Sight: 17 x 29.2 cm (6 ⅝ x 11 ½ in.)

Hong Kong Museum of Art, *AH84.8*

濠江艇戶   1838

法國，奧古斯特・波塞爾　(1808－1877)

附有畫家署名及題識

鉛筆紙本

17 x 29.2 厘米　(6 ⅝ x 11 ½ 吋)

香港藝術館　*AH84.8*

Two figures, perhaps engaged in business over a basket of fish, are shown in this view. Three men have stopped their activities to watch; one observes from the steps leading to a boat dwelling. Behind them another, carrying a fishing pole, walks by a dwelling perched high upon a stone wall in the background. This is one of two drawings of the exact same scene by Borget.[17]

Described by Borget as "aquatic streets", he was fascinated by these villages of old junks and sampans hauled ashore. In his writings he described how such communities are formed, how they were so crowded that, "It was impossible for a European, even when he sees it, to imagine how so many people can exist in such a narrow space". Yet, he also observed that there were flowers everywhere, faces "beamed with joy", and that whenever they had spare time the inhabitants engaged in games. Certainly, the sympathy and romantic tone of the drawing clearly indicates his admiration of the people living in this environment.

Published: Gregory 1984 (38), pp. 5-6; Hong Kong Museum of Art 1985, pp. 80-81, no. 34, and 1991, p. 65.

Related works: Hong Kong Museum of Art 1985, pp. 79-80, no. 33, another pencil drawing of houseboats in Macau, this one later lithographed by E. Ciceri; Hutcheon 1979, p. 7, another version of the same scene, Sotheby Parke Bernet, sold at auction, Hong Kong, December 4, 1978.

圖中二人蹲在地上，許是為面前的一簍魚兒議價。另外三人佇足觀看，其中一位正站在通往船屋的梯級上。遠方一位則揹著魚杆，在靠著高聳的石牆而興建的棚屋旁邊走過。波塞爾繪有另一幅素描作品，都是描寫相同景象。[17]

波塞爾目睹這些以舊帆船及舢舨堆砌而成的棚屋，深受吸引，並形容它們為「水上的街道」。他曾撰文記載這些住家艇的組成及其擠迫的狀況，他記道：「即使是親眼目見，歐洲人仍然無法想像得到這狹小的空間，竟能容納那麼多人居住。」 然而，他亦觀察到周圍種滿花卉，人們的面上總「帶著欣喜」，而當村民一有餘暇，即耍樂自娛。誠然，波塞爾對這些住家艇戶的欽佩之情，亦反映在他這幅帶有同情及浪漫調子的素描中。

刊載書目：格雷戈里，1984 (38)，頁 5－6；香港藝術館，1985，頁 80－81，編號 34 及 1991，頁 65。

相關作品：香港藝術館，1985，頁 79－80，編號 33，另一幅繪畫澳門住家艇戶的素描，後來給西塞里刻印為石版畫；哈其森，1979，頁 7，同一景象的另一版本，於 1978 年 12 月 4 日香港蘇富比拍賣行賣出。

---

[17] Hutcheon 1979, p. 7; the drawings are similar enough and yet disparate enough to warrant questioning whether or not both drawings are actually by Borget.

[17] 哈其森，1979，頁 7；兩幀素描雖然十分相似，但亦有很多不同之處，使人懷疑是否兩幀都出自波塞爾之手。

The Misericordia and Senate Square   1832
England, George Chinnery (1774 – 1852)
Pencil on paper
Sight: 11.7 x 17.8 cm (4 ¹/₂ x 6 ⁷/₈ in.)
Hong Kong Museum of Art, *AH79.1*

澳門仁慈堂及議事廳前廣場   1832
英國・喬治・錢納利 (1774 － 1852)
鉛筆紙本
11.7 x 17.8厘米 (4 ¹/₂ x 6 ⁷/₈吋)
香港藝術館   *AH79.1*

The façade of St. Dominic's church, one of Chinnery's favorite subjects, is seen to the left, with the Santa Casa de Misericordia on the right, and on top of the distant hill is Monte Fort. Inscribed in longhand and in shorthand in the upper left is the title as above and the date, "January 28th 1832."

Published: Hong Kong Museum of Art 1983, p. 51, 1985, p. 54-55, no. 21, and 1991, p. 61. Related works: Bonsall 1986, p. 91, no. 33, in the Toyo Bunko Collection; Gregory 1993 (61), pp. 13-14, no. 13; Peabody Essex Museum, M14,680, a similar view in pencil; Conner 1993, pp. 184-185, pls. 114-115.

板樟堂的正門是錢納利喜愛的題材，位於此圖左方。右方是仁慈堂，大炮台就在遠方的山峯上。左上角有題識及速記寫的作畫日期「1832年1月28日」。

刊載書目：香港藝術館，1983，頁51，1985，頁54－55，編號21及1991，頁61。
相關作品：彭傑福，1986，頁91，編號33，東洋文庫藏品；格雷戈里，1993 (61)，頁13－14，編號13；皮博迪艾塞克斯博物館，M14,680，是一幅類似景象的鉛筆作品；康納，1993，頁184－185，圖114－115。

The Misericordia de bens ti Igreia
Macao + 5r 28. 1832.

20

View of the Praya Grande from a Doorway on Peñha Hill   1834

England, George Chinnery (1774 – 1852)

Oil on canvas

Sight: 29.2 x 25.4 cm (11 ¹/₂ x 10 in.)

Framed: 39.6 x 35.8 cm (15 ¹/₂ x 14 in.)

Peabody Essex Museum, Anonymous Gift, *M17,053*

從西望洋山的石門外遠眺南灣景色   1834

英國‧喬治‧錢納利 （1774 － 1852）

油彩布本

29.2 x 25.4 厘米 （11 ¹/₂ x 10 吋）

原框：39.6 x 35.8 厘米 （15 ¹/₂ x 14 吋）

皮博迪艾塞克斯博物館，無名氏捐贈 *M17,053*

This painting is inscribed "View of the Praya Grande, Macao, from a Doorway on Peñha Hill". The date 1834 appears on a small plaque in the arch over the door.

There is an ink sketch of this doorway and the entablature over the lintel, as well as a separate enlargement of the entablature in the Victoria & Albert Museum, London (Vol. D17,2277-1928). The plaque in the enlarged entablature reads: "Anno Dei 1834" and the shorthand colour notes read, "A ground on which the pattern is orange and a white streak between the orange of the brick./ Brick/ The pattern is white on an orange ground./ August 30th 1834". (translated by Geoffrey Bonsall, Hong Kong).

Provenance: Christie's London, March 18th, 1977, lot 135.

Published: Arts of Asia, Sept/Oct 1977, letter from Francis B. Lothrop

Related works: Gregory 1985 (40), p. 72, no. 117, a pencil drawing by Elizabeth Watson, wife of Dr. Thomas Boswall Watson, and dated November 28, 1846, is nearly identical and must be a copy after Chinnery, possibly his working drawing for this oil study, rather from the finished oil itself.

此畫附有標題，而門楣上一拱形內的牌匾，則記有1834這個年份。

錢納利另有一幅墨水素描，是繪寫這度石門和門楣上的楣構，還有一幅楣構的近寫，皆藏於倫敦的維多利亞博物院(編號D17,2277－1928)。放大了的楣構內的牌匾上題有「Anno Dei 1834」字樣，並附有以顏色筆書寫的速記，內容如下：「背地有橙色的花紋，磚石的橙色紋樣之間有一白色條紋。/磚石/橙色背地上有白色紋樣。/1834年8月30日。」(速記由彭傑福繙譯)

收藏歷史：倫敦佳士得，1977 年 3 月 18 日，編號 135。

刊載書目：《亞洲藝術》，1977 年 9 月 /10 月期號內載有佛朗西斯‧洛斯羅普的信札。

相關作品：格雷戈里，1985 (40)，頁 72，編號 117，見屈臣醫生之妻伊利沙伯一幅鉛筆素描，寫於 1846 年 11 月 28 日，所繪景物與此油畫差不多完全相同，極有可能是依照錢納利原先為油畫所作的素描腹稿而繪畫的。

21

Steps of St. Lawrence   1841

England, George Chinnery (1774 – 1852)

Pencil and ink on paper

Sight: 22.9 x 21 cm (9 x 8 ¼ in.)

Framed: 42.6 x 40.1 cm (18 ⅛ x 15 ¾ in.)

Peabody Essex Museum, Gift of Cynthia G. Blackwell, *M20.516J*

聖老楞佐堂的梯級   1841

英國，喬治‧錢納利 (1774 – 1852)

鉛筆及墨水紙本

22.9 x 21 厘米 （9 x 8 ¼ 吋）

原框：42.6 x 40.1 厘米 （18 ⅛ x 15 ¾ 吋）

皮博迪艾塞克斯博物館‧辛西亞‧布萊克偉爾捐贈   *M20.516J*

Several street gamblers are seen in this view, looking north, to the steps of St. Lawrence Church. This sketch was probably the cover sheet to an album of views of Macau as it is inscribed, "Sketches in Macao, GC", and is dated [March] 18, 1841. The church, its dramatic stone steps and stone cross were popular subjects for Chinnery, who lived on the opposite side of the church.

Provenance: Frederick Welles Williams; Mrs. Garsten Blackwell

Related works: Gregory 1991 (57), p. 11, no. 17, an oil on canvas by Chinnery; and referencing there, Museu Luis de Camões, *George Chinnery - Macau*, 1985, Lisbon collection no. 22 (printed in reverse); Conner 1993, pp. 208-209, colour plate 81 and plate 143, an oil on canvas in the Hongkong and Shanghai Banking Corporation and a pencil drawing in the Geographic Society of Lisbon.

此圖前方三人圍在一起，似在賭博。其後方便是通往聖老楞佐堂的梯級。這幀畫作題有「澳門速寫」及錢納利姓名的簡稱，又標有(3月)18，1841的日期，故有可能是一本描繪澳門的風景冊封面。錢納利就住在這座教堂的對面，喜以這些石級和教堂上的十字架作為繪畫題材。

收藏歷史：佛雷德里克‧偉爾斯‧威廉斯；加斯滕‧布萊克偉爾夫人

相關作品：格雷戈里，1991 (57) ，頁 11，編號 17，見錢納利的一幅布本油畫；可參見賈梅士博物館 1985 年出版之《錢納利 — 澳門》，里斯本藏品編號 22 (印在背頁)；康納，1993，頁 208 – 209，彩圖 81 及圖版 143， 分別是香港上海匯豐銀行所藏的布本油畫和里斯本地理協會藏的鉛筆素描。

SKETCHES
IN
MACAO.
G.C.

22

Street Scene   1840 – 1845

England, George Chinnery (1774 – 1852)

Watercolour on paper

Sight: 20 x 16.3 cm (7 ³/₄ x 6 ³/₈ in.)

Framed: 40 x 35.6 cm (15 ⁵/₈ x 14 in.)

Peabody Essex Museum, Museum purchase, *M3,810.84*

澳門街景   1840 － 1845

英國，喬治·錢納利 (1774 － 1852)

水彩紙本

20 x 16.3 厘米 (7 ³/₄ x 6 ³/₈ 吋)

原框：40 x 35.6 厘米 (15 ⁵/₈ x 14 吋)

皮博迪艾塞克斯博物館，館方購藏 *M3,810.84*

Above the street scene of vendors one can catch a glimpse of St. Dominic's church, a subject Chinnery depicted in numerous versions from various angles. This watercolour was originally in the group of Chinnery's work collected by the American China trade merchant, Augustine Heard of Ipswich, Massachusetts.

Provenance: Augustine Heard

街道上有各式小販，遠方隱約見到板樟堂。錢納利常常從不同的角度描寫這座教堂。從事中美貿易的商人奧古斯丁·赫德，居於麻薩諸塞州的易普威治市，他藏有一組錢納利作品，這水彩畫原是其中一幀。

收藏歷史：奧古斯丁·赫德

23

The Façade of St. Paul's Church   c. 1845
Germany/America, drawn by W. Heine (1827 – 1885),
published by P. B. Duval & Co., Philadelphia
Lithograph, coloured
Sight: 15 x 22.5 cm (5 ⅞ x 8 ⅞ in.)
Hong Kong Museum of Art, *AH64.419.1*

聖保祿教堂遺跡   約 1845
德國 / 美國・海因 (1827 — 1885) 繪畫
美國費城杜瓦爾公司印製
設色石版畫
15 x 22.5 厘米 (5 ⅞ x 8 ⅞ 吋)
香港藝術館 *AH64.419.1*

Titled, "The Jesuit Convent", this lithograph shows the façade of the Church of St. Paul in Macau. In this view a parade of Western men, led by a figure who carries a cross, walk up the centre of the long steps leading to the entrance. The significance of this event is unknown.

Published: Hong Kong Museum of Art 1991, p. 66.
Related works: Hutcheon 1975, p. 76, another by Chinnery in the Victoria and Albert Museum, London; Cuthbertson 1986, p. 59, another example in the Derwent Collection; Gregory 1987 (47), p. 52, no. 79, and Conner 1993, p. 188, plate 116, a very similar view in sepia and ink over pencil by Chinnery, dated October 18, 1834 in the Museu Luis de Camões, Macau; Gregory 1993 (62), p. 41, no. 68, a drawing in pencil, pen and ink, and watercolour by Alexander Rattray.

此石版畫原來的英文標題為「耶穌會修道院」，描繪聖保祿教堂的遺跡。圖中一列隊伍，由一手持十字架的人物率領，朝著教堂門樓的方向，沿著梯級緩步而上。至於正在舉行甚麼儀式，則有待考查。

刊載書目：香港藝術館，1991，頁 66。
相關作品：哈其森，1975，頁 76，倫敦維多利亞博物院藏的一幅錢納利作品；卡斯伯森，1986，頁 59，見德温特藏的另一例子；格雷戈里，1987 (47)，頁 52，編號 79 及康納，1993，頁 188，圖版 116，錢納利的一幅描繪相同景物的棕色墨及淡墨鉛筆作品，繪畫日期是 1834 年 10 月 18 日，澳門賈梅士博物院藏品；格雷戈里，1993 (62)，頁 41，編號 68，亞歷山大‧拉特雷一幅鉛筆、鋼筆、墨水及水彩作品。

24

View of Two Bays   c. 1830

China, unknown artist

Oil on canvas

Sight: 50 x 71.5 cm (19 ³/₄ x 28 ¹/₈ in.)

Framed: 65.4 x 86.5 cm (25 ³/₄ x 34 in.)

Peabody Essex Museum, Gift of Mr. Russell Sturgis Paine, *M9,751.2*

澳門的南灣與內港   約 1830

中國，畫家佚名

油彩布本

50 x 71.5 厘米 (19 ³/₄ x 28 ¹/₈ 吋)

原框：65.4 x 86.5 厘米 (25 ³/₄ x 34 吋)

皮博迪艾塞克斯博物館，拉塞爾 · 斯特吉斯 · 佩因先生捐贈   *M9,751.2*

The view is of the peninsula of Macau from the south-west toward the mainland, with the Chapel of our Lady of Peñha on the hill to the right, and just to its left in the distance is the Praya Grande. Across the Praya on the hill beyond is the chapel of Our Lady of Guia. To the left, the inner harbour, with five Western ships at anchor in a row, leads the eye to the distant, small Green Island.

Provenance: Russell Sturgis Paine

此圖是從西南方眺望澳門半島，右方山上是西望洋聖母教堂，對開海岸是南灣，遙望遠山峯巒隱約見到東望洋聖母教堂（聖母雪地殿教堂）。左方的內港海面上，停泊著五艘西洋帆船，一直排列往遠處的青州。

收藏歷史：拉塞爾 · 斯特吉斯 · 佩因

CANTON

Middle Pagoda

Town Lang

Great Ladrone W.ly

Lyoui Town or Pagoda

Pagoda

CHIAMSHAN

OUT-TE-HEN

Tygers Island

Fort which Battery is Level with the water

Fort

TEMAON Pagoda ISLAND

BOCA TIGRIS

Byron Isle

HAY-TAYMAN BAY

Sugan Island

SIN-GAN-HEEN

HYANG-SEAN HEEN

the White Island

Cable Land

De Lintin and BAY

B, Off Macao it Flows N. and S. or 12 Hours at Full and Change; at Wampoe N.E. & S.W. or 3 Hours, and at Canton N.E. by E. and S.W. by W. or 4 Hours.

ISLE OF MACAO

Jin-chien-T

Baxos II

Harbor of Ly D.gra

BULLUNTUM Remarkable Table Land

Road

Chau Chequ or the Nine Hands

Jaqra

LINTOP

the Three Brothers

MACAO

Chang Chau

Orianche

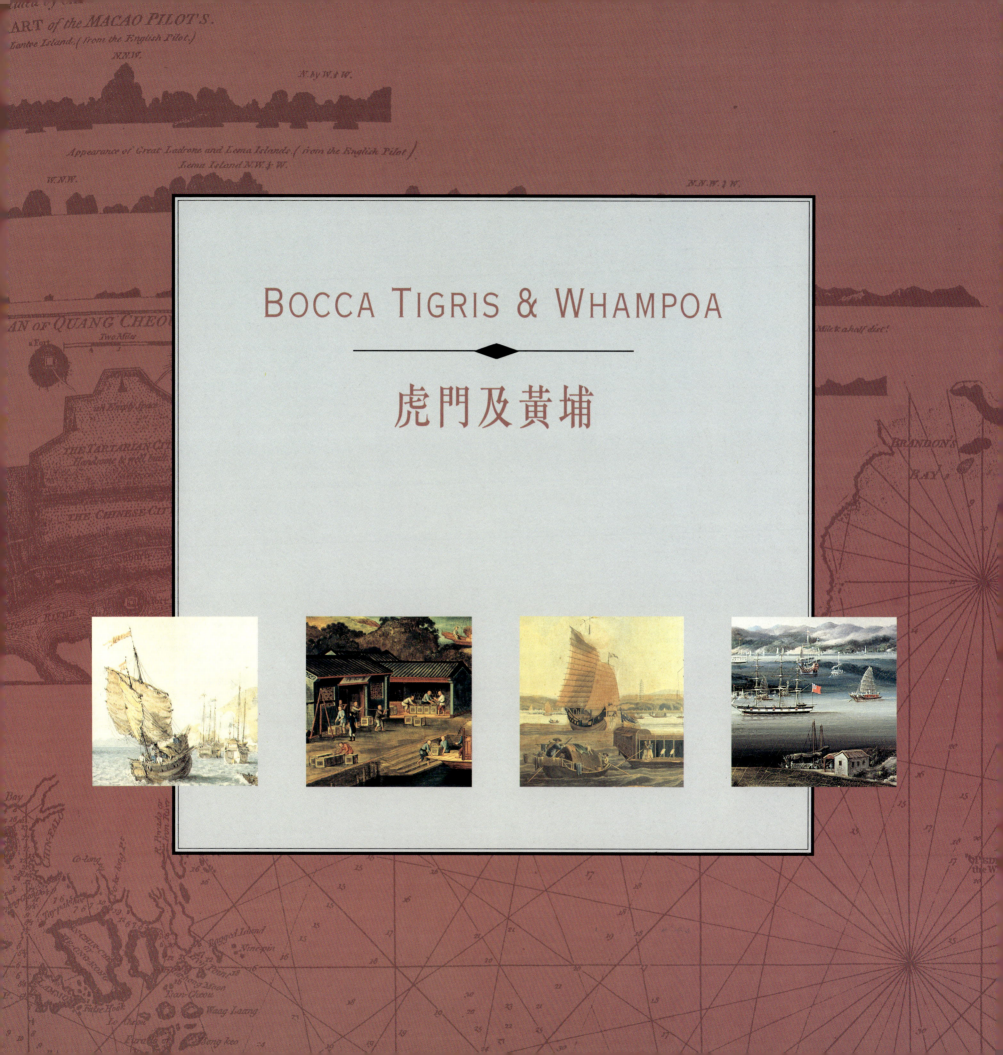

BOCCA TIGRIS & WHAMPOA

虎門及黃埔

III. BOCCA TIGRIS AND WHAMPOA

The island of **Whampoa** (Huangpu), which lies in the Pearl River seventy miles north of Macau and ten miles south of Canton, was the anchorage for all Western trading vessels at Canton. To reach the anchorage, Western ships passed a narrowing spot in the river called **Bocca Tigris** ("Tiger's Mouth", also known as the Bogue), thirty miles below Whampoa, on either side of which were the walled forts of North and South Wantong (to the west) and Anunghoy (to the east). The forts were there to protect the Chinese interests in shipping; and it was here that foreign ships would, before leaving Chinese waters, display for officials their permission-granting "grand chops". At Whampoa cargoes were loaded and unloaded and ships' crews were lodged while the captains and supercargoes resided at the Factories of Canton during the trading season. Most ships docked on the southern end of the island, although some small ships went as far as "Fiddler's Reach" in the vicinity of the Whampoa pagoda.

The Daniells, who visited the anchorage twice (in 1785 and in 1793) noted its "sweet, romantic scenery. Nothing indeed can exceed the beauty of the country in this vicinity".[22] In the 19th century, Osmond Tiffany, Jr., of Baltimore wrote: "This is about as unhealthy a quagmire as China affords, for the immense banks of alluvial mud, left dry at low water, give rise to pestilent, fever-breeding exhalations".[23] The paintings of the cemetery on nearby Dane's Island are a testament to those who succumbed to illness while there. But during their stay, "The foreign fleets form a sort of city in themselves...(the officers) visit and dine with each other, sail boats, amuse themselves with the Chinese, and brag of their ships".[24] By the middle of the 19th century the docks

and repair yards at Whampoa comprised the largest docking complex in East Asia, supported in particular by American companies. In 1846 John Couper, an Englishman, began to operate a dock on Fiddler's Reach for the newly-formed Peninsular and Oriental Steam Navigation Company; in 1856 Couper's son built a granite dry dock which still exists. Shortly after this, Western shipping was withdrawn from the dockyards. The docks, except for Couper's dock, were destroyed in January 1857 and never rebuilt which, in turn, only served to promote the development of Hong Kong.

One of the most notable and frequently depicted man-made landmarks in China was the **pagoda**; the pagodas visible along the Pearl River up to Whampoa and in the city of Canton would become familiar sites to all Westerners who traded with China. Nieuhof said, "China is very full of brave and Well-built Towers, whereof some are nine, others seven storeys high, many of which are only for Ornament....".[25] Although traditionally regarded by Westerners as a symbol of China, the pagoda form was derived from the stupa - an Indian Buddhist shrine known as a Dagoba, or Dhagoba, meaning "Relic Preserver". In China, where the first examples were constructed in the third century, pagodas have been erected in commemoration of unusual acts of devotion, as good omens, to improve the feng shui of the area, or merely as observation towers.[26] They were circular or octagonal buildings, generally of nine or seven storeys, and built of brick. The **Lotus Pagoda** (Lianhua Pagoda), constructed during the reign of Wanli (1573-1620), was a familiar view to sailors on the Pearl River, where it was visible through the ancient quarry which is now

[22] Conner 1986, p. 38.

[23] Christman 1984, p. 73.

[24] Ibid, p. 74.

[25] Nieuhof 1669, p. 227.

[26] Williams 1976, p. 305.

a garden and park land. The pagoda has been restored and is the centre of the mountain-top park. From the ship's log of the Marquis of Lansdown (1787-1788) we have this observation:

> As you go up the river you pass two pagodas or towers, first near Wampoa [sic] Town on your right, the other on the left about halfway. They have nine storeys and are octagons. The Chinese say they were as a Measure to the Roads, most probably they are watch towers, as they are built within sight of each other, all the way from Macau.[27]

The journal of sixteen-year old Caroline A. Stoddard, who accompanied her father on a voyage of the Kathay from New York to Sydney, Hong Kong, Canton and Shanghai between March and November 1856, she described her visit to a pagoda upriver from Shanghai:

> The Pagoda was but a little way off, and we soon reached it. It is seven storeys high, and one hundred and twenty steps up to the top. The stairs of course as you go up grow narrower and narrower until they are not much more than half a foot long, and the birds that have taken up their abode there, have rendered it, not the cleanest place in the world. But after you arrive at the top, I found I was repaid for my trouble. Oh! there was such a beautiful view, for miles and miles I could see, and it seemed as it were one vast garden. Not a spot but what was cultivated, as far as I could see, and in and out all over the land were little creeks running along, 'which lent the whole a charm.' Oh it was so beautiful I could have stayed hours looking [at] it, and there is hardly a tree to be seen, any where, but wher ever there is, it is considered such a luxury, that there is a perfect little village underneath it.[28]

Pagodas became perhaps the most easily recognizable symbols identified with the lure of China. Starting with the depiction of the so-called "porcelain pagoda" at Nanking (Nanjing) in an engraving of 1669 by Johan Nieuhof in *An Embassy... to China*, and ending with the inexpensive soapstone models made for the tourists of the later 19th century, the pagoda remains a popular motif with Westerners. The multi-storied buildings were replicated in many media including porcelain, mother-of-pearl, wood, various stones, and ivory. Full size pagodas were replicated in the West in many locations; the most famous, in England, is still standing at Kew Gardens and was executed after the original designs of William Chambers, while the "Chinese Pavilion of the Labyrinth Gardens" built in Philadelphia in 1823, is no longer standing.[29]

[27] Lansdown 1787, unpaginated.

[28] Stoddard 1856, unpaginated, entry for September 18, 1856.

[29] Conner 1979, pp. 92-93, 173.

III. 虎門及黃埔

黃埔是珠江河道上的一個小島，位處澳門以北七十哩，廣州以南十哩。所有外國商船往來廣州，都以此為泊碇所。在未到達此埠港前，外洋船須航經一狹窄的河道區域，名為虎門。虎門距離黃埔三十哩，左右築有炮台，西面有南北橫檔炮台，東面有威遠炮台，以保障中國在航運上獲取之利益。當外洋船離開中國水域時，須於此向海關關員呈閱附有印鑑的許可證明文件。在貿易季節期間，商船的貨物必須在黃埔起卸，船員亦須離開。只有船長及營運主管才可在廣州的商館區逗留。大部分船隻都停泊在黃埔的南端，體積較小的則泊往長洲島北岸，琶洲塔就在附近。

丹尼爾叔姪二人曾於1785年到訪黃埔，1793年重臨此地，他們形容這裡的風光「浪漫旖旎，無處可及」。[22] 然而在十九世紀時期，居於巴的摩爾的小奧斯蒙德・蒂法尼卻有如下看法：「這幅由中國提供的沼澤地，衛生欠佳，河堤上堆滿了沈積泥，潮退時則變得乾涸，致使熱病瘟疫叢生。」[23] 當時有不少的病逝者埋葬在附近的長洲島上，繪畫上出現的墳場就是最好的明證。但其實在他們有生之年，「外國船隊自成一閣……（官員）互訪及一同進膳、遊河、與中國人玩樂，又誇耀自己的船艇。」[24]

十九世紀中葉，黃埔擁有遠東地區最具規模的船塢，專門修理往來的船隻，美國公司在這方面貢獻良多。早於1846年，英國人約翰・柯拜在長洲北岸營建了一座船廠，主要承修大英輪船公司的船隻。1856年，其子建造了一座以花崗岩造成的大石塢，是現存的柯拜船塢遺址。後來，外洋船隻逐漸由黃埔撤離。除了柯拜船塢，其他的船廠都於1857年1月毀掉，而且不再重建。這樣便促成了香港的蓬勃發展。

神州大地，塔影處處。在通往黃埔的珠江河道及廣州市內，最為外國商人熟悉的莫如一座座矗立的古塔，它們是十分重要的陸標。據紐荷芙的記載：「中國遍佈宏偉而堅固的塔，塔高九層或七層，很多只是供人觀賞而已……」[25] 一向以來，外國人都把塔視為中國的一項象徵，但其實它是源自印度的佛塔，原文解作為「古蹟的保護者」。在中國建成的塔最早可追溯至第三世紀，用途廣泛，或為紀念某些豐功偉績而建，藉以改善當地風水，或只作為瞭望塔防守之用。[26] 塔身呈圓形或八角形，多為九層或七層高，以磚石築建。蓮花塔建於明萬曆年間（1573-1620），在珠江航行往來的海員可常常見到此塔。觀者可從一古石礦場處遙望覽賞，此石礦場現已改建成公園。蓮花塔曾重新修復，現高聳在公園的中央。

[22] 康納，1986，頁38。
[23] 克里斯曼，1984，頁73。
[24] 同上，頁74。

[25] 紐荷芙，1669，頁227
[26] 威廉斯，1976，頁305。

此外，我們可從"馬奎斯"號船 (1787-1788) 的日誌上獲悉下列資料：

> 沿江而上，你會遇到兩座塔，第一座出現在你的右方，近黃埔城，另一座在中途的左方。它們都是九層高，呈八角形。中國人說它們是用作丈量路途的遠近，而最大可能是作為瞭望塔之用，因從澳門的水道開始，二塔皆遙相對峙。[27]

卡羅琳·斯托達德於十六歲時曾跟隨父親乘搭"中國"號於紐約出發，途經悉尼、香港、廣州、上海等港口，時為1856年的3月至11月。她在日記中曾提及由上海沿河道上行時，曾遊訪一塔，其描述如下：

> 因路程不太遙遠，我們很快便到達此塔。塔高七層、共一百二十級石梯。梯級愈高愈窄，最後只剩約半呎闊。雀鳥到處築巢，也不免弄污了地方。可是，當你到達頂層時，你會發覺一切都是值得的。極目遠眺，外邊的景色是多麼的奇麗。無垠的平野，活像一個偌大的花園。一片片整齊無瑕的耕地，上有清溪縈繞，倍添意趣。如此美景，真箇百看不厭。周圍找不到一株樹木的蹤影，偶見一座小村落，已是十分難得的點綴品。[28]

塔往往使人聯想起中國。早於1669年，紐荷芙已繪有一幅南京瓷塔的畫作，並製成鐫刻版畫，刊印在《東印度公司使節團中國遊記》一書中。到了十九世紀後期，有以皂石製成的古塔造型，專供遊客購藏，價錢相宜。此後，以塔為題材的紀念品大受西方人士青睞。而製造這些模型的物料繁多，包括了瓷器、貝母、木、象牙及各種玉石等。亦有不少國家將塔原大仿製，最著名的莫如根據威廉·錢伯斯設計的一座，現仍佇立在英國的克佑花園內。至於在1823年建於費城的「迷宮花園內的中國亭台」，現已蕩然無存。[29]

[27] 蘭斯多，1787，無頁碼。
[28] 斯托達德，1856，無頁碼，1856年9月18日的日誌。
[29] 康納，1979，頁92-93及173。

Map of the Pearl River 1847

England, after Lieut. Martin, lithographed by T. Picken,

Lithograph

Sight: 47.7 x 32.5 cm (18 3/4 x 12 3/4 in.)

Hong Kong Museum of Art, *AH64.393.11*

珠江水域圖 1847

英國，根據馬丁上尉原稿刻製

石版畫，皮肯刻印

47.7 x 32.5 厘米　(18 3/4 x 12 3/4 吋)

香港藝術館　*AH64.393.11*

Titled in the lithograph, "SKETCH of the River CHOU-KIANG from the BOCA TIGRIS to CANTON", this map clearly depicts the landmarks that had been familiar to Western sailors since the official establishment of Canton as a trading centre by the Kangxi emperor. Additionally, set-in diagrams illustrate the city of Canton, the French Folly Fort and the destruction of the Keep on the 3rd of August 1847.

Lt. Martin was a member of the 42nd Madras Native Infantry and accompanied the British expedition during the hostilities of 1847. His drawings were published in 1848 as a series of eleven lithographs by Picken and entitled, "Operations in the Canton River in April, 1847."

圖上印有標題「從虎門到廣州的珠江流域簡圖」。自康熙將廣州開放成正式的通商港口後，珠江就成為西方人士航經之水道，圖上的航標已廣為人知。另外還包括廣州市圖、東水炮台圖和1847年8月3日某城堡被炸毀的圖樣。

馬丁上尉原是馬德拉斯當地步兵團第四十二分隊成員，在1847年英國強行進入廣州城事件中，他加入了英軍隊伍。馬丁上尉繪畫了一批素描，其中十一幅給皮肯刻印為石版畫，於1848年出版，題為「1847年4月於珠江的作戰行動」。

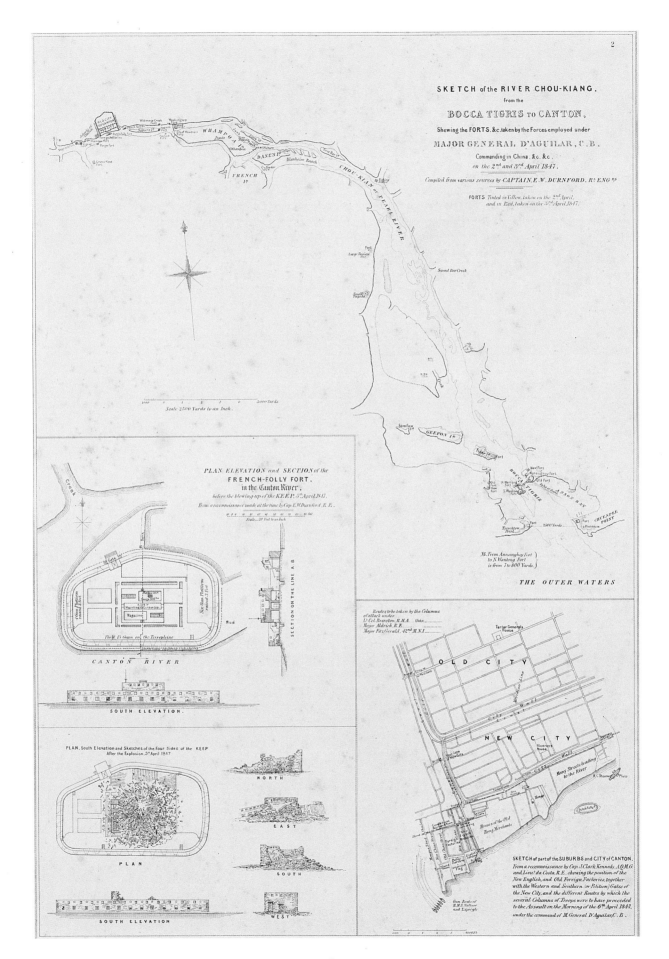

29

Dinner Plate c. 1745

China

Porcelain

22.5 cm (8 7/8 in.)

Peabody Essex Museum, Gift of Mr. Harry T. Peters, Jr., *E79,656*

餐碟 約 1745

中國

瓷器

22.5 厘米 （8 7/8 吋）

皮博迪艾塞克斯博物館，小哈里·彼得斯先生捐贈 *E79,656*

On the rim of this plate are two views, one of Plymouth Sound on the right, at three o'clock, and the other of the Pearl River on the left, at nine o'clock, each echoing the other in composition. The concept of using these two views most probably started with a service made for Commodore Anson in 1743 and was possibly designed by an artist accompanying his circumnavigation.[30] Plymouth Sound was originally illustrated with the lighthouse from Eddystone (destroyed by fire in 1756) relocated through artistic license to balance the composition.

Later versions of the Anson service, such as this example, depict these scenes in an altered form. The view of the Pearl River includes two pagodas, representing the larger Whampoa pagoda in the distance and the shorter pagoda on the island; there are seven Chinese vessels in the river and a group of ruins to the right. The central motif within the quatrefoil is most likely taken from a contemporary drawing of Fort St. George, Madras, the British entrepot between Plymouth and Canton.

This pattern was used in about twenty other services for the British market in the following decade, formulating the earliest export views of Whampoa. The arms at the base of the rim are of Mills impaling Webber, while the crest is of Mills. The service was probably made for the brother of William Mills of Clapham, Surrey, England.[31]

Provenance: Harry T. Peters, Jr.
Related works: Howard 1979, pp. 323-329.

碟沿繪有兩幀對稱的河道景貌。右方是普里茅斯海峽，時為下午三時正；左方是珠江景色，時為上午九時正。這項構思，可能始於海軍代將安森於1743年的環航旅程時，隨團藝術家為其餐具所作的新設計，[30] 為求畫面構圖對稱，此處的普里茅斯海峽加插了錯放位置的埃迪斯通的燈塔(於1756年燒毀)。

安森的餐具設計，後期款式就如此碟一般，兩幅圖象的位置是與前期的呈相反方向。珠江一景中有兩座古塔，遠方的是琶州海鰲塔，島上有另一小塔；河面停泊了七艘中國船艇，右方一堆頹垣敗瓦。碟心內的開光圖象應是依照當時一幅馬德拉斯港中的聖佐治炮台而繪，馬德拉斯港是普里茅斯及廣州之間的貿易轉口港。

在此後的十年，大概有二十件餐具採用這種款式，都是為英國市場而製，使我們得以欣賞到黃埔的早期風貌。碟沿的底部有一盾徽代表了米爾斯及韋伯兩個家族，紋章則是米爾斯家族的。這件餐碟相信是特別為英國薩里郡克拉罕市的威廉·米爾斯的兄長而訂製。[31]

收藏歷史：小哈里·彼得斯
相關作品：霍貨德，1979，頁 323 — 329 。

[30] Howard 1979, pp. 46-49, p. 325.
[31] Ibid., p. 325.

[30] 霍貨德，1979，頁 46 — 49，頁 325 。
[31] 同上，頁 325 。

The Forts of Anunghoy Saluting the *Lion* in the Bocca Tigris   1796

England, William Alexander (1767 – 1816),
signed and dated lower right. "W. Alexander 96"
Watercolour on paper
Sight: 25.4 x 39.8 cm (9 7/8 x 15 1/2 in.)
Hong Kong Museum of Art, *AH91.4*

馬戛爾尼使節團撤離虎門情景   1796

英國・威廉・亞歷山大 (1767 － 1816)
右下方有作者署名及年款
水彩紙本
25.4 x 39.8 厘米 (9 7/8 x 15 1/2 吋)
香港藝術館   *AH91.4*

This view is identified with an inscription on an old mount in an early hand: "View of the Boca Tygris, or entrance of Canton River. The *Lion* with Lord Macartney on board saluted by the Chinese Forts, on her passage to Macao."

William Alexander, official draftsman on the first British embassy to reach China (1792-1794) recorded in his diary that on 11 January 1794, the embassy's three ships passed by the forts of the Bocca Tigris en route from Canton to Macau, "the Lion saluting each Fort with 3 guns, which was returned by each and also the war junks". The Ambassador, Lord Macartney, was himself aboard the *Lion*, from whose cannon smoke is seen emerging; the smaller brig is to the right of the *Jackall*, and the view is presumably taken from the deck of the other brig, *Clarence*, on which Alexander was sailing at the time. The watercolour and its companion view of the *Lion* off Macau are perhaps Alexander's finest seascapes, combining breadth of composition with a sharp eye for detail.[32]

Published: Gregory 1977 (18), no. 6, 1981, no. 55 and 1991 (57), p. 20-21, no. 48; Legouix 1980, p. 80.
Related works: Legouix 1980, p. 80, a companion view of the *Lion* off Macau.

此畫作原本的舊裝裱上有如下記載：「這是一幅珠江河口虎門的景色，馬戛爾尼特使正在乘坐軍艦"獅子"號往澳門，岸上的中國炮台鳴炮致敬。」

威廉・亞歷山大是馬戛爾尼使節團的隨團畫家，這是英國第一次派遣使臣往中國，期間為1792至1794年。根據威廉・亞歷山大1794年1月11日的日記，使節團的三艘艦隻由廣州出發，經虎門往澳門，「"獅子"號向沿途的每一座炮台鳴炮三響致敬，並獲得各炮台和其他戰艦的回禮。」馬戛爾尼特使當時正在"獅子"號上，炮火的濃煙在船上冒出；在其右方是體積較小的兩桅帆船"積克柯爾"號。此圖取景的位置，應是在亞歷山大乘坐的另一艘兩桅帆船"克拉倫斯"號的甲板上。這幀水彩和其他描繪"獅子"號從澳門歸航的畫作，視野廣闊，筆觸細膩，可算是亞歷山大最好的海景作品。[32]

刊載書目：格雷戈里，1977 (18)，編號6；1981，編號55及1991 (57)，頁20－21，編號48；洛卡，1980，頁80。
相關作品：洛卡，1980，頁80，另一幀描繪"獅子"號撤離澳門的相連作品。

[32] Gregory 1991, p. 20, where it is noted that Lord Macartney's account of this event is published in J. L. Cranmer-Byng (ed.), *An Embassy to China*, 1962, pp. 217-218; the watercolour and its companion view are illustrated in Susan Legouix, *Image of China: William Alexander*, 1980, p. 80.

[32] 格雷戈爾，1991，頁20，記載馬戛爾尼特使曾在他的日記題及此事，克蘭默賓為其日記編輯及出版為《英使謁見乾隆紀實》，1962，頁217－218；這幀水彩和其他有關畫作，見於蘇珊・洛卡《威廉・亞歷山大的中國畫象》，1980，頁80。

31

The China Tea Trade   1790 – 1800

China, unknown artist

Oil on canvas

Sight: 119.7 x 182.2 cm (47 ⅛ x 71 ¾ in.)

Framed: 143 x 205 cm (56 ¼ x 80 ¼ in.)

Peabody Essex Museum, Museum Purchase with funds donated anonymously, *M25,794*

中國的茶葉貿易   1790 － 1800

中國，畫家佚名

油彩布本

119.7 x 182.2 厘米　(47 ⅛ x 71 ¾ 吋)

原框：143 x 205 厘米　(56 ¼ x 80 ¼ 吋)

皮博迪艾塞克斯博物館，館方以無名氏基金購藏　*M25,794*

Highly unusual because of its subject matter and enormous size, this synoptic depiction of the countryside and Whampoa Island illustrates all the stages of production in the tea industry, as well as shipping from the anchorage at Whampoa Island. The entire process of tea production is illustrated in story-book fashion. The landscape area is possibly meant to represent the Bohea Hills of Fukien Province, the primary tea-producing. Thomas Allom, wrote of this area: "Celebrated for the culture of the most delicious description of tea......"[33] At left foreground is a tea trading post. The horizontal tablets on the gate say Yihe Company. Four British ships are at anchor at Whampoa. The larger role of the British traders reflected in the painting echoes the role British trade took in tea sales. The East India Company of Great Britain exported more than 27,000,000 pounds of tea during the 1810 trading season, almost ten times more than the Americans.[34] This is one of three such works known of comparable size and is the only one known which depicts the entire process of tea trade in a single view. [35] Tea, the most popular and most profitable luxury goods, had always been a commodity and subject of great interest to Westerners. Watercolour albums of various sizes had already been produced for European merchants when this painting was executed.

Provenance: Found in England; The Gallery of Modern Art (The Huntington Hartford Collection), New York; Robert P. Holding, Jr., North Carolina; purchased from private American collection

Published (partial list): Choi 1979, p. 35, fig. 1; Berry-Hill Galleries 1979, cover and detail on p. 9; Howard 1984, no. C102, pp. 103 and 125; Keswick 1982, p. 109.

Exhibited: "Merchants, Mandarins and Mariners: 19th Century Paintings of the China Trade", Berry-Hill Galleries, New York, 1979; "19th Century China Trade Paintings", Berry-Hill Galleries, New York, 1983; "New York and the China Trade", The New-York Historical Society, 1984

Related works: Choi 1979, p. 34, a view by William Daniell (1769-1837), in the Yale Centre for British Art; Conner 1986, pp. 64-66, nos. 81-82.

[33] Allom 1843, pp. 175-176.

[34] Choi 1979, p. 35.

[35] See the painting of the same size in the Peabody Essex Museum (M25,000) depicting the production of porcelain, and most likely made as a companion piece to this view of tea production.

這是一幅珍貴的油畫鉅作，描述了在鄉間及黃埔島上的各種製茶工序，以及經黃埔水道運茶往珠江口的景象。整個過程以故事形式順序繪畫出來。圖中繪畫的地方應是福建省著名的產茶區武夷山。托瑪斯‧艾林曾盛讚此區出產了最優質的茶葉。[33]

此圖的左前方是一茶葉轉運站，上有一商舖名叫「義和行」。黃埔河道中正泊有四艘英國船，反映出英國在中西茶貿裏佔著一重要位置。事實上，英國東印度公司在1810的貿易季節裏，出口了多於27,000,000磅茶葉，差不多是美國出口數量的十倍。[34]

茶葉是外國人最喜歡的貿易商品，利錢亦最為豐厚。在這幀油畫出現之前，已有不少專為歐洲商人繪製的水彩冊頁。同類體積的畫作，共有三件，但描繪整個產茶及運輸過程的大型作品，現時只此一幀。[35]

收藏歷史：最早於英國發現；現代藝術畫廊 (亨廷頓‧哈特福德藏品)，紐約；小羅拔‧霍爾丁，北卡羅萊納州；於美國私人藏家處購藏。

刊載書目 (部分)：蔡，1979，頁35，插圖1；貝里‧希爾畫廊，1979，封面及頁9的局部圖象；霍貨德，1984，編號C102，頁103及125；凱瑟克，1982，頁109。

展覽：「商人、官員及航運者」：十九世紀中國貿易畫，紐約貝里‧希爾畫廊，1979；「十九世紀中國貿易畫」，紐約貝里‧希爾畫廊，1983；「紐約與中國貿易」，紐約歷史學會，1984。

相關作品：蔡，1979，頁34，威廉‧丹尼爾 (1769－1837) 的作品，耶魯中心英國藝術部藏；康納，1986，頁64－66，編號81－82，有關製茶及燒瓷的畫作，英奇凱普洛卡藏。

[33]　艾林，1843，頁175－176。

[34]　蔡，1979，頁35。

[35]　皮博迪艾塞克斯博物館有一幀同樣大小的畫作 (M25,000)，描繪陶瓷的製作過程，可能是此幅茶貿畫的相連作品。

32

The Lianhua Pagoda   c. 1793
England, Thomas Daniell, R. A. (1749 – 1840)
Watercolour on paper
Sight: 31.7 x 53 cm (13 ⅝ x 20 ⅝ in.)
Hong Kong Museum of Art, *AH88.40*

蓮花山城及蓮花塔   約1793
英國，托瑪斯·丹尼爾 (1749 － 1840)
水彩紙本
31.7 x 53 厘米 (13 ⅝ x 20 ⅝吋)
香港藝術館 *AH88.40*

Western merchants would have been familiar with this view from sailing past on the Pearl River as they pulled in to anchor at Whampoa. Here the artist has approached the Lianhua (Lotus) Pagoda through the ancient quarry, now a garden and park. Another watercolour of Whampoa by Thomas Daniell is inscribed "the Canton river. Taken in September 1793. Whampoa, Half Way and Canton Pagodas appear".

In 1787, the surgeon of the *Marquis of Lansdown* wrote in his journal:

As you go up the River, you pass two Pagodas or towers, first near Wampoa Town on your right, the other on the left about halfway. They have nine stories & are octagons. The Chinese say they serve as a Measure to the Roads, most probably they are watch Towers, as they are built within sight of each other, all the way from Macau. The Distance from the Shipping at Whampoa to Canton is about sixteen Miles.[36]

Published: Hong Kong Museum of Art 1991, p. 75.

西方商人應對此景象十分熟悉，因這是他們沿珠江航運而上往黃埔港泊碇前必經之道。此圖作者在古石礦場這一方繪畫蓮花塔，礦場現已成為公園。托瑪斯·丹尼爾另有一幅類似的水彩作品，他在畫中題識道：「珠江。繪於1793年9月，往黃埔的途中出現有中國式的塔。」

1787年，"馬奎斯"號船上的外科醫生在日記中寫道：

沿江而上，你會遇到兩座塔，第一座出現在你的右方，近黃埔城；另一座在中途的左方。它們都是九層高，呈八角形。中國人說它們可以用作丈量路途的遠近，而最大可能是作為瞭望塔之用，因從澳門的水道開始，二塔皆遙相對峙。由黃埔至廣州的航道約長十六哩。[36]

刊載書目：香港藝術館，1991，頁75。

---

[36] Lansdown 1787, p. 7.

[36] 蘭斯多，1787，頁7。

33

Whampoa Pagoda on the Pearl River   1830
England, Anthony Vandyke Copley Fielding (1787 – 1855)
Signed and dated lower left, "Copley Fielding 1830", inscribed on the reverse,
"Chinese Pagoda, between Canton and Whampoa/C. Fielding."
Sepia wash and watercolour on paper,
Sight: 11.6 x 18 cm (4 $^{9}/_{16}$ x 7 $^{1}/_{16}$ in.)
Hong Kong Museum of Art, *AH87.18*

珠江塔影   1830
英國，安東尼‧菲爾丁 （1787－1855）
附有畫家署名及畫背有題識
水彩及棕色墨紙本
11.6 x 18 厘米 （4 $^{9}/_{16}$ x 7 $^{1}/_{16}$ 吋）
香港藝術館　*AH87.18*

The Whampoa (Huangpu) Pagoda, built during the reign of Wanli (1573-1620), was one of the traditional "eight beautiful scenes" of Canton and a focus of attraction in the Panyu County in the Qing dynasty. Fielding has created a sensitive testament to the beauty of the structure and its setting; today it awaits restoration.

Fielding, one of the leading English watercolourists of his time, did not visit China himself. He, like other professional artists, was sometimes employed in re-drawing sketches made by amateur artists who travelled abroad. In this instance, the drawing was done from a sketch by Captain Robert Elliot, R.N., and from this an engraving was made by Thomas Jeavons which appears in Elliot's *Views of the East: India, Canton, and the Shores of the Red Sea*.[37] The description, derived from other sources as stated in the introduction, reads in part,

> The Pagoda that forms the subject of this Plate stands on the banks of a small creek that is connected with the main stream of the Canton river, and is situated about half way between the city of Canton and Whampoa, a distance of ten or twelve miles. By the Europeans at Canton, this building is recognized by the name of the Half-way Pagoda, in allusion to the situation which it occupies. There is something very graceful in the form of the Chinese pagodas, and they are usually placed in conspicuous situations, as if more intended for ornament than use.[38]

Published: Gregory 1987 (47), p. 63, no. 99; Hong Kong Museum of Art 1991, p. 85.
Related works: Hutcheon 1975, p. 108, a drawing by George Chinnery in 1831.

[37] Elliott 1833, Vol. II, opposite p. 1 under "Pagoda".
[38] Ibid., "Pagoda between Canton and Whampoa".

琶洲海鰲塔建於明代萬曆年間（1573－1620），琶洲砥柱是清代羊城八景之一，也是番禺縣著名的古蹟。菲爾丁以敏銳的觸覺刻劃了這座古塔的造型結構及四周思古幽情的氣氛。現時這座塔正待修復。

菲爾丁是當時首屈一指的英國水彩畫家，他未曾到訪中國。一如其他職業畫家一般，他也間中受聘重繪一些由旅居外地的業餘畫家所畫的素描作品。即如此圖，原本是羅拔‧埃利奧特的素描，後來由托馬斯‧杰馮斯製成版畫，印刊於《東方風貌：印度、廣州及紅海沿岸》一書中。[37] 他對此塔有如下的描述：

> 此圖的主要景象琶洲塔，座落於一小溪旁，溪水連接珠江的主流。塔位於廣州城與黃埔路程的中間，兩邊距離約十至十二哩，因此歐洲人又稱它為「中途塔」。中國的塔式造形古雅，常建於當眼之處，多用作觀賞，實際作用不大。[38]

刊載書目：格雷戈里，1987 (47)，頁63，編號99；香港藝術館，1991，頁85。
相關作品：哈其森，1975，頁108，錢納利於1831年繪畫了一幅相同景象的素描。

[37] 埃利奧特，1833，第二冊，頁一之對頁「塔」的部分。
[38] 同上，「廣州與黃埔之間的塔」部分。

34

Model of a Pagoda   c. 1800
China, unknown artist
Soapstone, nephrite, wood, brass, silk
56.5 x 20 cm (22 ³/₁₆ x 7 ³/₄ in.)
Peabody Essex Museum, Gift of Capt. Nathaniel Ingersoll, *E9,659*

古塔模型   約 1800
中國，畫家佚名
皂石，角閃石，木，黃銅，絲
56.5 x 20 厘米　(22 ³/₁₆ x 7 ³/₄ 吋)
皮博迪艾塞克斯博物館，納撒尼爾‧英格索爾上尉捐贈　*E9,659*

This model of a pagoda is one of the earliest Chinese objects presented to the East India Marine Society (the forerunner of the Peabody Essex Museum) by one of its members. The seven-story model, donated in 1801, is carved from soapstone. The brightly painted figures, Buddha lions, columns supporting each roof and ornate roof tiles which support the gilded wooden bells, are made of nephrite (white jade).

Very little is known about the donor, Nathaniel Ingersoll, who was from one of the first families to settle in Salem, Massachusetts. In 1801 he gave the museum "A beautiful model of a Chinese Pagoda" (no. 450), "a model of the foot of a Chinese lady of fashion" (no. 242), a Chinese box compass (no. 546), and another Chinese compass with calendar.[39] He was elected a member of the East India Marine Society in 1801 but is recorded as having left the Society very shortly thereafter.[40] The Ingersoll genealogy lists many Nathaniels, two of which are the most likely to be the one in question: one was baptized in 1778 and died before 1832 (no. 205, who had two children who died young) and another, who was unmarried and for whom there is no death date, born before 1744.[41] The earliest model of a pagoda brought to the United States was a four foot high model in ivory collected by Samuel Shaw, the supercargo of the first American ship to go directly to China, the *Empress of China*, which left in 1784 and returned in 1785.[42]

Provenance: Nathaniel Ingersoll
Published: Crossman 1972, p. 188, no. 157 and 1991, p. 305, colour plate 104.

[39] East India Marine Society Catalogue, 1821, cat. nos. 173-176, 242, 546, 617, and 650.
[40] Whitehill 1949, p. 161.
[41] Avery 1926, p. 26, no. 87 and p. 62, no. 205.
[42] Christman 1984, p. 68, in the Metropolitan Museum of Art.

這座古塔模型是東印度海事學會（皮博迪艾塞克斯博物館的前身）的會員於1801年的捐贈，亦是該會最早收到的中國藏品之一。此模型塔高七層，以皂石（壽山石）雕刻而成。塔內的彩繪人物、石獅、支撐著每一層屋簷的小圓柱及懸掛鍍金木鈴的飛簷，皆以角閃石（軟玉）雕製。

捐贈者納撒尼爾‧英格索爾是最早移居往麻省賽倫市的家族成員之一，生平不詳。根據記載，他於1801年捐贈給博物館的物品包括有「一座美麗的中國古塔模型」（編號450）、「一位趨時的中國婦女的足部模型」（編號242）、一個中國盒式羅盤（編號546）及另一件附有曆法的中國羅盤。[39] 他於1801年曾遴選為東印度海事學會會員，但未幾便離開該會。[40] 英格索爾家族史上曾出現過多位納撒尼爾，其中有兩位可能便是這位捐贈者：其一是於1778年接受領洗儀式，並於1832年前逝世（編號205，有兩子女早年夭折）；另外一位則出生於1744年之前，未婚，卒年不詳。[41]

最早運往美國的古塔模型是一件象牙製品，高四呎，由塞繆爾‧蕭收藏。塞繆爾是首隻往中國的美國商船"中國皇后"號的營運主管，商船於1784起航並於翌年回程。[42]

收藏歷史：納撒尼爾‧英格索爾
刊載書目：克羅斯曼，1972，頁188，編號157；及1991，頁305，彩圖104。

[39] 東印度海事學會目錄，1821，目錄編號 173－176，242，546，617 及 650。
[40] 懷特希爾，1949，頁161。
[41] 埃佛里，1926，頁26，編號87，及頁62，編號205。
[42] 克里斯曼，1984，頁68，紐約大都會博物館藏。

35

Covered Vegetable Tureen   c. 1812

China

Porcelain

16.6 x 29 x 26 cm (6 $^1/_2$ x 11 $^3/_8$ x 10 $^1/_8$ in.)

Peabody Essex Museum, Gift of Mrs. Gordon Abbott, *E63,199AB*

連蓋蔬菜湯盤   約 1812

中國

瓷器

16.6 x 29 x 26 厘米 （6 $^1/_2$ x 11 $^3/_8$ x 10 $^1/_8$ 吋）

皮博迪艾塞克斯博物館，戈登·阿博特夫人捐贈　*E63,199AB*

The service from which this tureen comes is unique in that the central motif is a pagoda. The standard central motif of the so-called "Fitzhugh" pattern is a pomegranate, although variations were numerous and popular, especially in the United Kingdom and the United States.

This service was made for Samuel Cabot, Jr. (1784-1863) and Elizabeth Perkins who were married November 2, 1812. Samuel Cabot, who was engaged in the China trade, became an active partner in the firm of his father-in-law (James and Thomas H. Perkins' Sons & Co., later Perkins and Company). Elizabeth was the daughter of Colonel Thomas Handasyd Perkins who also went to China in 1789, as a supercargo.[43]

Provenance: Samuel Cabot and Elizabeth Perkins; Mrs. Gordon Abbott
Related works: A platter and cover (E79,065AB) are in the Peabody Essex Museum; for other examples from the service see, Mudge 1962, p. 111, no. 39, in the Museum of Fine Arts, Boston.

此湯盤原屬一套餐具，中央的花紋是一座塔，風格獨特。常見的花紋應是一種所謂「菲茨休」的石榴果紋樣，有多種變化，是英美兩地的時尚設計。

這套餐具是為小塞繆爾·卡伯特(1784－1863)及伊利莎伯·珀金斯訂製，他們於1812年11月2日結婚。塞繆爾·卡伯特從事中國貿易，曾加盟其岳丈的公司（詹姆斯及托馬斯·珀金斯父子公司，後成為珀金斯公司），是一活躍的合夥人。伊利莎伯的父親托馬斯·珀金斯是營運主管，1789年往中國貿易。[43]

收藏歷史：塞繆爾·卡伯特及伊利莎伯·珀金斯；戈登·阿博特夫人
相關作品：皮博迪艾塞克斯博物館另藏有一個連蓋大淺盤(E79,065AB)；這套餐具的其他組件可參看馬奇，1962，頁111，編號39，　波士頓美術館藏品。

[43] Crawford 1930, p. 198.

[43]　克勞福德，1930，頁198。

Whampoa in China   1835

England, after a painting by William John Huggins (1781 – 1845)

Engraved by Edward Duncan (1804 – 1882)

Aquatint, hand-coloured

Sight: 36.7 x 59.8 cm (14 ³/₈ x 23 ¹/₂ in.)

Hong Kong Museum of Art, *AH64.405*

黃埔帆影   1835

英國，根據威廉・哈金斯 (1781 － 1845) 原作

愛德華・鄧肯 (1804 － 1882) 刻印

著色飛塵蝕刻版畫

36.7 x 59.8 厘米 (14 ³/₈ x 23 ¹/₂ 吋)

香港藝術館   *AH64.405*

Inscribed at the bottom, "WHAMPOA IN CHINA. Taken on the Spot by Mr. W. J. Huggins, Marine Painter to His Majesty and Printed expressly for John Morice Esq. This Plate is most Respectfully Dedicated to the Commanders & Officers in the E. I. Company's Service & also to the Commanders & Officers of the Ships trading in India. This View is taken from Danes Island looking towards Canton embracing Whampoa and Junk Rivers with the surrounding picturesque scenery and including Whampoa Pagoda and those near Canton". Many ship portraits by Chinese artists were taken from this same vantage point, with the pagoda usually placed to the left of the ship, just before its bow.

Huggins had sailed to China in 1812 and 1824, in the employ of the East India Company, before establishing himself as a professional painter of marine subjects. The oil painting from which this acquatint is derived was exhibited at the Royal Academy, London, in 1822.

Related works: Orange 1924, p. 156, no. 15, illustrated p. 175; Lee 1984, p. 33, another example in the Philadelphia Maritime Museum.

在圖版的下方，刻印有下列文字：「在中國的黃埔港，由皇家海景畫家哈金斯實地繪畫及專誠為約翰・莫里斯先生刻印。並誠意獻給東印度公司的軍官及官員，和在印度經商的船務部軍官及官員。此圖是自長洲島遠眺廣州，其中包括了黃埔及附近美麗的河道景色。圖中可見琶洲塔及鄰近廣州的塔。」中國畫家亦喜愛從此角度取景繪畫港口船艦景貌，並經常把塔的位置繪畫在船的左方，在船桅之側。

哈金斯曾受聘於東印度公司，於1812年及1824年往中國，他後來才成為職業的海景畫家。他的油畫原作於1822年在倫敦皇家美術學院展出。

相關作品：奧林奇，1924，頁156，編號15，解說於頁175；李，1984，頁33，另一件作品，屬費城海事博物館藏品。

37

View of Dane's Island Foreign Cemetery c. 1840

China, Sunqua (active 1830 – 1870), signed lower right

Oil on canvas

Sight: 34.5 x 82.5 cm (13 ⅝ x 32 ½ in.)

Framed: 46.4 x 93.4 cm (18 ⅛ x 36 ¾ in.)

Peabody Essex Museum, Museum purchase with funds donated anonymously, *M20,543*

長洲島外國人墳場一景 約 1840

中國，新呱 (活躍於 1830 － 1870)

右下方附畫家署名

油彩布本

34.5 x 82.5 厘米 (13 ⅝ x 32 ½ 吋)

原框：46.4 x 93.4 厘米 (18 ⅛ x 36 ¾ 吋)

皮博迪艾塞克斯博物館，館方以無名氏基金購藏 *M20,543*

This is a view of the cemetery and monument on Dane's Island with two American ships at anchor in the Whampoa anchorage and the pagoda at the far right. The large obelisk in the centre is the monument erected by the Governor over the remains of the Hon. Alexander H. Everett, the first United States Commissioner to China who died at Canton June 28, 1847 and was interred on the island June 29th. Many Westerners perished in the semi-tropical conditions of the Pearl River during the extended stays. Christian Westerners were given permission to bury their dead at this location, while not too far away was a second cemetery for Muslims. Today nothing remains of the stones in the Western cemetery except for two toppled obelisks, one that of Everett. The Chinese government is attempting to repurchase the tombstones which were removed for construction over the past century by nearby villagers. A few recovered stones now rest at the bank of the river, including several for Salem natives, awaiting funds for restoration.

While this painting and two similar examples may be signed or labelled Sunqua, the stylistic differences between them preclude the possibility that they are by the same artist. It appears that Sunqua created the master painting from which various examples were copied in his studio, where his name would then be added. While compositionally identical to the other two, this example has in the middle ground, below the obelisks, a long low tomb with a small pyramidal top. It is not known what this feature represents, and it may be a mistake of the artist copying an original.

Provenance: Kurt Dieninger, Boston

Published: Brewington 1968, p. 93, no. 415; Crossman 1991, p. 126, plate 46.

Related Works: Choi 1979, p. 44, an identical view also signed Sunqua, then in the possession of The Dietrich Brothers Americana Corporation; another in the Peabody Essex Museum, c. 1850, signed lower right, Sunqua.

圖中景象是長洲島上的墳場及碑石。黃埔港中停泊了兩艘美國商船，右邊遠方可見古塔一座。中央的尖方柱石碑是為紀念亞歷山大・埃佛里特而建，他是來華的第一任美國專員，於1847年6月28日在廣州逝世，並於翌日安葬在此島上。

很多西方人士因不能適應珠江流域的亞熱帶氣候，往往逗留此地過久而死亡。外籍基督徒被允准在此地安葬，離此不遠是一座回教墳場。現時在此座西式墳場內，除了兩台倒塌了的碑石外（其一為埃佛里特的一座），其他的已蕩然無存。有些是給鄰村的居民取去建房舍，而中國政府亦嘗試去購回這些墓碑。另一些則在河堤發現，其中包括了賽倫市的市民的墓碑，現正等待修復。

雖然此幅油畫與另外兩幅近似的畫作都有新呱的署名或標籤，但風格的不同，可明證出它們並非出自同一畫家手筆。亦有可能是新呱先繪一幅，再由其畫室的其他畫工依樣繪畫，再加上他的名字。這三幅畫佈局相同，而此圖中央則出現有一長形墓石，上有金字塔形頂，用途不詳，也許是抄繪時的錯誤。

收藏歷史：庫爾特・迪寧查，波士頓

刊載書目：布魯因頓，1968，頁93，編號415；克羅斯曼，1991，頁126，圖版46。

相關作品：蔡，1979，頁44，亦是一幅附新呱署名的畫作，景物相同，後來由迪特里希兄弟美國公司所擁有；皮博迪艾塞克斯博物館另藏有一幅約1850年的新呱作品，署名在右下方。

38

Whampoa Anchorage   c. 1850

China, Youqua (active 1840 – 1880s)

Labelled "YOUQUA" on reverse stretcher

Oil on canvas

Sight: 68.6 x 111.8 cm (27 x 44 in.)

Framed: 81 x 124.9 cm (31 ³/₄ x 49 ¹/₈ in.)

Peabody Essex Museum, Gift of Mr. Walter H. Trumbull, *M4,478*

黃埔船塢   約 1850

中國，煜呱 (活躍於 1840 － 1880 年代)

畫背支架上有畫家標籤

油彩布本

68.6 x 111.8 厘米 (27 x 44 吋)

原框：81 x 124.9 厘米 (31 ³/₄ x 49 ¹/₈ 吋)

皮博迪艾塞克斯博物館，沃爾特·特朗布爾先生捐贈 *M4,478*

In this panoramic view from Dane's Island, with the Protestant Cemetery in the centre ground, British, American and French vessels are seen anchored in Whampoa Reach. It has been suggested that the American ship with the red stripe in the middle distance could be the *Sea Witch* or the *Samuel Russell.* Beyond is Whampoa Island with its warehouses, town and pagoda. On the shoreline are the "bankshalls" or storehouses allotted to five trading nations, left to right, Britain, the Netherlands, Denmark, Sweden and Austria. To the left is French Island.

The composition of this view from Dane's Island was first used in the 1760s, in gouache on silk scrolls.[44] In early views the masts are stepped as required by Chinese authorities, as an indication that the ships would not easily leave port without paying customs duties. Ships with full masts must have been preparing to anchor or weigh anchor. By mid-century this was apparently no longer necessary.

Youqua painted several monumental port scenes with meticulously defined river, harbour and ocean waters; his delineation of boats and buildings was particularly distinctive. This work, one of a set of four highly important port paintings, has been described as one of the key works in the identification of Youqua's fine port paintings.[45]

Provenance: Walter H. Trumbull

Published: Brewington 1968, pp.91-92, no. 413; Crossman 1991, p. 137.

Related works: Gregory 1989 (53), p. 55, no. 101, a Chinese export gouache painting.

此圖是從長洲島遠望開去的黃埔景全圖，圖中央是基督教墳場，海港內則泊碇了美國及法國的商船。曾有人推斷中央紅色橫紋的美國船是 " 海上女巫 " 號或 " 塞繆爾·拉塞爾 " 號。海港後面便是黃埔島，島上可見岸邊的倉棧及遠方的市鎮及古塔。岸邊的倉庫分配予五個通商國家，由左至右分別是英國、荷蘭、丹麥、瑞典及奧地利。左方是"法國人島"。

此圖的取景方式，最早見於1760年代的水粉絹本畫上。[44] 在早期的畫作上，可見船桅上的帆大多放下，這種做法是順應清政府的規定，以防止船隻在未付清關稅前離開港口。如船桅上滿帆的，多是剛進港或正準備離開。但到了十九世紀中葉應再無此現象。

煜呱有多幅海港景象鉅作，精細地描繪了河流、港口及海洋不同的水域景貌；對於船隻及建築物的刻劃尤其了得。此畫原屬一組四件的油畫作品，在鑑定煜呱優秀的海港畫方面來看，此佔十分重要位置。[45]

收藏歷史：沃爾特·特朗布爾。

刊載書目：布魯因頓，1968，頁 91 － 92，編號 413；克羅斯曼，1991，頁 137 。

相關作品：格雷戈里，1989 (53)，頁 55，編號 101，一幅中國外銷水粉畫。

[44] For example, see Gregory 1987 (47), no. 33.

[45] Crossman 1991, p. 137.

[44] 例子見於格雷戈里，1987 (47)，編號 33 。

[45] 克羅斯曼，1991，頁 137 。

39

Fan   c. 1850

China

Lacquer, wood, white metal, paper, gouache

28 x 52.5 cm (11 x 20 ⁵/₈ in.)

Peabody Essex Museum, Gift of Miss Esther Oldham, *E46,494*

摺扇   約 1850

中國

水粉紙本、漆、木、白金屬

28 x 52.5 厘米 (11 x 20 ⁵/₈ 吋)

皮博迪艾塞克斯博物館，埃絲特‧奧爾德姆女士捐贈   *E46,494*

The obverse of this fan is decorated in gouache colours with a panoramic view of Dane's Island at Whampoa Reach, with East Indiamen anchored below. The village of Whampoa, with its two pagodas, is plainly visible in the background. On the reverse, fifty Chinese figures with applied ivory faces attend a theatrical performance. The fourteen sticks and two guard sticks are of black lacquered wood with gilt decoration.

Provenance: Miss Esther Oldham
Published: Crossman 1991, discussed p. 326, illustrated p. 325, colour plate 116.

此扇扇面以水粉顏料繪畫黃埔長洲島的全景，東印度公司的船隻在其下方的黃埔港口內泊碇，遠方可見到黃埔城的兩座塔。扇的背面有另一幅畫象，描繪了一群中國人正在欣賞戲劇表演，五十張臉孔以象牙繪製。首尾及中間十四條木扇骨皆以黑漆製成，並飾以描金花卉人物。

收藏歷史：埃絲特‧奧爾德姆女士
刊載書目：克羅斯曼，1991，詳述於頁 326，插圖頁 325，彩圖 116。

CANTON

◆

廣州

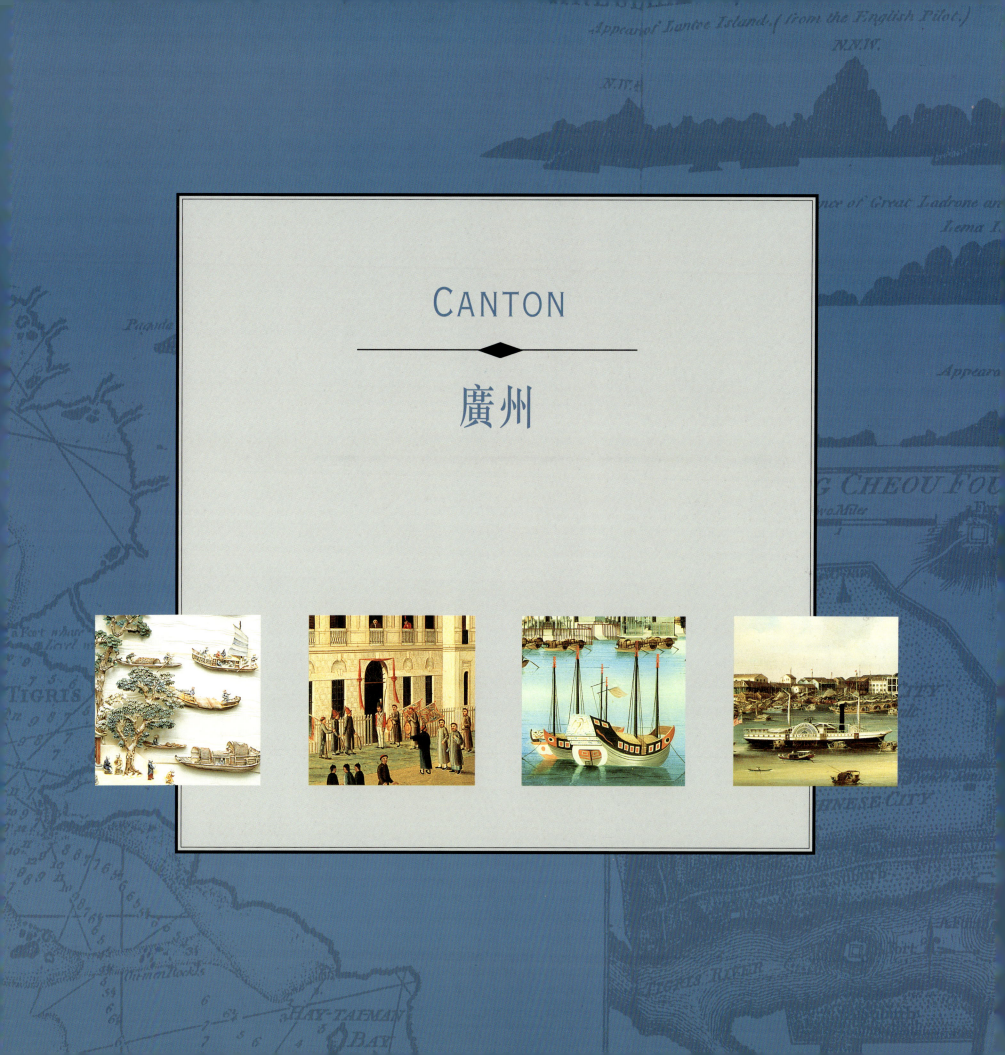

IV. CANTON

Perhaps the earliest view of Canton (Guangzhou) is the engraving after the 1655 drawing by Nieuhof, where the town was identified as "Quang Chew Fu, or Kanton". One of the earliest Chinese views of Canton documented in the West is the ink and colour Chinese painting in the Chinese Pavilion at Drottningholm, recorded as having been in the collection by 1777, and dating to before 1748, when the European warehouses were first built. This view shows the walled city from Honam Island with its two forts, later to be known as the Dutch and French Folly Forts, in the Pearl River.[46] Prominently depicted in both the Nieuhof print and the Chinese painting are the three major landmarks of Canton: the Mohammedan Tower, the Flowery Pagoda and the Five Storey Watchtower. A later scroll painting in gouache (c. 1760, in the collection of the museum at Göteburg) portrays the foreign Factories, while other sets, now cut into multiple elements, are in several collections, including the Peabody Essex Museum.

Canton had been, since the Tang dynasty, an important trading centre. Nieuhof described it thus:

> Canton is... surrounded toward the East, West, and North, with very Fruitful and Delightful Hills, and borders toward the South so very much upon the Sea, that on that side there is no part in all China so commodious to Harbour Shipping, where they likewise arrive daily from all quarters of their World, with all manner of Goods, wherewith they make a considerable gain... For three miles upon this River is this City of Canton walled in, and some places adorned with rich and populous Suburbs...[47]

In 1756 an imperial edict established what became known as the "Canton system". Foreigners were officially allowed to trade only at Canton, confined to a quarter mile tract on the river, to the south of the old city, outside the city walls. This area was described by Auguste Borget as "...the little spot which the sublimity of the Emperor has conceded to the barbarians". William Hunter described the area in the 1820s:

> The space occupied by the foreign community at Canton is about 300 feet from the banks of the Pearl River, eighty miles from Macau, sixty miles from Lintin, forty miles from the Bogue Forts and ten miles from the Whampoa anchorage. In breadth from east to west it was about 1,000 feet. On it stood the Factories which comprised the dwellings and places of business of each nation... The lower floors were occupied by counting-rooms, go-downs and storerooms, by the rooms of the Compradore, his assistants, servants and coolies, as well as by a massively built treasury of granite, with iron doors, an essential feature, there being no banks in existence. The second floor was devoted to dining and sitting rooms, the third to bedrooms.[48]

The thirteen two- and three-storey buildings rented by a country or trading company from the Chinese merchant who was responsible for them, were home, business and entertaining centre for the captains, supercargoes and other officers who stayed there during the trading season. The Hongs (the Chinese name for the buildings), also known as warehouses or Factories (after the business "factor" or agent who worked there) were rented annually for the

[46] Setterwall et al 1974, pp. 206-207.

[47] Nieuhof 1669, p. 36.

[48] Hunter 1882, pp. 20-21, 24.

duration of the trading season, usually about six months, although it was common to hire the same building year after year. The flags of their respective countries flew in front of the buildings. They were all destroyed by the fire of 1822 which started in a bakery and spread quickly. This devastating fire was a subject for local artists who produced "before, during and after" versions.

The Hongs were rebuilt immediately after the fire. The **Protestant Church**, which figures prominently in the landscape views, was built on land bought in May 1847. But the Hongs were burnt yet again in December 1856. The Westerners then moved to Honam Island (Henan, Honan), across from the former foreign Factory site where they worked out of the Godowns, or long storage facilities. Several years later they moved again, across the river to **Shamian** (Shameen, or "sand surface") Island, where an English and French concession was granted and European-style buildings once again were constructed for the conducting of trade. The French Catholic church, **Sacred Heart Church**, was built of granite between 1863 and 1888, on what is still the main boulevard.

Views of Canton were the most popular subjects with both Western and Chinese artists working for the Western market, not surprisingly inasmuch as this was the only city of China most Westerners would come to know and it was where they made their fortunes. Aside from the expected views on paper and canvas, images of this city can be found on porcelains (punch bowls and entire services), fans, lacquer and silver products. Not until the 1840s, after the first Opium War, were native street scenes commonly depicted by Westerners, although there had been a thriving trade for such illustrations by Chinese artists for about fifty years.

The three most prominent and permanent structures visible to the Westerner were the Mohammedan Tower, Flowery Pagoda and Five-Storey Watchtower. These, along with the folly forts, were invariably visible whenever the town was portrayed. Rarely were they depicted independently.

The **Mohammedan Tower** (Guang ta, also known as the Plain or Smooth Tower) was erected in the tenth century as a minaret for the Huai Sheng Mosque which, according to tradition, had been built in 627 AD by a disciple (and possibly an uncle) of Mohammed. One hundred and sixty feet in circumference at the base, the tower is an impressive reminder of the large number of Moslem traders who established the first sea-borne commercial relations between China and the West in the seventh century.

The **Flowery Pagoda**, a 270-foot high, nine-storey octagonal structure was erected by a priest in the sixth century and was originally topped by a copper pillar. According to legend, the Buddhist saint Bodhidharma, a missionary monk from India, and founder of the Zen sect, spent a night in the pagoda. Since then it is said to be miraculously free of the mosquitoes that plague the rest of Canton.

The **Five-Storey Watchtower** (Zhen hai lou, Pavilion Overlooking the Sea), was originally built in 1380 during the Ming dynasty. It burned and then was rebuilt in 1686 as a lookout post by the Chinese. In 1857 it was seized and used for that purpose by British and French troops and is now a museum of the history of Canton. The only existing portion of the old city wall can be found behind the museum, situated in Yuexiu Park. From here one can see the White Cloud Mountains to the north, often depicted in old views of Canton. Little remains today, other than these three major monuments, to remind one of the early days of the China trade.

A river fort built by the Chinese, a half mile down-river from the location of the Hongs, was known by the Chinese as "Pearl of the Sea". It had been occupied by Dutch crews during their embassy to China in 1655 and from that time it may have derived its common name of the **Dutch Folly Fort**. From the 1780s to the wars of 1856-7 it was often the subject of artists who visited Canton. It was dismantled after the battle of 1856-7 and the site is now reclaimed land, as is the site of the **French Folly Fort** (the origin for its name is not known).

The original site of the Hongs is now the People's Park. Several side streets such as Hog Lane and New China Street still exist, but the White Swan Hotel now occupies the later area of the Western trading concession on Shamian Island where it is surrounded by buildings in the French and English style which to this day give an idea of what it might have been like in the 19th century.

IV. 廣州

　　一幀名為"廣州城遠眺"的鐫刻版畫，可能是外國人繪畫廣州最早期的作品，它是參照紐荷芙於1655年所作的素描而繪製的。至於中國畫家採用廣州景物為題的作品，據西方文獻記載，是一幅自1777年便藏於瑞典德羅廷格爾摩一中國庭館內的設色水墨畫，繪畫年期更可追溯至1748年，當時歐洲人已開始在廣州設立商館。此幀中國水墨畫中的景物，是從河南島上眺望築起了城牆的廣州城，及珠江河上的海珠炮台及東水炮台。[46] 而在兩件作品中都清晰可辨的建築物是光塔、花塔及五層樓。隨後亦有一幅約繪於1760年的水粉畫卷，描寫外國商館景貌，現藏於瑞典越特堡的博物館內。至於其他集冊，已流散各地，其中部分為皮博迪艾塞克斯博物館收藏。

　　遠溯至唐代，廣州已是一重要商業貿易中心。紐荷芙有如下記載：

　　　　廣州是……給東西北三方壯麗的山川圍繞著，南端瀕海，利於
　　　航運，其有利位置非中國其他城市所及。每天外洋船接踵而至，貨
　　　品名目繁多，利錢豐厚……沿河行走三哩，可達廣州城，此外村落
　　　無數，皆繁盛富庶……[47]

　　清政府於1756年實行新措施，規限外國商人只許在廣州貿易，並只能在舊城以南城牆以外沿岸一帶地方活動，全長只有四分一哩。波塞爾

形容此為「大清皇帝賜與夷人的一小片土地。」而威廉‧肯特對這1820年代的商館區則有如下描述：

　　　　這一幅外國人佔用的地區，離近珠江堤岸約三百呎，距澳門八
　　　十哩、伶仃島六十里、虎門四十哩及黃埔港約十哩。由東至西此地
　　　約佔一千呎寬，上建有商館，供給外商作居住及貿易之用……下層
　　　作會計室及貨倉，亦設有主管、其助手、僕人和縴夫的房間，此外
　　　另有一間以花崗岩建成的錢庫，裝上鐵閘，以充替當時仍未設立的
　　　銀行。二樓設有飯廳及客廳，三樓則是臥房。[48]

　　這些兩三層高的建築物，是中國行商的物業，以租借給外國官員或商行作為商住用途。那些來華的船長、營運主管及其他官員在貿易季節便居住於此。這些「行」又稱為「商館」，每年在貿易季節的六個月便租借出去，大多數公司都會繼續租用同一座建築。商館外飄揚的旗幟，代表其所屬國家。1822年，商館因鄰近餅店失火而被波及，這場火災成為了中國畫家的描繪題材，並分為幾個不同的階段，有「大火初起」、「焚燒中的商館」及「火勢熄滅」等各種景象。

　　商館於大火後立即重建。畫中常見一基督教堂，建於一塊在1847年5月買下來的土地上。1856年12月，商館區再次被焚毀，外國商人惟有

[46] 塞特沃爾等人，1974，頁206-207
[47] 紐荷芙，1669，頁36
[48] 肯特，1882，頁20-21及24。

搬往對岸的河南貨倉區繼續經營。後來他們於1861年再遷往**沙面**，這是他們新取得的英法租界區，並於其上建造歐式洋房，作商貿之用。其後在該區的主要大道上，建有一座以花崗岩建成的法國天主教堂，名為**聖心教堂**，建築年期由 1863 至 1888。

廣州的景物，是最受中外畫家鍾愛的外銷繪畫題材。因廣州是大部分外國人唯一熟悉的中國城市，亦是外商賺取豐富利潤的地方。除了布本或紙本的畫作外，我們亦可在瓷器、餐具、摺扇、漆器及銀器上找到廣州的景貌。到了第一次鴉片戰爭後的1840年代，西方畫家才開始繪畫廣州的街道景色，而中國的外銷畫家早半個世紀前已大量繪製以街景為題的作品。

對外國人而言，廣州最惹人注目及最易辨認的建築物是光塔、花塔和五層樓，它們大多會與附近的炮台一同出現在畫作上，但描繪個別建築物的作品，則較為罕見。

光塔（又稱穆罕默德塔）於公元十世紀時興建，原屬懷聖寺旁的一所尖塔，以供報時人站立呼喚回教徒祈禱之用。相傳此寺院是由穆罕默德的弟子（或他的叔父）於公元 627 年建成。塔座圓周為一百六十呎。這座宏偉的塔樓令人回想起公元七世紀時，大量的回教商人到中國洽商貿易，拓立了中國早期與西方的海貿關係。

花塔是一僧侶於公元六世紀時興建，塔呈八角形，外觀九層，共二百七十呎高，塔頂原有銅製剎柱。相傳印度的達摩禪師曾在此塔中渡宿，自此廣州便免除了蚊患所帶來的疫症。

五層樓（又名鎮海樓），始建於明代1380年，經歷一次大火後於1686年重建成一防哨站。1857年，英法聯軍佔據了五層樓作瞭望守衛之用。現時該樓為廣州博物院所在。而現時僅存的舊廣州城的城牆遺跡可在博物院的後方得見，位於越秀公園內。從這裡向北眺望，可見到舊廣州風景畫中常出現的白雲山。除了上述提及的三座重要的古跡外，可供緬懷過去中外貿易的輝煌歷史的建築遺物，已所餘不多了。

在離開商館區下游約半哩長，有一座中國人興建的炮台，名為**海珠炮台**。在荷蘭使節團於1655年來華時，荷蘭船隊曾佔領此炮台，所以外國人多稱之為「荷蘭人炮台」。自1780年代至第二次鴉片戰爭（1856—1857）的一段時期，到來廣州的畫家都喜繪畫這座炮台，它於戰爭中被摧毀，該處現已填為平地。**東水炮台**（洋人稱為法國人炮台）亦遭同一命運。

商館區現已成為廣州文化公園，不少當時的街巷如新荳欄街和同文街仍然存在。往昔為外國人佔用的沙面租界區已興建成白天鵝賓館，但周圍仍見英法式建築，可令人懷緬十九世紀時期的風貌。

41

The City GUANG CHEW FU, or KANTON   after 1669
England, after a drawing by Johan Nieuhof (1618 – 1672)
Engraving
Sight: 18 x 29 cm (7 x 11 ¼ in.)
Hong Kong Museum of Art, Donated by Sir Catchick Paul Chater, *AH64.111*

廣州城遠眺   1669 以後
英國，根據紐荷芙 (1618 － 1672) 素描而刻印
鐫刻版畫
18 x 29 厘米 （7 x 11 ¼ 吋）
香港藝術館，遮打爵士捐贈   *AH64.111*

The dramatic view places Dutch ships in the most prominent position, as if to stress their importance and their greater familiarity to the artist, and may possibly represent the Dutch ambassador's ship *Roukerken*. In the distance the seemingly impenetrable city is surrounded by its crenelated wall with only three landmarks easily visible: the Mohammedan Tower, the Flowery Pagoda and, in the distant hills, the Five-story Watchtower. These three architectural wonders would become forever the visual references which would define views of Canton. The view itself dates to c. 1655 when Nieuhof visited China with the Dutch Embassy, which started at Batavia. The original book, in Dutch, was published c. 1665 where this scene is titled only "KANTON". This print's longer title is followed by "from Nieuhoff", and is probably from a volume on voyages published after the 1669 English edition titled, *Embassy from East-India Company of the United Provinces to the Grand Tartar Cham.*

The city gate forms the central focus for the scene as it was through these gates that all Westerners would pass to conduct trade; and it would be here, later in the following century, that the Western-style Hongs were built when Canton was designated as the trading centre for Westerners. To the right, in an area known later as Jackass Point, outside the walls of the city, close to the water, are the small buildings which may have been used initially as Factories, described by Peter Osbeck in 1751 as "... a general denomination of the houses built towards the river, or over it upon piles, and which are let by the Chinese to the Europeans during their stay". It may be these buildings which are depicted with some frequency on porcelains, as with the view depicted on the Lee of Coton service (no. 42).

Provenance: Sir Catchick Paul Chater
Published: Orange 1924, discussed p. 222, illustrated, p. 243.
Related works: Another example, in the original volume, London edition of 1669, the Peabody Essex Museum, Phillips Library.

畫家將荷蘭的船艦戲劇化地繪在圖中的最當眼處，以顯示其重要性，此船相信是荷蘭使節團所乘的＂勞克肯＂號。遠方見到的廣州城，給重重有城垛的城牆包圍，貌狀不能進入。而辨認得到的陸標有：光塔、花塔及遠山的五層樓，這三座古建築日後就成為廣州圖象的指標。

此圖原繪日期約是1655年，紐荷芙於是年跟隨荷蘭使節團，由巴達維亞出發往中國。後來他將沿途所見所聞刊印成書，最早的荷文版約於1665年印行，此圖當時的標題只是「廣州」，而這幅版畫的標題則較為詳盡，說明是參照紐荷芙一畫而作，應於是1669年英文版出版後才繪製的，書本的名稱是《東印度公司使節團訪華紀實》。

中央的城門是此圖的焦點，通過這度城門，西方商人便可進入中國進行貿易。一個世紀後，廣州正式成為通商口岸，西式建築的商館亦在此興建起來。在其右方城牆外河邊名為「牡驢尖」的一小片土地，可見一些小房舍，可能原先作為外國商行之用。1751年，彼得・奧斯伯克有如下的記述：「河岸上築建了一排排的房子，是中國人租借給逗留此地的歐洲人的。」

有些瓷器上的屋子圖樣繪畫的可能就是這裡的景象，其中一個例子是展品編號42的李氏餐具。

收藏歷史：遮打爵士
刊載書目：奧林奇，1924，詳述於頁222，插圖見頁243。
相關作品：另一作品可參見1669年倫敦出版的原冊，現存皮博迪艾塞克斯博物館菲利普斯圖書館。

The City QUANG CHEW FU, or KANTON *from Nieuhof*

42

Soup Plate c. 1733

China

Porcelain

4.1 x 22.7 cm (1 ⁵⁄₈ x 8 ⁷⁄₈ in.)

The Peabody Essex Museum, The Munson Campbell Collection, *E83,683*

湯盤 約 1733

中國

瓷器

4.1 x 22.7 厘米 （1 ⁵⁄₈ x 8 ⁷⁄₈ 吋）

皮博迪艾塞克斯博物館，芒森‧坎貝爾藏品 *E83,683*

A view of Canton, downstream from the Hongs with a folly fort and which predates the construction of Wesern buildings, is repeated twice in ink-colour on the rim, as is the view of London across London Bridge, with St. Paul's Cathedral figured prominently. The two views were compared by William Hickey, a visitor to Canton in 1769:

> The scene upon the water [in Canton] is as busy as the Thames below London Bridge, with this difference, that instead of our square-rigged vessels of different dimensions you have junks... Nothing appears more extraordinary to the eyes of a stranger at Canton than the innumerable boats of different sizes with which the river is covered for many miles together.[49]

The black enamel was developed at Jingdezhen by 1730 and was called by the Chinese *mocai*, or ink-colour; in that year the list of wares sent to the Yong Zheng emperor included "porcelain painted in ink colour". Technically, ink colour enamel is based on the German *schwarzlot*, an enamel decoration also inspired by engravings and used on European faience and glass during the last quarter of the 17th century. The technique has been previously referred to in the West as Jesuit ware, *en grisaille, encre de chine* or penciled ware. In the well of the plate are the arms of Lee of Coton quartering Astley of Staffordshire.[50] The service was made for Eldred Lancelot Lee (1650-1734), of Coton, who died in 1734, or his son Lancelot.

Provenance: Eldred Lancelot Lee of Coton, or his son; Heirloom and Howard, Ltd.; Munson Campbell
Related works: Howard 1974a, p.329, no. 35; Howard 1974b, fig. 4a; Howard and Ayers 1978, Vol. 1, pp. 204-205, the Mottahedeh Collection; Howard 1994, p. 68, no. 46, the Hodroff Collection; Godden 1979, frontispiece; Conger and Rollins 1991, pp. 256-258, no. 156, Diplomatic Reception Rooms of the U.S. State Department; Phillips 1956, pp. 12-13, Metropolitan Museum of Art, New York.

[49] Phillips 1956, pp. 12-13.
[50] Howard 1974a, p. 329; Howard and Ayers 1978, vol. 1, pp. 204-205

此湯盤沿邊以墨彩繪了兩幀相同的廣州珠江下遊景色，岸上可見早期的商行，其時仍未有西式建築出現，河上有一座炮台。另外兩幀重複的景物則是倫敦市景貌，聖保祿教堂十分顯眼，倫敦橋就在前方。威廉‧希基於1769年訪遊廣州城時，曾對這兩個城市作出下列比較：

> （廣州）河道景色，就如倫敦橋下的泰晤士河一般繁盛，唯一不同的是我們有的是不同大小的橫帆船，而你們有的是中國帆船…對剛抵廣州的新訪客來說，長河上綿延千里的無數大大小小的船艇景貌，令人歎為觀止。[49]

黑彩琺瑯是於1730年在景德鎮開始燒製，稱為「墨彩」，是年進貢雍正的瓷器包括「墨彩繪瓷」。這種墨彩技法，源自德國，那是一種十七世紀末期受鐫刻版畫影響而應用於歐洲彩陶和玻璃器皿的琺瑯裝飾。昔日西洋人稱之為「教士琺瑯」、「單灰色琺瑯」、「墨色琺瑯」或「鉛芯色琺瑯」。湯盤中央紋飾為科都李氏家族的盾徽，他們居於斯塔福德郡的阿斯特尼。[50] 這套餐具可能是為埃爾德雷德‧李（1650－1734）或其子蘭斯洛特燒製。

收藏歷史：埃爾德雷德‧李或其兒子；霍貨德公司；芒森‧坎貝爾。
相關作品：霍貨德1974a，頁329，編號35；霍貨德，1974b，圖4a；霍貨德及艾爾斯，1978，第1冊，頁204－205，莫特赫德藏品；霍貨德，1994，頁68，編號46，霍佐夫藏品；戈丹，1979，卷首插圖；康格及羅林斯，1991，頁256－258，編號156，現存美國州政府外交接待室；菲利普斯，1956，頁12－13，紐約大都會博物館。

[49] 菲利普斯，1956，頁12－13。
[50] 霍貨德1974a，頁329；霍貨德及文爾斯，1978，第一冊，頁204－205。

43

Punch bowl   c. 1788

China

Porcelain

16 x 40.5 cm (6 ^{1}/$_4$ x 15 ^{7}/$_8$ in.)

Peabody Essex Museum, Gift of the Estate of Mr. Harry T. Peters, Jr., *E81,407*

水果酒盌   約1788

中國

瓷器

16 x 40.5 厘米 (6^1/$_4$ x 15^7/$_8$ 吋)

皮博迪艾塞克斯博物館，小哈里・彼得斯捐贈   *E81,407*

Punch bowls decorated with the foreign Factory site at Canton were popular between about 1760 and 1800.[51] Commonly called "Hong bowls" today, the only period reference we have is the 1785 invoice for the purchase by Captain Green of the *Empress of China*, of "4 Factory painted Bowles @ 5 ^{1}/$_2$p - $22." [52] On these bowls, the foreign area was depicted either as a continuous view or in panels, mostly in polychrome enamels and very rarely in ink-colour, as with the other bowl in this exhibition (no. 45). This example displays a continuous view of the Hongs. The Dutch and British flags are seen in front of their respective Factories, while various Westerners observe from balconies, enter or leave various Factories and one strolls in the walkway in front with his pet dog. The continuous scenes came into fashion about 1780. The small boats used for transporting goods to the ships at Whampoa line the dock, and the pilings on which everything has been built are easily visible. Although such scenes must be somewhat idealised, life in this compact community has no doubt been well documented.

Provenance: Harry T. Peters, Jr.

Exhibited: "Winter Antiques Show: China Trade Edition", 1983, cat. no. 7, p. 34; "Highlights of the China Trade Museum", Peabody Museum of Salem, October 1984 - May 1985.

Related Works: Scheurleer 1974, fig. 54; Palmer 1976, p. 31, fig. 3, in the Winterthur Collection; Schiffer 1980, p. 193; Mudge 1981, p. 135, figs. 41a-c; Lee 1984, p. 206, no. 230; Le Corbeiller 1974, pp. 115-117, no. 49; Howard 1994, p. 200, no. 233, in the Hodroff Collection. See Choi 1979, pp. 48-50, where there is discussed a very similar bowl with the interior decorated with a ship with an American flag aft and the monogram BGE above the ship, for Benjamin George Eyre, who served with George Washington at the Battle of Princeton.

在1760至1800年期間，繪有廣州商館景貌的水果混合酒盌十分流行，[51] 外國人通常稱它們為「行盌」。唯一可作年份參考的文件是一幀1785年的發票，是「中國皇后」號格林船長所購買的「四個商館紋樣的盌，每個五仙半至廿二元」。[52] 盌上的商館紋樣，以相連或開光形式繪畫，大多以彩色琺瑯料繪製，甚少採用墨色（如另一展品，編號45）。此盌上的商館圖樣圍繪在碗身上，荷蘭及英國的國旗在其所屬的商行前飛揚。洋人在遊廊上上下顧盼，而下層各人則自由進出，通道上有人帶著小狗漫步。這種迴環式的紋樣設計，於1780年前後最為流行。河上的小艇整齊地排列著，準備運載貨物以接駁停泊於黃埔港的大船。層層疊疊的貨品清晰可見。雖然此等景象在畫中給美化了，無疑地繁忙熱鬧的商埠百態已活靈活現地繪錄下來。

收藏歷史：小哈里・彼得斯
刊載書目：冬季文物展：中國貿易篇，1983，頁34，編號7。
展覽："中國貿易博物館精選"，塞林市皮博迪博物館，1984年10月至1985年5月。
相關作品：謝爾里爾，1974，圖54；帕爾默，1976，頁31，圖3，溫特費爾藏品；希佛，1980，頁193；馬奇，1981，頁135圖41a－c；李，1984，頁206，編號230；科比利，1974，頁115－117，編號49；霍貨德，1994，頁200，編號233，霍佐夫藏品；參見蔡，1979，頁48－50，一件類似的盌專為本傑明・艾爾訂製，他曾在普林斯頓一戰中，為華盛頓總統服役。此盌面繪有一船，船尾掛上美國國旗，船上有本傑明・艾爾名字簡稱（BGE）。

---

[51] Howard and Ayers 1978, p. 209, discuss the history of Canton scenes on punch bowls; Hervouët et al 1986, pp 23-29 for illustrations of the range of styles.

[52] Mudge 1962, p. 95.

[51] 霍貨德及艾爾斯，1978，頁209，詳述水果酒盌上廣州景物的源流；赫維特，1986，頁23－29，圖解不同的風格。

[52] 馬奇，1962，頁95。

44

Tureen, Cover and Stand   c. 1780

China

Porcelain

Tureen: 21.1 x 33.2 x 21.9 cm (8 $\frac{1}{4}$ x 12 $\frac{3}{4}$ x 8 $\frac{3}{4}$ in.)

Stand: 35.9 x 27.3 cm (14 $\frac{1}{8}$ x 10 $\frac{5}{8}$ in.)

Peabody Essex Museum, Museum purchase with funds donated anonymously, *E80,322ABC*

蓋盌連托盤   約 1780

中國

瓷器

蓋盌：21.1 x 33.2 x 21.9 厘米 （8 $\frac{1}{4}$ x 12 $\frac{3}{4}$ x 8 $\frac{3}{4}$ 吋）

托盤：35.9 x 27.3 厘米 （14 $\frac{1}{8}$ x 10 $\frac{5}{8}$ 吋）

皮博迪艾塞克斯博物館，館方以無名氏基金購藏   *E80,322ABC*

This tureen and stand are from a possibly unique dinner service decorated in underglaze blue with a view of the city of Canton. Beyond the crenelated wall surrounding the city can be seen the important landmarks of Canton: to the left is the nine-storeyed Flowery Pagoda, in the middle ground is the Mohammedan Tower, while the Five-storey Watch Tower can be seen in the hills to the right. The view would seem to be an incorrect one in that the Flowery Pagoda appears to be to the left of the Mohammedan Tower as one faces the city, rather than to the right.

Decorated in Jingdezhen, the artisan may not have had first-hand knowledge of Canton and has depicted the town in a highly stylized manner, while retaining all the necessary landmarks. The view leaves out the Hong sector, an odd omission for porcelain obviously intended for the export market. Small boats are on the Pearl River in front of a few buildings on stilts outside the city walls. Just left of centre is a building displaying the characters for the word "acme" or "zenith".

Provenance: Purchased from William Ferrell, Dallas, Texas

Published: Forbes 1978, pp. 784-787.

Exhibited: "Porcelain to Ping-Pong" (E80,288) Monmouth Museum, NJ, March 15, 1983 - June 25, 1983.

Related Works: There are two plates from the same service in the Peabody Essex Museum, E80,288.1,.2; Howard and Ayers 1978, pp. 207-208, no. 206, a blue and white octagonal underdish with a view of a folly fort.

此附有托盤的蓋盌，原屬一套青花餐具，飾以廣州城景物紋樣，風格獨特。廣州城處於圍築有門垛的城牆後，重要的陸標包括了左方九層高的花塔、中間的光塔及右方後山的五層樓。然此圖花塔的位置可能錯誤，它應位處光塔的右方。這套器皿在景德鎮燒製，此地的畫工可能並未曾親往廣州知悉當地景貌，故此只作一概括的描繪，但亦保留了所有重要的建築。對陶瓷外銷市場而言，商行是十分重要的一環，但在此碗上卻不慎地繪漏了。在城牆外河邊也築有一些房屋，建在木製的高台上，其中一間寫有「天」、「元」二字。前方珠江河道上數隻小舟緩緩而過。

收藏歷史：購自德克薩斯州達拉斯市的威廉‧費雷爾

刊載書目：福布斯，1978，頁 784－787。

展覽："從陶瓷到乒乓球"（E80,288），新澤西州蒙茅斯博物館，1983 年 3 月 15 日至 1983 年 6 月 25 日。

相關作品：皮博迪艾塞克斯博物館亦藏有同一套餐具中的另外兩只盤（E80,288.1,2）；霍貨德及艾爾斯，1978，頁 207－208，編號 206，有一青花八角形托碟，繪有炮台一景。

45

Punch bowl   c. 1785

China

Porcelain

14.8 x 36.5 cm (5 ³/₄ x 14 ⁵/₁₆ in.)

Peabody Essex Museum, Gift of Mr. William A. Coolidge, *E75,076*

水果酒盆   約1785

中國

瓷器

14.8 x 36.5 厘米 (5 ³/₄ x 14 ⁵/₁₆ 吋)

皮博迪艾塞克斯博物館，威廉·庫利奇先生捐贈   *E75,076*

A detailed and continuous view of the Hongs at Canton decorates the exterior of this bowl and shows from left to right, the flags of Holland, France (white), Imperial Austria, Sweden, Great Britain and Denmark. A fence has been built in front of the Hongs, with gates opening to the waterfront. This change occurred by 1780 as seen in a print published in 1789.[53] As with a similar example in the British Museum, this bowl shows the verandas of the English and Dutch Factories restyled with heavy half-round arches at the street level, which occurred around 1785.[54] The absence of the American flag, which was first flown in 1788, indicates the view dates just prior to this.

This is a rare example of a Hong bowl decorated entirely in ink-colour with some detailing in gilding; the technique not only replicates the quality of, but may be copied from, an engraving. The latest recorded view of the Hongs on porcelain are the pair of large punch bowls (22.7cm H x 22.5cm W). Both bowls came on the American Ship *Peacock* to Boston in 1834 after the completion of a two-year diplomatic voyage during which Edmund Roberts of Portsmouth, New Hampshire, attempted unsuccessfully to negotiate a commercial agreement with China.[55] The views of the Hongs are within medallions on the interior well of the bowl, surrounded on the sides by a continuous scene of Chinese figures. Large shields containing the inscriptions are on the exteriors and are surrounded by panels of Chinese figures and borders and ground work of flowers and butterflies.

Provenance: Purchased at The Art Exchange, New York; William A. Coolidge

Related Works: Schiffer 1980, p. 194; Temple Newsam House, Yorkshire, England; Art Institute of Chicago; Beurdeley 1962, fig. 7., in the British Museum; Choi 1979, p. 49, an underglaze blue water-bottle with a view of the Hongs.

[53] Orange 1924, pp. 224-225, no. 6.

[54] Choi 1979, p. 49.

[55] Crossman 1967, p. 170.

此盆外壁飾以廣州商館近景，描繪細緻，由左至右的旗幟分別為荷蘭、法國（白色）、奧地利、瑞典、英國及丹麥。商館外邊設有圍欄，在河畔置有關閘。在1789年印製的一幅版畫上可看見1780年時的轉變。[53] 大英博物館藏有另一件相類的盆，圖中可見英國和荷蘭商館遊廊外新建的圓拱形支柱，時約1785年。[54] 美國國旗是於1788年首次出現，故此這個景象應早於1788年。

此盆壁上的圖象主要以赭墨描繪，再加描金圍飾，這種技巧較為罕見，可能是受鐫刻版畫的形式所影響。文獻上有記載的繪有商行景貌的陶瓷製品，最晚期的為一對大型水果酒盆（22.7厘米（高）x 22.5厘米（闊）），由美國商船"孔雀"號於1834年運回波士頓。居於新罕布什爾州樸次茅斯的埃德蒙·羅伯茨就是乘搭此船往中國洽談通商條件，但兩年的外交工作最後亦白費了，無功而回。[55] 器心內以圓框圍繪商館景貌，旁邊堆滿了中國人物。而刻有題識的盾徽則繪於外壁，周圍有開光中國人物和花蝶圖案鑲邊及作地紋。

收藏歷史：購藏自紐約藝術交易行；威廉·庫利奇

相關作品：希佛，1980，頁194；英國約克郡紐塞姆樓；芝加哥美術學院；伯特里，1962，圖7；大英博物館藏；蔡，1979，頁49，有一青花水瓶以廣州商館為題。

[53] 奧林奇，1924，頁224－225，編號6。

[54] 蔡，1979，頁49。

[55] 克羅斯曼，1967，頁170。

46

Canton Factory Site   c. 1785

England, William Daniell (1769 – 1837)

Soft-ground etching

Sight: 41 x 77.5 cm (16 x 31 in.)

Framed: 59 x 95.8 cm (23 $^1/_8$ x 37 $^3/_4$ in.)

Peabody Essex Museum, Gift of Mr. Stephen Wheatland, *M10,474*

廣州商館區　　約1785

英國，威廉・丹尼爾 (1769 － 1837)

軟防蝕劑蝕刻版畫

41 x 77.5 厘米　(16 x 31 吋)

原框：59 x 95.8 厘米　(23 $^1/_8$ x 37 $^3/_4$ 吋)

皮博迪艾塞克斯博物館，斯蒂芬・惠特蘭先生捐贈　*M10,474*

This view from the Pearl River shows the foreign Factories which, from left to right, are the Danish, French (Bourbon), Spanish, Swedish, British and Dutch. The drawing on which this print was based may have been executed in 1785 when Thomas and William Daniell visited Canton en route to India, rather than in 1793-1794 on their return journey, as the American flag is absent. This view was published as a coloured print by Daniell on June 1, 1805. The same angle and alignment of buildings appears in the oil on canvas (no. 49), although the arrangement of small boats and larger ships has changed.

Provenance: Stephen Wheatland

Related works: Orange 1924, p. 224, no. 7, illustrated p. 247, the same view as a completed print, inscribed: "Drawn, engraved and published by William Daniell", and described there as a mezzotint.

此圖是從珠江河上眺望商館區的景貌，由左至右可見丹麥、法國（波旁）、西班牙、瑞典、英國及荷蘭國旗。原作是一幅素描，應是托瑪斯及威廉・丹尼爾於1785年往印度經遊中國時所繪，而非在1793至1794年回程時所作，因此時美國商館的旗幟仍未見掛上。此圖後來於1805年給丹尼爾印製成一設色版畫。展品編號49的油畫與此圖有著相同的取景角度，然而各大小船隻的布局編排則有所分別。

收藏歷史：斯蒂芬・惠特蘭

相關作品：奧林奇，1924，頁224，編號7，插圖見頁247，景象相同，題識註明由威廉・丹尼爾繪畫、刻版及印行，又形容此為一件磨刻版畫。

47

View of the Hoppo Returning   late 18th century

China, unknown artist

Watercolour on silk

Sight: 56 x 75 cm (22 x 29 ¹/₂ in.)

Hong Kong Museum of Art, *AH64.196*

市舶司回府   18世紀晚期

中國，畫家佚名

水彩絹本

56 x 75 厘米 (22 x 29 ¹/₂ 吋)

香港藝術館 *AH64.196*

This view may have been part of a scroll depicting the continuous view of the Pearl River from the Whampoa anchorage to the foreign Factories. An intact example of such a scroll, measuring twenty-six feet in length and dating to about 1760, is in the British Museum, and another example of equal length is in the Historical Museum, East India House, Stockholm, Sweden. The number of existing individual views of this type indicate that there were other scrolls which have been, since their production, cut into individually framed pictures; as many as twelve separate views seem to have been cut from the scrolls.

The Hoppo of Canton was the Imperial Commissioner of Customs with head-quarters at Canton whose term of office generally lasted three years. Usually only one individual held this title, although occasionally his subordinates would use the title and in the later 19th century there were two officials of this rank. The Hoppo would arrange for two boats to be made fast to the ship, one on each side, to prevent smuggling. After measuring a ship and levying duties, the Hoppo would give the ship's captain a Chop granting freedom of access for merchants coming to trade with the supercargo, as well as Chops for permission to come and go to Canton. A Hoppo was, therefore, a powerful and important individual in the world of international trade at Canton.

Related works: Individual pictures on silk in the Peabody Essex Museum.

此圖可能是一長卷畫的部分，全卷相信是描繪珠江河道上由黃埔船塢至廣州商館的景色。大英博物館藏有一卷完整無缺的相類畫作，全長廿六呎，時約1760年。另外一卷則藏於瑞典斯德哥爾摩東印度樓歷史博物館，長度相約。其他現存的是散頁，可知這類型的長卷畫在繪製之後，很多都分割開來獨立裝裱，有些更分成十二幀之多。

廣州的市舶司是海關處的欽命監督，總口設於廣州，任命年期大多為三年。粵海關監督通常只有一位，但有時亦有其他下屬可採用此名銜，故此在十九世紀晚期有兩位監督主理關務。他們會派遣兩艘艇船迅速駛往要課稅的商船兩旁以防止走私販毒。當丈量好船貨及徵收稅銀後，船長便可取得蓋鑑給予外商進入廣州貿易的權利。因此，在廣州的國際貿易來說，市舶司是一舉足輕重的人物。

相關作品：皮博迪艾塞克斯博物館藏有其他相類的絹本畫散張。

Fan 1790 – 1800

China

Ivory, paper, gouache

26.3 x 43.5 cm (10 $\frac{1}{4}$ x 17 $\frac{1}{8}$ in.)

Peabody Essex Museum, Gift of Mr. and Mrs. John E. Rogerson, *E80,202*

摺扇 1790 － 1800

中國

水粉紙本、象牙扇骨

26.3 x 43.5 厘米 （10 $\frac{1}{4}$ x 17 $\frac{1}{8}$ 吋）

皮博迪艾塞克斯博物館，約翰‧羅格森先生夫人捐贈 *E80,202*

This paper fan is decorated with a charmingly naive painting of the foreign Factory site at Canton with (left to right) the Danish, Spanish (the Philippine Company), American, Swedish, British and Dutch flags. Of particular interest is the inclusion of the fort in the lower right-hand corner. The reverse shows three European-style floral sprays. The eighteen sticks and two guard sticks, all of ivory, have pierced geometric decoration lacking the delicacy of earlier ivory fans.

Similar fans, of which a few are recorded, were certainly sold individually as souvenirs for those officers and sailors looking for a memento of Canton to bring their loved ones. Other paper fans which depict the Pearl River Delta include those with views of Whampoa and composite views of Canton, Whampoa, Macau and/or Hong Kong (no. 1). Fans were exported in bulk throughout the 18th and 19th centuries but shipping records rarely indicate the specific decoration for "painted fans", possibly indicating a more common style of decoration, such as flowers or birds, while the majority were listed by material such as palm leaf, bone, sandalwood, lacquer, or feather.[56]

Provenance: Mr. and Mrs. John Rogerson
Published: Nelson 1984, pp. 50-51.
Exhibited: "Directly from China", Feb. 1985 - Sept. 1985, Peabody Museum of Salem.
Related works: Crossman 1991, p. 328, colour plate 118. Interestingly, this fan is supposed to have belonged to Abigail Brown Francis (1766-1821) a daughter of John Brown, the Providence, Rhode Island, merchant who was in Canton between 1787 and 1789; the fan was later offered by the Oriental Art Gallery, London, and illustrated in their catalog, December 1995, p. 68, no. 137, and dated to c. 1785.

[56] Crossman 1991, pp. 322-337.

這把紙扇上的廣州商館風貌繪圖，充滿拙趣。商行門外的旗幟由左至右依次為丹麥、西班牙（菲律賓公司）、美國、瑞典、英國及荷蘭。值得留意的是右下角的炮台。扇的另一面繪有三種歐洲式的花卉連枝。首尾扇骨及十八枝小骨都是以通雕幾何圖案的象牙製成，手工不及早期象牙扇那般精緻。

有不少外國官員和水手都喜購買這類型摺扇，作為紀念品送給摯愛親友，以留住他們在廣州的美好回憶，有些還有文獻記載。其他繪有珠江景色的紙扇包括有黃埔風景及組合廣州、黃埔、澳門或香港數處景物（如展品編號1）等類別。在十八、十九世紀期間，有大量的扇銷往外地，然而船運紀錄上很少特別註明"彩繪扇"上的圖樣，也許它們只是普通的花鳥紋飾，至於扇的物料則大多有闡明，如棕櫚葉、骨、檀香木、漆或羽毛。[56]

收藏歷史：約翰‧羅格森先生夫人
刊載書目：內爾遜，1984，頁 50 － 51。
展覽："直接來自中國"，賽倫市皮博迪博物館，1985 年 2 月至 1985 年 9 月。
相關作品：克羅斯曼，1991，頁 328，彩圖 118，此扇應原屬阿比蓋爾‧佛朗西（1766 － 1821），她的父親是居於羅德島的約翰‧布朗，曾在 1787 年至 1789 年期間在廣州貿易；此扇後來在倫敦的東方藝廊出售，並刊登於目錄中，1995 年 12 月版，頁 68，編號 137，系年約 1785。

[56] 克羅斯曼，1991，頁 322 － 337。

View of Canton   c. 1800

China, unknown artist

Watercolour and gouache on paper

Sight: 60.8 x 118.1 cm (23 $^7/_8$ x 46 $^1/_2$ in.)

Framed: 71.2 x 128.5 cm (28 x 50 $^5/_8$ in.)

Peabody Essex Museum, Museum purchase with funds donated anonymously, *E79.708*

遠眺廣州城   約 1800

中國‧畫家佚名

水彩及水粉畫紙本

60.8 x 118.1 厘米   (23 $^7/_8$ x 46 $^1/_2$ 吋)

原框：71.2 x 128.5 厘米   (28 x 50 $^5/_8$ 吋)

皮博迪艾塞克斯博物館‧館方以無名氏基金購藏   *E79.708*

The great port city of Canton is seen in this unusual, panoramic bird's-eye view, with all the standard landmarks clearly visible. The most prominent of the mountains in the background is White Cloud Mountain *(Bai yun shan)* whose highest peak rises fourteen hundred feet above sea level. The only other panoramic view of Canton known is the oil painting (no. 69) done in the latter part of the century.

The quality of the painting is superb: the details have been executed with great precision in a very difficult medium. Undoubtedly this is one of the most "Western" of early Chinese paintings for the export market.

Provenance: Kennedy Galleries, New York
Published: Choi 1979, p. 43; Christman 1984, cover illustration and p. 39; Forbes 1978, p. 785.
Exhibited: "The China Trade: Romance and Reality", De Cordova Museum, June 22 - September 16, 1979; "Adventurous Pursuits: Americans and the China Trade 1784-1844", National Portrait Gallery, Feb. 1, 1984 - Sept. 30, 1984, cover illustration.

這是一幅罕見的廣州城鳥瞰全圖，很多著名的陸標都清晰可見。遠處的山峰便是白雲山，高度是海拔一千四百呎。另外唯一的一幀廣州城全景的作品，是一幅作於較後期的油畫（展品編號69）。

此圖是一幅十分優秀的早期中國外銷畫，描繪技巧精確細緻，對顏料水份的控制尤其精到，並且吸納了不少"西方風格"。

收藏歷史：紐約肯尼畫廊
刊載書目：蔡，1979，頁43；克里斯曼，1984，封面插圖及頁39；福布斯，1978，頁785。
展覽："中國貿易：浪漫與現實"，科多瓦博物館，1979年6月22日至1979年9月16日。"探險歷奇：1784－1844年間的中美貿易"，美國國家肖像畫廊，1984年2月1日至1984年9月30日，此圖是該展覽目錄的封面插圖。

51

The Foreign Factory Site c. 1805

China, unknown artist

Reverse painting on glass

Sight: 39.4 x 59.8 cm (15 $\frac{1}{2}$ x 23 $\frac{1}{2}$ in.)

Framed: 50.2 x 70.9 cm (19 $\frac{3}{4}$ x 27 $\frac{3}{4}$ in.)

Peabody Essex Museum, Gift of the Misses Rosamond and Aimee Lamb, *E78,680*

廣州商館區 約 1805

中國‧畫家佚名

玻璃畫

39.4 x 59.8 厘米　(15 $\frac{1}{2}$ x 23 $\frac{1}{2}$ 吋)

原框：50.2 x 70.9 厘米　(19 $\frac{3}{4}$ x 27 $\frac{3}{4}$ 吋)

皮博迪艾塞克斯博物館‧羅莎蒙德及艾梅‧拉姆女士捐贈　*E78,680*

From left to right are the flags of Denmark, Spain, the United States, Sweden, England and the Netherlands. The Danish Hong is the last on the left of the Factory grounds and is separated from the non-Western district by a high wall, also seen in the ink-colour punch bowl (no. 45). The white flag of the French monarchy was replaced by the tricolour of the Republic and was first hoisted in Canton on January 16, 1803 by Jean Baptiste Piron, Commercial Agent of the French Republic. It was removed at the death of Piron twenty-one months later, in February of 1805, and was not flown again until the return of the French in 1832.[59] The British Union Jack of 1800 is flying and the fence, which was thought to have been removed by 1800, is still intact.[60] This painting was brought to America by the Boston China trade merchant Thomas Lamb (1753-1813). Many views of Canton dating to this period survive, but few are painted with such detail; fewer still are known to have such a well-documented family origin.

Eglomisé was a technique of decorating on the obverse side of a glass panel, in reverse of the normal method of painting and was introduced into China in the 17th century by the Jesuit missionaries. The term is derived from the name of Jean-Baptiste Glomy, a frame maker in Paris during the late 18th century, although the first reverse glass paintings were done in Italy late in the 13th century. After 1850, the production of reverse paintings declined everywhere including in China.

Provenance: Thomas Lamb; by descent to the Misses Rosamond and Aimeé Lamb

Exhibited: "Highlights of the China Trade Museum", Peabody Museum of Salem, October 1984-May 1985

Related works: Gregory 1992 (59), pp. 42-43, no. 83, a view dated c. 1803; Crossman 1991, p. 425, no. 6, Peabody Essex Museum, another view dated 1800-1803.

[59] Morse 1926-1929, Vol. II, pp. 408, 423.

[60] Crossman 1991, p. 425.

此圖的旗幟由左至右分別代表了丹麥、西班牙、美國、瑞典、英國及荷蘭等國家，丹麥行位於商館地帶最左方。再往左行，便是中國人居住的地區，兩方以一高牆相隔，此景象亦見於另一件墨繪水果酒盌（展品編號45）。代表法國皇朝的白色旗幟，後來由法國共和國的三色旗代替。1803年1月16日，法國的商貿代表瓊‧皮朗首次掛起此面三色旗，但廿一個月後，皮朗於1805年2月逝世，國旗卸下，直至法國人於1832年再到中國時才又懸掛起來。[59] 至於英國國旗則自1800年便開始出現，而商館前面的欄杆，原應在1800年便拆除，但英國館門外的仍保持原狀。[60] 這幅畫是由居於波士頓的中美貿易商人托瑪斯‧拉姆（1753－1813）購返美國，雖然同期亦有不少廣州景貌的畫作，但少有這般刻劃入微，而更罕見的是附有詳細的家族收藏史。

玻璃畫的技法是繪畫在一片玻璃鏡片的背面，其繪畫方向是與一般畫法相反，最早由傳教士於十七世紀時傳入中國。其名稱是取自瓊‧巴普蒂斯特‧格洛米，他是十八世紀晚期巴黎一位製框工匠，但其實最早期的玻璃畫發源自意大利十三世紀晚期。繪畫的次序與平常的作畫方法相反，例如先畫細緻的部分及最後才畫背景。1850年以後，這種繪畫方法在世界各地逐漸式微。

收藏歷史：托瑪斯‧拉姆並相傳至羅莎蒙德及艾梅‧拉姆女士

展覽："中國貿易博物館精選"，塞林市皮博迪博物館，1984年10月至1985年5月。

相關作品：格雷戈里‧1992 (59) ‧頁42－43，編號83，一幅約1803年的作品；克羅斯曼‧1991‧頁425，編號6，皮博迪艾塞克斯博物館藏的另一幅作品，繪於1800年至1803年期間。

[59] 莫爾斯‧1926－1929‧第二冊‧頁408及423。

[60] 克羅斯曼‧1991‧頁425。

52

View of Canton　　1750 – 1800

China

Ivory, paint and gilt

Framed: 73.5　x　107 cm (29　x　42 in.)

Peabody Essex Museum, Museum purchase with funds donated anonymously, *E82,856*

廣州城一覽　　1750 － 1800

中國

象牙、彩繪及鍍金

原框：73.5 x 107 厘米　(29 x 42 吋)

皮博迪艾塞克斯博物館，館方以無名氏基金購藏　*E82,856*

This bas-relief of Canton is perhaps unique, composed of ivory with details painted and gilded; other composite pictures of ivory are known but no other bas-relief view of Canton has been recorded.[61] This view includes some of the buildings of Honam Island in the lower left section, in addition to the more typical scene of the Hongs, Flowery Pagoda, Dutch Folly Fort and, in the upper right, the Five-Storey Pagoda. The picture is comprised entirely of ivory, including the ground work which consists of sheets of ivory pegged to a wooden backing. Details, in some cases, are extraordinary; minuscule bells actually dangle from the corners of the Flowery Pagoda, while a lantern hangs from a ring on the porch of a building to the far right - this was carved from a single piece of ivory, not attached later. Recent conservation work has restored the relief as close to its original condition as can be determined, though it had undergone considerable repainting at some time in its existence. The picture retains its original frame and one of the brass hangers. On the reverse of one element of the construction (the third group of buildings from the right), is a five-character vertical inscription which unfortunatley is mostly illegible, and only several numbers can be read.

The Pearl River is filled with a veritable dictionary of Chinese rivercraft, including a flower vendor and a small, canopied boat with eight rowers transporting a Westerner. Of the many Chinese boats in the harbour, the surgeon of the *Marquis of Lansdown* reported in his 1787 journal, "Sampans of burthen are the largest Boats, in these the Cargo of the Ship is transported to & from Shore. Whole families are born, marry, & die in these Boats. They are sent by pairs to the Ship, which they call a Chop. The two Boats generally carry about 800 Chests of Tea."[62]

Provenance: Massachusetts family; Northeast Auctions, November 11, 1989, lot 121.

Related works: Spink & Son Ltd., *The Minor Arts of China III*, April 1987, no. 49, a late 18th century landscape of ivory on painted glass.

[61] For other ivory relief pictures see: Spink & Son Ltd., The Minor Arts of China III, 1987, no. 49, appliquéd painted glass and dated to the late 18th century.

[62] Lansdown 1787, unpaginated.

這幅淺浮雕象牙廣州圖十分別緻，細部繪上顏色及鍍金；其他象牙浮雕有各類不同類型的圖象，但以廣州為題的則未有所聞。[61] 除了一般常見的景物如商館區、花塔、海珠炮台及右上角的五層樓外，左下方還加添了河南島上的房舍。此件作品主要以象牙製成，裡地是以象牙片拴釘在木板上。有些細部的手工異常精巧；花塔的飛簷上掛有精緻的小鈴，可發出清脆的鈴聲。最右端的一所樓房，栓廊上懸掛上一盞以圓環扣著的燈籠，是以一塊完整的象牙雕成，非後來加上。此件作品雖曾作修補，但已盡量保持原狀，只有部分重新上彩。原來的框架及一隻銅掛鈎現仍保持完整。在背面其中一支架上刻有一行文字，除了幾個數字外，其他字體因太模糊而難以辨認。

珠江河上佈滿了各式各樣的中國船艇，有販賣花卉的，也有一蓋上船篷的小舟，八個船伕正在載運一位外國人，有關這些中國船艚，「馬奎斯」號船上的外科醫生在他1787年的日記有如下記載：「舢舨可算是是最大的貨艇，它們將貨品從岸邊及大洋船不停地往來轉運。由出生、嫁娶以至死亡的一天，艇戶人家就是在這些小船上渡過，通常它們是一對一對的駛往大商船處，並帶備蓋章。一般來說，兩艘舢舨可載運八百箱茶葉。」[62]

收藏歷史：麻省一家族；「東北拍賣行」，1989 年 11 月 11 日，編號 121。

相關作品：斯平克父子公司，《中國工藝品 III》，1987 年 4 月，編號 49，是一幅十八世紀彩繪玻璃上的象牙風景圖。

[61] 其他的象牙浮雕作品可見斯平克父子公司《中國工藝品 III》，1987，編號 49，一幀 18 世紀晚期的彩繪玻璃。

[62] 蘭斯多，1787，無頁碼。

53

A Close View of the Foreign Factories   c. 1807

China, attributed to Spoilum

Oil on canvas

Sight: 73 x 100 cm (28 ³/₄ x 39 ¹/₂ in.)

Hong Kong Museum of Art, Donated by Sir Robert Ho Tung, *AH64.28*

廣州商館區一角   約 1807

中國，傳史貝霖畫

油彩布本

73 x 100 厘米　(28 ³/₄ x 39 ¹/₂ 吋)

香港藝術館，何東爵士捐贈　*AH64.28*

From left to right are the Imperial, Swedish, Old English and Chow-chow Factories with the New English Factory at the extreme right. Observing from the balconies of all the Hongs are Western merchants. Below on the esplanade, called the Respondentia, two Mandarins in sedan chairs arrive in a procession to the old English Factory where a British soldier, two Chinese drummers, and a festooned doorway await their arrival. Behind, in front of the Chow-chow Factory, four Western sailors watch, while groups of Chinese gather to observe as well.

This is one of a pair in the Hong Kong Museum of Art, the other depicting the interior of the English Factory. Another of these pairs exists in the National Maritime Museum, London; while one set is divided between the Peabody Essex Museum and Winterthur.

Published: Hong Kong Museum of Art 1981, p. 32, no. 17, and 1987, p. 42, no. 6.
Related works: Connor 1986, p. 33, no. 27.

畫中建築物由左至右順序為：帝國館、瑞典館、舊英國館及諸洲館，最右方是新英國商館。外國商人在商館的遊廊上倚欄張望，而廣場內兩位滿清官員正乘著轎子，在儀仗隊的護送下前往舊英國館，飾有彩帶的門外已有一英國士兵及中國鑼鼓手肅立歡迎。諸洲館的前方站有四名海員，其他亦有很多中國人在圍觀。

此畫原是一對，香港藝術館藏有另一幀舊英國館的內貌。現知倫敦國家海事博物館亦藏有另一對相同的作品；再有另一對則分別藏於美國的溫特費爾博物館(外貌)及皮博迪艾塞克斯博物館(內貌)。

刊載書目：香港藝術館，1981，頁 32，編號 17 及 1987，頁 42，編號 6。
相關作品：康納，1986，頁 33，編號 27。

Panoramic View of Canton Across the Rooftops of the Foreign Factories c. 1810

China, unknown artist, possibly Tonequa

Gouache on paper, mounted on canvas, varnished

Sight: 66.6 x 122.5 cm (26 ¼ x 48 ½ in.)

Framed: 84.3 x 140 cm (33 ¾ x 56 in.)

Hong Kong Museum of Art, *AH89.2*

從集義行 (荷蘭館) 頂樓眺望廣州全景　約 1810

中國，畫家佚名，可能是通呱

水粉紙本，裝裱在帆布上並塗上清漆

66.6 x 122.5 厘米　(26 ¼ x 48 ½ 吋)

原框：84.3 x 140 厘米　(33 ¾ x 56 吋)

香港藝術館　*AH89.2*

The front of the busy harbour, just before the Hongs, cannot be seen from this unusual perspective, probably viewed from the terrace of the Danish Factory. There is a sense of solitude and quiet uncommon in most depictions of the harbour and streets surrounding the Hongs. Only the tops of the stalls on Hog Lane and the two lone figures, hanging clothes out to dry, hint at the bustle going on below. Hog Lane's chief attraction for Western sailors was the *sam shu* or rice liquor available there.[63]

To the far left is the creek which marked the eastern limit of the foreign concessions. In the background is the island of Honam, with the Honam (Haichuang) Temple complex at the extreme left and the Red Fort at the water's edge between the Dutch and British flags. The pagoda of the Macau Passage fort appears in the far distance.[64]

For further discussion of this painting see the essay by Patrick Conner in this catalogue where it is suggested that such a view would have served as the basis for a panorama of Canton painted by Robert Burford for his *Panorama* off Leicester Square in London, in 1838. The text of the visitor's brochure for the *Panorama* suggests the viewer would feel transported to "a terrace on the summit of the British Factory", and that it was based on work by "Toonequa, a native of Canton".

Published: Gregory 1989 (53), p. 49, no. 93; Hong Kong Museum of Art, 1991, p. 80.

[63] Gregory 1994 (64), p. 52.

[64] Gregory 1989 (53), p.49.

此畫描繪了從荷蘭商館的陽台上眺望河南地區及繁忙的珠江河道景色，因取景角度特別，商館下望的景物都遮蓋了。屋頂層層疊疊，只有新荳欄街的木棚上兩個中國人在晾曬衣物。畫中散發著一種不尋常的孤清感，有別於其他大多表現商館區熙來攘往景象的畫作，觀者或可想象下面街道上也許另有一番熱鬧景況。新荳欄街最吸引外國水手的地方就是這裏售賣的「三蘇」，意指中國的米酒。[63]

左端的小溪名西濠，是商館區東面的界限。後方便是河南島，島上最左方有海幢寺。紅炮台就築在河堤邊（畫中荷蘭旗與英國旗之間的位置）。遠方可隱約見到澳門河段的古塔。[64]

至於有關此畫的詳細敘述，可參閱康納在此目錄中撰寫的文章。文中指出羅拔·伯福特可能曾參照是畫用以繪畫一幅廣州全景壁畫，於1838年在倫敦萊斯特廣場他開設的"全景畫廊"內展出，場刊內的文字形容此壁畫可令觀者感覺到他是置身於英國商館外的陽台上，而此畫是根據廣州畫家通呱的作品而繪。

刊載書目：格雷戈里，1989 (53)，頁 49，編號 93；香港藝術館，1991，頁 80。

[63] 格雷戈里，1994 (64)，頁 52。

[64] 格雷戈里，1989 (53)，頁 49。

Canton Foreign Factories - Start of the Fire   1822

China, unknown artist

Oil on canvas

Sight: 27.5 x 38 cm (10 ³/₄ x 15 in.)

Hong Kong Museum of Art, Donated by Sir Robert Ho Tung, *AH64.31*

廣州商館 － 大火初起   1822

中國，畫家佚名

油彩布本

27.5 x 38 厘米 (10 ³/₄ x 15 吋)

香港藝術館，何東爵士捐贈   *AH64.31*

In this dramatic depiction of the fire of 1822, the full moon is shining brightly as the fire begins its devastating course from the Chinese section of the city to the back of the Hongs. Anxious inhabitants have gathered in the promenade with lanterns, while to the left others arrive with buckets of water to help to extinguish the flames. Others, in the enclosed yard (later to become the American garden) and in small boats, point to the oncoming danger. The Chinese artist has aptly played upon our own fears as spectators by lighting the site dramatically and drawing our full attention to the fiercely burning buildings, while framing the scene in the darkness of the waterfront and the smoke-filled sky.

A brief description of the progress of the fire is given by Morse: at half-past nine on the evening of November 1, the Western merchants received word that a fire was raging a mile and half to the north. The following morning, at three o'clock, when it became obvious that the fire was headed for the Hongs, Western ships and sailors were summoned to help salvage goods from the Factories; they arrived at seven. By nine o'clock the British Factories were in flames at five or six points and the line of fire embraced the whole of the foreign Factories from the creek to Mowqua's Hong on the far side of Old China Street.[67]

Published: Hong Kong Museum of Art 1982, p. 48

是圖描寫了1822年廣州商館大火初起的情景，天空上一輪明月，商館後街的中國樓房上火焰初升。居民們都提著燈籠趕來幫忙，左方有人肩揹著水桶到來救火，廣場內及船艇上的人都指往火場。這位中國畫家巧妙地把觀畫者代入這些觀火的群眾裡面，令我們如置身這火場之中，給黑漆一片的海面及佈滿濃煙的夜空包圍。

莫爾斯曾記述這場大火的過程：「十一月一日黃昏九時半，外國商人接到消息，北面約一哩半的地點失火。凌晨三時，火勢明顯地向商行這邊蔓延。洋船及水手們被召令到商行區搶救貨物；他們於七時到達。到了九時，英國館內已有五、六個火場，而整個商館區由小溪至靖遠街茂官的商行都被火焰包圍著。」[67]

刊載書目：香港藝術館，1982，頁48。

[67] Morse 1926, pp. 64-66.

[67] 莫爾斯，1926，頁 64－66。

The Canton Fire of 1822   c. 1822

China, unknown artist

Oil on canvas

Sight: 43.8 x 57.8 cm (17 1/4 x 22 3/4 in.)

Framed: 54 x 68 cm (21 1/4 x 26 11/16 in.)

Peabody Essex Museum, Museum purchase with funds donated anonymously, *M22,764*

廣州商館 — 烈火蔓延   約1822

中國，畫家佚名

油彩布本

43.8 x 57.8厘米 (17 1/4 x 22 3/4 吋)

原框：54 x 68厘米 (21 1/4 x 26 11/16 吋)

皮博迪艾塞克斯博物館，館方以無名氏基金購藏   *M22,764*

This painting depicts the fire of 1822, with the Factory buildings fully engulfed in flames. A large expanse of smoke blackens the afternoon sky; by three o'clock on the afternoon after the fire started, the staffs of the Factories and the sailors sent to assist them, were driven by the flames into boats in the river. In the foreground, the small boats usually present in this typical view of Canton are, as ever, portrayed, but for this event are laden with onlookers who can do little at this point but observe the destruction. Although Chinese losses were enormous — over 7,000 shopkeepers were burned out — the Hong merchants commenced rebuilding almost immediately.

Interestingly there seems to be very little in the way of first-hand accounts of the fire. John Richardson Latimer, an American merchant who arrived in Canton only a few days before the fire, wrote to his family: "You will have heard from our Mother to whom I usually address my letters, of my safe arrival here, of our being houseless, made so by the fire and in one of my letters I mention something about China Ware being destroyed." [68]

Provenance: Elinor Gordon; H. A. Crosby Forbes

此圖描繪1822年商館區被熊熊烈火包圍的情景。是日下午，天空上籠罩著黑煙；商行職員及水手於三時抵步協助滅火，但猛烈的火勢卻把他們趕回船上。很多畫作中常見的小船，此刻則站滿了圍觀者，他們對於這場大火帶來的破壞，愛莫能助。此次大火期間，超過七千名店主從商舖逃出，財物損失甚為嚴重，然而行商很快就進行了商館的重建工程。

關於這場大火的第一手資料並不多見。美國商人約翰·拉蒂默於大火數天前才抵達廣州，他給家人的一封信寫道：「你們應從我給母親的信中知悉我已平安到步，但因那場大火，我們已經無家可歸，前信提及的那些中國瓷器亦被燒毀了。」[68]

收藏歷史：埃莉諾·戈登；克羅斯比·福布斯

[68] Thill 1973, p. 119.

[68] 蒂爾，1973，頁119。

View of Canton from the Foreign Factories   c. 1825

China, unknown artist

Oil on canvas

Sight: 113.7 x 168.6 cm (44 ³/₄ x 66 ³/₈ in.)

Hong Kong Museum of Art, *AH92.8*

從商館區眺望廣州景色   約1825

中國，畫家佚名

油彩布本

113.7 x 168.6 厘米 (44 ³/₄ x 66 ³/₈ 吋)

香港藝術館 *AH92.8*

This detailed and highly unusual view is taken from the roof of one of the Factories of Canton, looking south with the Red (or West) Fort in the background. The fenced-in yard contains chickens, sheep, goats, and a cow for dairy products (not customarily consumed by the Chinese). Interestingly, it is known that John Richardson Latimer, a Philadelphia merchant, had kept a cow at Canton which he gave to Mrs. Thomas Richardson Colledge, wife of a Scotsman, who served as assistant surgeon to the Honorable East India Company at Canton. Latimer used the cow for the milk it provided to go with his favourite supper dish — peach pie.[69]

On the quayside, to the left, is a great diversity of porters, vendors and figures of all kinds. In the crowded river, the covered boat elaborately decorated in blue and red, with a canopied entrance amidships, is the official craft of one of the Chinese Hong merchants, with whom the Westerners conducted their business.

The buildings on the right are adorned with pot-plants, inscriptions and various decorative motifs. The Chinese characters inscribed on the tall structure near the right-hand margin translate as "See Chong (Constant Prosperity) charcoal storage and distribution"; to its left, near the skyline, another inscription gives the name of an inn "Sun Tien Woo."[70] For a further discussion of this painting and its relationship to cat. no. 54, see the essay in this catalogue by Patrick Conner.

Published: Gregory 1992 (59), pp. 46-47, no. 88.

此圖是從廣州其中一商館屋頂上眺望珠江景色，背後可見在南面的紅炮台（或西炮台）。平台上的圍欄裡面飼養的家畜有雞隻、羊及乳牛（應非供應給中國人食用）。軼聞一則，謂費城商人約翰‧拉蒂默在廣州養有一頭牛，後來贈予托馬斯‧郭雷樞夫人，她的丈夫是蘇格蘭人，是廣州東印度公司的外科醫生。拉蒂默以自己飼養的牛隻擠牛奶烹製他最喜愛的食物 ── 桃子餡餅。[69]

左方的碼頭旁邊繪有各式各類的人物，有挑夫和小販等。在擠擁的河道上，有一隻髹上紅藍兩色並裝飾得很漂亮的船艇，中間有篷蓋入口，是其中一行商的 " 花艇 "，用以與外商洽談生意。右方屋頂的石欄上種有盆栽，屋簷上飾以雕花，有些牆壁外更寫上商舖招牌，如右邊灰色牆上有一招貼寫上 " 時昌柴炭批 （？）發零售 "，左面有一間旅店的名稱為 " 新天和 "[70]，有關此畫的研究及其與編號54的展品比較，可參看本目錄內康納一文。

刊載書目：格雷戈里，1992（59），頁46－47，編號88。

[69] Forbes 1984, p. 18.

[70] Gregory 1992 (59), p. 46.

[69] 福布斯，1984，頁18。

[70] 格雷戈里，1992（59），頁46。

60

The Factories of Canton 1825 – 1835

China, attributed to Lam Qua

Oil on canvas

Sight: 47 x 72.3 cm (18 $^1/_2$ x 28 $^1/_2$ in.)

Framed: 56.2 x 81.5 cm (22 $^1/_8$ x 32 $^1/_8$ in.)

Peabody Essex Museum, Museum purchase, *M3,793*

廣州商館側貌 1825 － 1835

中國，傳是啉呱所作

油彩布本

47 x 72.3 厘米 （18 $^1/_2$ x 28 $^1/_2$ 吋）

原框：56.2 x 81.5 厘米 （22 $^1/_8$ x 32 $^1/_8$ 吋）

皮博迪艾塞克斯博物館，館方購藏 *M3,793*

This unusual view was painted from the upper end of the Factory site looking downriver toward the American, British and Dutch Factories. This painting shows the influence of the English artist George Chinnery on Chinese artists working for the Western market. This view complements the Hong Kong Museum of Art view (no. 59) of, apparently, the same enclosed yard, shown here with goats.

Provenance: Augustine Heard

Published: Brewington 1928, p. 81, no. 347; Crossman 1991, p. 99, colour plate 31 and p. 429, no. 13.

這是從一斜視角度繪畫東面盡頭的商館區，向江邊望過去可見美國、英國及荷蘭商館。此圖是中國畫家為迎合西方市場而作，畫風襲錢納利。這個景象與對上一幅香港藝術館藏品（編號59）可算是相輔相成，兩幅畫中建有圍欄的院子應是同一建築，這幅的院子內則飼養有山羊。

收藏歷史：奧古斯丁・赫德

刊載書目：布魯因頓，1928，頁81，編號347；克羅斯曼，1991，頁99，彩圖31及頁429，編號13。

61

Dutch Folly Fort   c. 1832

England, George Chinnery (1774 – 1852)

Ink and watercolour on paper

Sight: 20.2 x 28.6 cm (8 x 11 1/2 in.)

Hong Kong Museum of Art, *AH80.7*

海珠炮台   約 1832

英國，喬治‧錢納利 (1774 — 1852)

墨水及水彩紙本

20.2 x 28.6 厘米 （8 x 11 1/2 吋）

香港藝術館   *AH80.7*

The Dutch Folly Fort was an oval fort built on a sand bar in the Pearl River. It was guarded by forty soldiers with twenty-six cannons, and contained a temple built in memory of Li Maoying, a distinguished mandarin of the Song dynasty (960-1279).

Chinnery visited Canton a number of times after 1825 and sketched the Hongs and the Dutch Folly Fort which lay to the east of the Factories. In this drawing the pagoda roof of Mingqua's Factory, which was built after the fire of 1822 and removed by 1832, is at the extreme left. This south-west view was also used by Thomas and William Daniell whose 1810 engraving of this scene is in the collection of the Hong Kong Museum of Art (AH64.357).

The two forts, the other being the French Folly Fort, were frequently mentioned by travellers but less frequently depicted, at least independently, by either Chinese or Western artists. The French Folly Fort was guarded by thirty soldiers and twenty cannons and was situated on the eastern passage to Canton.

Published: Hong Kong Museum of Art 1981, p. 37, no. 22, and 1985, pp. 56-57, no. 22.
Related works: Hong Kong Museum of Art 1981, p. 30, no. 15, and p. 84, colour plate, a Chinese export gouache on silk picture of the fort; and 1987, p. 38, no. 4, a watercolour of the Dutch Folly Fort by Chinnery, in the collection of Mr. and Mrs. P. J. Thompson.

海珠炮台是築於珠江海珠石上的一個橢圓形炮台。炮台內有四十名士兵把守，設有二十六台炮，島上並建有一祠廟紀念宋朝（960－1279）名官李昂英。

錢納利在1825年後曾造訪廣州多次，也畫了不少商行及位於其東面的海珠炮台速寫。在此圖的左方可見中和行的樓頂，建於1822年大火前，並於1832年拆掉。托瑪斯及威廉‧丹尼爾也曾以此西南景色為題，於1810年製成鐫刻版畫，現存香港藝術館(AH64.357)。

海珠炮台及東水炮台，雖然有不少的旅遊記述，但中外畫家都甚少以它們為繪畫題材，尤其是只畫取炮台景貌的更為罕見。東水炮台有三十名士兵駐守、二十台炮，位於往廣州的東面通道。

刊載書目：香港藝術館，1981，頁37，編號22及1985，頁56－57，編號22。
相關作品：香港藝術館，1981，頁30，編號15，彩圖於頁84，是一幅外銷的水粉絹本畫，圖中有海珠炮台；另1987，頁38，編號4，錢納利繪畫該炮台的水彩作品，湯普森先生夫人藏。

ᐉ 62 ᐊ

Standing Cup c. 1839

China, Cutshing

Silver

Mark: CU (Cutshing) and pseudo-London hallmarks

26.9 cm (10 ⅝ in.)

Peabody Essex Museum, Gift of Mrs. Edward W. Moore, *E79,772AB*

蓋杯 約1839

中國，吉星店

銀器

刻記：CU 及假冒的倫敦標記

26.9厘米 （10⅝吋）

皮博迪艾塞克斯博物館，愛德華‧穆爾夫人捐贈 *E79,772AB*

One of the most important presentation pieces made for the American market, this magnificent cup, with its unusual sea-dragon handles, depicts a "pulling" (i.e., rowing) race among Westerners on the Pearl River at Canton. An engraved inscription indicates that the cup was presented by the Hong merchants of Canton to Joseph Coolidge, a partner in the American firm of Russell and Co. from 1834 to 1839. This may indicate it was made and given in 1839 as Coolidge left Canton to return to Boston in that year. Coolidge was well known to Houqua II (1769-1843). Engraved in script on the front reserve: "Presented to Joseph Coolidge Esqre/as a token of respect from his friends/ Houqua Mouqua Pounkeyqua./Kingqua Linchong. Gouqua./Mongqua. Souqua Pounhoyqua./Samqua Thouching Quinching./ Sounching & Cumvor [sic]/Hong Merchants." Coolidge died in Boston in 1880.

Rowing was a popular sport which relieved the boredom of the business season. The Canton Regatta Club was founded in 1837, only two years earlier than the production of this cup. In 1852, Sir Harry Parkes wrote:

> Our only public amusement, a regatta, came off ten days ago, and it attracted many visitors from Hong Kong, both ladies and gentlemen, we had one or two very pleasant evening parties, graced by about eighteen ladies, a sight, I assure you for Canton, which during a large portion of the year, cannot boast a single petticoat![71]

Provenance: Presented to Joseph Coolidge by Chinese merchants; descended to the recipient's granddaughter, Mrs. Edward W. Moore

Published: Forbes 1975, p. 104, no. 58, fig. 39, 117a,b

Exhibited: "Tradition of Splendor: Chinese Silver for the West", China Trade Museum, 1981, ill., cover in detail and on the reverse in full; New York Antiques Show 1983, also ill.; "A Legacy of Luxury 1984-1987", IEF Traveling Exhibition, 1984-1986.

此杯雙耳以龍為飾，杯身雕有洋人在珠江賽艇一景，取材特別，是一件十分有價值的紀念品。它是廣州眾行商贈予美國商人約瑟‧庫利奇的禮物。庫利奇曾於旗昌洋行任職，任期為1834年至1839年。由此推算此杯是在1839年由行商訂送給是年離職返回波士頓的庫利奇。他與行商浩官二世（怡和行商伍紹榮1769－1843）十分熟稔。杯上刻有銘文：「送給約翰‧庫利奇先生，友人浩官、茂官、潘啟官、經官、鰲官、明官、秀官、海官、爽官、（安昌）及（孚泰）等行商敬贈。」庫利奇於1880年在波士頓逝世。

在貿易季節裡，外國人的節目並不多，划艇遂成為他們日常的消遣活動。他們在1837年組成了"廣州划船俱樂部"，是此杯製造日期的前兩年。哈里‧帕克斯於1852年曾為文記道：

> 我們唯一能在公共場所的消閑活動－划艇－在十日前舉行，它吸引了不少從香港來的觀眾，有先生和士女。我們舉辦了一兩個氣氛融洽的晚間聚會，共約十八位女士蒞臨，這個場面，我可肯定，在廣州年中大部分的時間並不多見![71]

收藏歷史：中國商人贈與約瑟‧庫利奇的禮品；世代相傳至庫利奇的曾孫女愛德華‧穆爾夫人。

刊載書目：福布斯，1975，頁104，編號58，插圖39，117ab。

展覽："輝煌的傳統：外銷中國銀器"，中國貿易博物館，1981，此杯的細部用作該展覽目錄的封面，而封面內頁則刊登全圖；紐約文物展，1983，並有圖錄；"豐盛的遺產1984－1987"，IEF 巡迴展覽，1984－1986。

[71] Stanley Lane-Poole, *The Life of Sir Harry Parkes, KCB, GCMG*, 1894, quoted in Gregory 1985 (41), p. 8.

[71] 格雷戈里，1985（41），頁8，節錄自斯坦利連普爾《哈里‧帕克斯的一生》一書，1894。

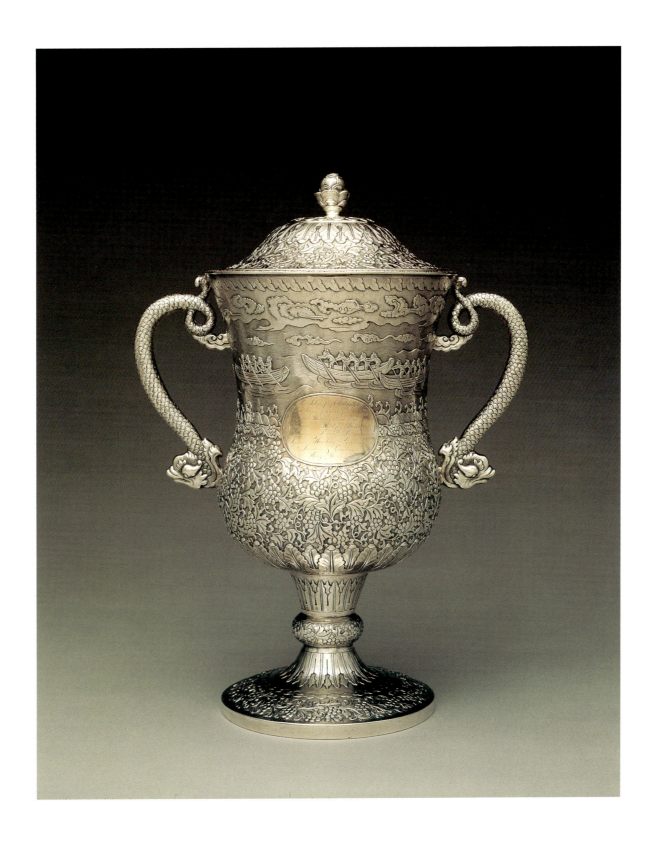

63

Mug 1840

China, unknown artist

Silver

Maker: "LEO", impressed on base

15.3 cm (6 in.)

Peabody Essex Museum, Gift of the Estate of Esther Pace Kuna, *E82,520*

杯 1840

中國，作者不詳

銀器

刻記：" LEO " 於底部

15.3 厘米 （6 吋）

皮博迪艾塞克斯博物館，埃絲特・庫娜基金捐贈　*E82,520*

This dragon-handled presentation mug is inscribed in a shield opposite the handle: "Presented to Dr. Field / by the Stewards of the / S.S. *Australia* ". The exterior shows a scene of Chinese Hongs to the right of the shield and to the left, the city wall of Canton behind which are the Flowery Pagoda, Mohammedan Tower, and Five-Storey Watchtower. Along the bottom of the mug is a continuous scene of the boat-filled Pearl River with the roof-tops of buildings on Honam Island visible at the very bottom edge. The interior is gold-washed. This mug is one of only three currently known which depict the Hongs in the 1840s. A smaller example, with the Dutch Folly Fort, is currently on loan to the Peabody Essex Museum, and is also marked by the maker "LEO". A third mug carves with soldiers parading in front of the Hongs and the 1846 Church prominent on the ground.[72] These three mugs and the Isaac Bull salver [73] (made by Khecheong and dated 1847) at the Metropolitan Museum of Art, New York, are the only known pieces of Chinese export silver depicting the Hongs.[74] Nothing is yet known about the silversmith. Only two other pieces are recorded by him: a cylindrical mug in the Bernice P. Bishop Museum, Honolulu, Hawaii; and a dessert spoon on loan to the Peabody Essex Museum.[75] A Salem native, Andrew Shales Waters, Jr. (b. 1833) made several voyages in the ship *Australia*, between about 1852 and 1857; this may be the same ship.[76]

Provenance: Ralph M. Chait Galleries, Inc., NY; Ester Pace Kuna

Published: Kiernan 1985, p. 123, no. 116.

Exhibited: "Connecticut Yankee in the Celestial Empire", Connecticut River Museum, Essex, CT, October 1988-March 1989.

Related works: Peabody Essex Museum, another example lent by Mr. Miles A. Fish III.

[72] Oriental Art, Spring 1990, No. 1, p. 3.

[73] Choi 1979, pp. 52-54.

[74] This information was taken from research by Richard Capurso in the Capurso papers at the Peabody Essex Museum; the mug is now owned by Miles Fish III and is on loan to the Peabody Essex Museum.

[75] Forbes 1975, p. 131, nos. 178 and 179.

[76] Putnam 1924, pp. 148-149.

此龍耳紀念杯有銘文刻於耳把對開的盾形上：「送予菲爾茲醫生，" 澳洲 " 號船上服務員敬贈。」盾形之右方刻有商館景貌，左方是廣州城，城牆後可見花塔、光塔及五層樓。沿著杯的底部是船艇雲集的珠江河岸，近邊緣處可見到河南島上樓房的屋頂部分。杯的內壁鎏金。在1840年代刻有商館圖樣的杯，傳世作品暫時知道的只有三個，此為其中之一。另外一個刻有海珠炮台及製造者的名稱 " LEO "。現時由私人借藏皮博迪艾塞克斯博物館。第三個杯子刻有在商行前方操練的軍隊，亦見到1846年才興建的教堂。[72] 現存描繪商館風貌的中國外銷銀器，已知的包括此三隻杯子及紐約大都會博物館藏的一件伊薩布爾的托盤[73]（由奇昌號（？）製造，系年1847）。[74] 有關這位銀匠的資料，現時仍未有所聞。有他的署名的作品還有兩件，一件是夏威夷火奴魯魯的伯尼斯主教博物館藏的杯子；另外是一隻甜食匙，暫借存於皮博迪艾塞克斯博物館。[75] 而關於上述 " 澳洲 " 號船，曾有記載賽倫市居民安德魯・沃特斯（生於1833）在1852年至1857年期間，乘坐 " 澳洲 " 號多次，二者可能是相同的一艘船。[76]

收藏歷史：紐約拉爾夫・蔡特畫廊；埃絲特・庫娜

刊載書目：基爾南，1985，頁123，編號116。

展覽："大中國裡的康乃狄格美國人"，康乃狄格海河博物館，艾塞克斯，康乃狄格州，1988年10月至1989年3月。

相關作品：皮博迪艾塞克斯博物館有另一件相類杯子，由邁爾斯・菲什三世先生借出。

[72] 《東方藝術》，1990年春季，第1期，頁3。

[73] 蔡，1979，頁52－54。

[74] 這些資料取自里查德・卡普索所作的 " 卡普索文書 "，現存皮博迪艾塞克斯博物館；此杯由邁爾斯・菲什擁有，現借存予皮博迪艾塞克斯博物館。

[75] 福布斯，1975，頁131，編號178及179。

[76] 帕特南1924，頁148－149。

64

The American Garden   1844 – 1845

China, unknown artist

Pen and ink, watercolour on paper

Sight: 34.5   x 34.5 cm (13 ⅝ x 17 ⅛ in.)

Peabody Essex Museum, Museum purchase *E82,881 (M10,915)*

美國花園   1844 – 1845

中國，畫家佚名

鋼筆及墨水、水彩紙本

34.5 x 34.5 厘米 (13 ⅝ x 17 ⅛ 吋)

皮博迪艾塞克斯博物館，館方購藏   *E82,881   (M10,915)*

This is a view of the American garden after the fire of May 22-23, 1841 and before 1856 when the Danish, Spanish and French Hongs to the left of the American garden were burned. As Crossman points out, it is impossible to know from this important drawing if the British, Dutch and Creek Factories had been rebuilt after the 1841 fire.[77] The area had been a previously undeveloped open space known as Respondentia Walk; Old China Street is to the left, Hog Lane to the right.

This appears to be a documentary drawing recording the original planting scheme of the garden; many of the plants have been identified and it has been noted that the cotton is in bloom and has no leaves, indicating that the drawing was taken during the winter months.[78] Crossman also notes that the garden is young here, compared to that illustrated on a silver salver, by the Chinese silversmith Khecheong (active in Canton 1840-1870) and given to Isaac Bull, which is discussed with the silver mug exhibited in this collection (no. 63).

Provenance: Louis Pappas, San Francisco
Published: Brewington 1968, p. 77, no. 332; Crossman 1991, p. 443, no. 21.
Related works: A rare view of the garden from the window of the American Hong was offered by Christie's New York, February 23, 1984, lot 44; Gregory 1993 (83a), p. 52.

是圖描畫了1841年5月22日至23日大火後的美國花園，其後於1856年商館區發生另一次大火。花園左方的丹麥館、西班牙館及法國館都化為灰燼。即如克羅斯曼指出，從這件重要的作品中根本無法知悉英國館、荷蘭館及小溪館（義和行）是否於1841年大火後曾經重建。[77] 這個花園從前是一個開放的海濱廣場，但未經開發。左方是靖遠街，右方是新荳欄街。

此件畫作似乎把整個花園原來的種植計劃都記錄下來，園中很多花木都可辨認。木棉樹正在盛放花朵，葉子已經掉落；相信已屆入冬時分。[78] 克羅斯曼亦指出此時花園內的林木應剛剛開始種植，可與編號63文中提及的一個銀托盤比較，它是中國銀器工匠奇昌（活躍於廣州1840至1870年）特為伊薩·布爾刻製。

收藏歷史：路易斯·帕帕斯，三藩市
刊載書目：布魯因頓，1968，頁77，編號332；克羅斯曼，1991，頁443，編號21。
相關作品：紐約佳士得曾拍賣一罕見的作品，描繪從美國商館窗外所見的花園景色，1984年2月23日，編號44；格雷戈里，1993 (83a)，頁52。

---

[77] Crossman 1991, p. 434.

[78] Richard Capurso, letters on file, Peabody Essex Museum.

[77] 克羅斯曼，1991，頁434。

[78] 里查德·卡普索檔案中的信札，皮博迪艾塞克斯博物館存。

65

The American Garden and Anglican Church   1848 – 1856

China, unknown artist, possibly Tingqua (active 1840 – 1870s)

Gouache on paper

Sight: 26.2 x 35.6 cm (10 $^1/_2$ x 14 in.)

Peabody Essex Museum, Museum purchase, *E83,532.3*

美國花園和聖公會教堂   1848－1856

中國，畫家佚名，可能是庭呱 (活躍於1840－1870年代)

水粉紙本

26.2 x 35.6 厘米 （10 $^1/_2$ x 14 吋）

皮博迪艾塞克斯博物館，館方購藏   *E83,532.3*

This unusual view, looking west, documents the newly constructed church near Jackass Point (1847) and the two large Factories in the so-called "Shanghai" style of China Coast architecture built on the site of the old English and Dutch Factories.[79] The garden was probably originally laid out in 1840. After surviving the fire of 1841, it was developed into the mature garden depicted here.

This drawing came from an album of 56 paintings once in the collection of John Heard, a descendant of the China trade merchant Augustine Heard of Ipswich, Massachusetts. The Peabody Essex Museum acquired other albums from the Heard estate which include views of Hong Kong and Canton (including the Heard & Company building at Canton), river craft, birds and flowers, a series of men and women from the Philippines, tradesmen and other subjects done in pen and ink.[80]

Provenance: Augustine Heard; John Heard

Published: Brewington 1968, p. 56, no. 246; Choi 1979, p. 54; Crossman 1991, p. 190, plate 92.

Related works: Howard 1984, pp. 126-127, no. C105C, colour ill. p. 99, an identical view in oil in the New-York Historical Society, one of a set of three views (1946.80-1946.82).

此畫景象並不常見，圖示在牡驢尖附近新建的教堂（1847年建）。在舊英國館和荷蘭館的舊址上，興建有兩座中國沿海常見的"上海式"大型建築，作為商館用途。[79] 美國花園原先在1840年拓建，經歷翌年大火後，可見圖中花園的樹木已茂盛起來。

這幅作品原屬一本共五十六幀畫的畫冊，曾由約翰·赫德收藏，他是麻省易普威治市的中美貿易商人奧古斯丁·赫德的後裔。皮博迪艾塞克斯博物館亦有從赫德家族處購藏其他畫冊，內容包括香港及廣州風貌（其中有位於廣州的赫德公司樓址）、河艇、花鳥、一系列的菲律賓人物、商人及其他題材的鋼筆墨水畫。[80]

收藏歷史：奧古斯丁·赫德；約翰·赫德。

刊載書目：布魯因頓，1968，頁56，編號246；蔡，1979，頁54；克羅斯曼，1991，頁190，圖版92。

相關作品：霍貨德，1984，頁126－127，編號C105C, 彩色插圖於頁99，紐約歷史學會藏一幀相類的油畫作品，是三幅畫中的其中一件（1946.80－1946.82）。

[79] Choi 1979, p. 54.

[80] Crossman 1991, pp. 191-192.

[79] 蔡，1979，頁54。

[80] 克羅斯曼，1991，頁191－192。

The Hongs of Canton   c. 1852

China, Tingqua (active 1840 – 1870s)

Gouache on paper

Sight: 19 x 25.7 cm (7 ¹/₂ x 10 ¹/₈ in.)

Framed: 23 x 30.5 cm (9 x 12 in.)

Peabody Essex Museum, Gift of Miss Clara Curtis, *E83,553*

從河南眺望十三商館   約 1852

中國，庭呱 (活躍於 1840 － 1870 年代)

水粉紙本

19 x 25.7 厘米 (7 ¹/₂ x 10 ¹/₈ 吋)

原框：23 x 30.5 厘米 (9 x 12 吋)

皮博迪艾塞克斯博物館，克拉拉‧柯蒂斯女士捐贈   *E83,553*

The Canton waterfront is depicted from Honam Island where workers load a sampan with chests of tea. The Protestant church, which figures prominently in this view, was built in 1847 and burned with the Hongs in 1856. In front of the church is anchored the steamer *Spark*, which was brought to Canton by Capt. Robert Bennet Forbes in 1849. Captain Forbes, an important China trade merchant from Boston, with the firm of Russell & Co., owned another example of this gouache, which was keyed by him so that all the buildings can be identified. Also on that example is an inscription on the reverse which reads in English, "A Chinese painting of the Foreign Factories at Canton by Tinqua [sic] of 16 New China Street, Canton, January, 1855."

Provenance: Misses Clara and Amy Curtis

Published: Crossman 1991, p. 195, plate 96.

Related works: An example acquired by R. B. Forbes, once exhibited at The Forbes House Charitable Trust, Milton, Massachusetts; another example in the Peabody Essex Museum (E82,532.28); Hong Kong Museum of Art, 1982, p. 37, no. 14.

此圖前方是河南貨倉區，一位挑夫正把一箱箱的茶葉運往舢舨上，對岸便是廣州城的河堤。1847年興建的基督教堂清晰可見，它後來在1856年被燒毀，教堂前方泊碇了一艘蒸汽輪船"火花"號，是由羅拔伯特‧福布斯船長於1849年駛往廣州。他是從波士頓來華的一位十分重要的商人，任聘於旗昌洋行。他藏有另一幅相同的水粉畫，並親自註有各建築物名稱，以供辨認。此畫背後附有英文題識：「一幅描繪廣州商館的畫作，由廣州同文街十六號的庭呱繪，1855年1月記。」

收藏歷史：克拉拉及埃米‧柯蒂斯女士

刊載書目：克羅斯曼，1991，頁 195，圖版 96。

相關作品：福布斯購藏有一件類似的作品，曾於麻省米爾頓的福布斯慈善信託基金大樓展出；皮博迪艾塞克斯博物館有另一件相類畫作 (E82,532.28)；香港藝術館，1982，頁 37，編號 14。

Godowns in Honam   1857 – 1861

China, unknown artist

Oil on canvas

Sight: 53.5 x 146 cm (21 x 57 $^1/_2$ in.)

Hong Kong Museum of Art, Donated by Sir Robert Ho Tung, *AH64.43*

河南貨倉區   1857 － 1861

中國，畫家佚名

油彩布本

53.5 x 146 厘米 (21 x 57 $^1/_2$ 吋)

香港藝術館, 何東爵士捐贈   *AH64.43*

The godowns on Honam Island, on the south side of the Pearl River, opposite the site of the old Factories, were built after the destruction of the Hongs in 1856; the godowns remained there until Shamian Island was leased to the Westerners in 1859. The damaged Red Fort can be seen near the centre of the painting. The *Willamette*, flying an American flag, belonged to Russell & Company and sailed between Hong Kong and Canton during the months of January to October in 1856, and from 1858 to 1861.[81]

Several views of the godowns on Honam are very similar but with different sidewheelers depicted in each, while others show an array of Chinese vessels, giving the impression that perhaps the paintings are meant to be as much about the vessels as about the harbour. This would stand to reason as the architecture of Honam was not as distinctive as that of the Factory site.[82]

Published: Hong Kong Museum of Art 1981, p. 39 and 1991, p. 84.
Related works: Hong Kong Museum of Art 1982, pp.38-39, c. 1858, attributed to Tingqua, gouache on paper, 51.5 x 116 cm, donated by Sir Robert Ho Tung, AH64.42. In the middle of the picture is the old French Folly Fort, and just to the right before it is the *Whitecloud*, an American sidewheeler; and Gregory 1991 (57), p. 53, no. 104, c. 1858, gouache on paper.

河南島上的貨倉區在珠江南面，對岸為舊商館區，在1856年商館區嚴重焚毀後，商館的貨倉便搬移到此地，直至1859年外國人租借沙面為止。中央是已毀壞了的紅炮台，河上的＂威廉梅茨＂號豎起美國旗幟，它是旗昌洋行的輪船，於1856年1月至10月及1858至1861年行駛港穗兩地。[81]

描繪河南起卸貨物區的畫作也不少，景物大致相同，但每幅的輪船都有分別，有些則畫有列陣的中國船艇，可見畫家都很著重描寫河道和船艇的風貌，對於河南岸上的樓房建築反而不及舊商館區那麼鮮明易辨。[82]

刊載書目：香港藝術館，1981，頁39及1991，頁84。
相關作品：香港藝術館，1982，頁38－39，約1858年，一幅傳為庭呱所畫的水粉畫，51.5 x 116 厘米，為何東爵士捐贈 (AH64.42)，圖中有水炮台，前方是＂白雲＂號美式輪船；格雷戈里，1991(57)，頁53，編號104，一幅約1858年的紙本水粉畫。

---

[81] Hong Kong Museum of Art 1991, p. 84.
[82] For example see, Crossman 1991, p. 435, a view with only Chinese vessels, and the Hong Kong Museum of Art view with the *Whitecloud* (AH64.42).

[81] 香港藝術館，1991，頁84。
[82] 這些畫作的例子可參見克羅斯曼，1991，頁435，畫上只有中國船；香港藝術館藏有的一幅，上有＂白雲＂號美式輪船 (AH64.42)。

69

View of Canton   1865

China, unknown artist

Oil on board

Sight: 64.4 x 105.2 cm (25 $^3/_8$ x 41 $^3/_8$ in.)

Framed: 80.3 x 121 cm (31 $^9/_{16}$ x 47 $^5/_8$ in.)

Peabody Essex Museum, Museum Purchase,

through funds donated by Museum Friends and Fellows, *M10,867*

廣州城   1865

中國，畫家佚名

木板油畫

64.4 x 105.2厘米 (25 $^3/_8$ x 41 $^3/_8$ 吋)

原框：80.3 x 121厘米 (31 $^9/_{16}$ x 47 $^5/_8$ 吋)

皮博迪艾塞克斯博物館，館方以博物館之友基金購藏 *M10,867*

By the date of this work, photographs were beginning to replace paintings of topographical views; the unusual perspective, unattainable in photography at the time, may have been the impetus for this painting. This extraordinary view of the entire city of Canton, depicts Shamian Island in the lower left and steamboats in the river.

Shamian Island, a reclaimed mudbank adjacent to the western suburb of Canton, was one-half mile in length and one-quarter mile wide and comprised forty-four acres. It was once an area for wealthy Chinese to anchor their flower boats for entertainment, and in 1859 was leased to the British and French after the destruction of the Hongs. The island was divided into 82 lots, which were put up for auction on September 2, 1859; six lots were reserved for the British consulate and offices, and another lot for the church which still stands. In the painting, Shamian is very prominently painted as the main interest to the purchaser.

The walls of the city, once forty feet high, are the most evident landmarks from this view; all but a fragment of the walls behind the Five Storey Watchtower are now gone. To the far right, in the river, stands the remainder of the island on which the Dutch Folly Fort, destroyed in 1856, was built; this would soon be reclaimed by the expanding waterfront.

Provenance: Childs Gallery, Boston

Related works: Gregory 1989 (53), p. 64, no. 110 for a c. 1860 view in oil by an unknown Chinese artist; Gregory 1994 (64), p. 62, no. 130, a c. 1870 gouache on canvas by an unknown Chinese artist; Hong Kong Museum of Art 1987, pp. 50-51, a watercolour by Marciano Baptista.

此圖的作畫時期，正值攝影作品逐漸流行，並開始取代一些風景地形畫作。然而這幅畫取景角度特別，憑當時的攝影技術，應不能達到這種效果，畫家可能因此而創作此圖。圖中可見整個廣州城左下方的沙面及河上的蒸汽輪船。

沙面是位於廣州西郊旁的一幅填土泥澤區。全長半公哩，闊四分一哩，面積有四十四頃。這裡曾是中國富戶人家泊碇花艇娛賓作樂的地方，在商館燒毀後，它於1859年曾成為英國及法國的新租界。這個區分割成八十二個地段，於1859年9月2日拍賣，六個地段是預留給英國領事館及辦事處，另一地段用作興建教堂，現仍保存。這幀畫作特別著墨於沙面的描寫，以迎合顧客的需求。

廣州城的城牆，高四十呎，是此圖惹人注目的一環，城牆現已拆掉，只剩餘五層樓後面一小幅殘垣。在右方的河面上，可見海珠炮台所在的小島遺跡，炮台於1856年被炸毀。此島很快便因擴展海濱區而填為平地。

收藏歷史：蔡爾茲藝廊，波士頓。

相關作品：格雷戈里，1989 (53)，頁64，編號110，一幅約1860年的油畫，畫家佚名及1994 (64)，頁62，編號130，另一幅約1870年的布本油畫，佚名的中國畫家所繪；香港藝術館，1987，頁50－51，一幅巴普蒂斯塔的水彩畫。

CANTON.

Hong Kong

香港

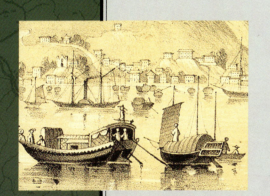

V. HONG KONG

Hong Kong (officially known as Victoria) is an island at the eastern side of the wide mouth of the Pearl River, 76 miles south-east of Canton. When the British first arrived in the late 18th century there were some 5,000 Chinese inhabitants, mostly fishermen and quarrymen. The British were attracted to the island by the fresh water supply from the waterfall at Aberdeen (Shek Pai Wan). Shortly after 1843, when the Treaty of Nanking formally ceded the island to the British, the Chinese population had expanded to 12,000 and a new Chinese town had developed near the British-built town of Victoria. By 1855 Hong Kong and Shanghai had surpassed Canton as the main centres of China's import-export trade.

Clark Abel, in his book on Lord Amherst's Embassy published in 1818, said: "As seen from the ship, this island was chiefly remarkable for its high conical mountains, rising in the centre and for a beautiful cascade, which rolled over a fine blue rock into the sea. I took advantage of the first watering boat to visit the shore and made one of these mountains and the waterfall the principal objects of my visit". Future artists would be impressed by these same geographical landmarks. **Victoria Peak** and the silhouette of the mountains which comprise the island of Hong Kong were the leitmotif for many artists depicting the island, as the Praya Grande was of Macau and the Hongs were of Canton. The **Waterfall at Aberdeen** on the southwest coast of Hong Kong Island, at Shek Pai Wan, is still visible near the present Wah Fu Housing Estate, but the flow of water was greatly reduced when the Pokfulam Reservoir was constructed.

Aside from the standard scenes of the island from Kowloon, views were taken from various angles of the Hong Kong waterfront. However, without a resident artist of the caliber of Chinnery to promote interest in picturesque detail, depictions of Hong Kong tended to be more documentary than artistic. Part of the reason for this may have been the introduction and broader use of photography beginning in the mid-19th century, as well as the more hectic pace of trading that formerly took place seasonally in Canton. At this time, the most frequently documented scenes were offices, godowns, and residences. **Flagstaff House**, illustrated in this exhibition as the residence of Lt. Gov. the Hon. Major General D'Aguilar, was originally called Headquarter House and was completed prior to 1846. Long known as Flagstaff House because of the flag of the British East India Company which flew from its staff, it is now the oldest residential structure standing on the island and is the home, since 1984, of the Flagstaff House Museum of Tea Ware. **St. John's Cathedral** (1849) was described ungraciously by Charles Wirgman (1832-1891), to accompany his drawing of a military band playing on the Parade Ground, published in the *Illustrated London News*, 15 September 1857: "Before you is the Church or Cathedral, an unsightly pile, quite destroying the Oriental appearance of the place". Recognized today as an important landmark building, it is preserved and still functions as a church. Other landmark buildings include: the **Pedder Street Clock Tower** (1862); the **Bishop's House** (1851); the twin-turreted **Roman Catholic Church** (1851); the **Goverment House** (1855); and the **Signal Station** (1861) on the Peak. **Causeway Bay** (Tung Lo Wan, or Copper Gong Bay), now mostly reclaimed, was once a fishing harbour and site of godowns.

V. 香港

香港（昔日正式名稱是維多利亞城）是位於珠江口東面的一個島嶼，距廣州東南七十六哩。當英國人於十八世紀晚期初次涉足此地時，島上約有五千名中國居民，他們大多數是漁民及打石工人。英國人最喜往香港仔（石排灣）附近的瀑布汲水補碇。未幾，於1843年簽訂的南京條約將香港島正式割讓予英國，而島上的中國居民人口亦增至一萬二千人，他們的居住範圍亦擴展至英人所建的維多利亞城附近。1855年，香港和上海兩個城市已取代了廣州，成為中國進出口的貿易中心。

克拉克・埃布爾在其1818年的阿美士德使節團遊記一書曾記述：「從船上所見，島上佈滿尖角形的山巒，由中央高聳起來，又見一條美麗的瀑布，在一塊藍色的石上流轉，最後奔流入海中。我乘搭第一艘載水艇登岸，並選擇了其中一個山巒及這條瀑布作為主要的駐腳點。」其後這些景物也吸引到不少畫家。太平山及其他組成香港島的山脈的剪影，就成為了畫家筆下的香港景色主要的題材，一如澳門的南灣和廣州的商館，都是代表當地的特徵。**香港仔附近的瀑布**位於港島西南岸的石排灣，現時華富邨的公園內的位置，但在薄扶林水塘建成後，已因水流減弱而變為一條山溪。

除了一般從九龍眺望港島的景色外，亦有不少畫作是在港島沿岸各處所見之景物。然而，如沒有了錢納利這位天才橫溢的畫家致力推動繪畫的風氣，描繪香港景物的畫作便流於紀錄價值大於藝術價值了。可能是因為十九世紀中葉攝影術已逐漸普及，而且昔日於廣州季節性的商業活動已逐漸遷移至香港，並日益頻繁。此時，最常見的畫作題材記錄了各洋行、貨倉及住宅的實地景貌。**旗桿屋**即德己立少將官邸，亦是今次展覽的其中一項選材，竣工於1846年，因懸掛有東印度公司的旗幟，所以得名。它應是現存香港最具歷史價值的西式建築物，自1984年開始改建成茶具文物館。查爾斯・沃格曼曾繪有一幅**聖約翰教堂**（建於1849）的素描，一隊軍樂團在練兵場上奏樂，此畫刊登於1857年9月15日的《倫敦畫報》，其中並附有沃格曼的評語：「在你眼前就是這座教堂，一間難看的大型建築，破壞了這塊地方的東方風味。」如今聖約翰教堂仍是一十分重要的大教堂。其他在畫中常見的建築物有：**畢打街鐘樓**（1862）；**會督府**（1851）；**羅馬天主教堂**（1851）；**督憲府**（1855）及山頂的**訊號台**（1861）。昔日的**銅鑼灣**是一漁港及貨倉區，現時大部分已填成平地。

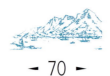
Hong Kong Harbour Above Causeway Bay   1845

England, drawn by Lt. Thomas Bernard Collinson (1821 – 1902)

Lithograph, Published by Dickson & Co.,

Sight: 43 x 85 cm (17 x 33 ½ in.)

Hong Kong Museum of Art, *AH84.29*

從銅鑼灣眺望海港景色   1845

英國・托馬斯・柯林森畫 (1821 － 1902)

石版畫，迪克森公司刻印

43 x 85 厘米 (17 x 33 ½ 吋)

香港藝術館   *AH84.29*

A topographical and panoramic view of Hong Kong harbour, with the twenty important landmarks identified in the lower margin of the print, illustrates the newly settled harbour. To the left, in the foreground is East Point of Causeway Bay and the godowns of Jardine, Matheson & Co., with only a few structures built along the waterfront of Victoria. The section of the peninsula of Kowloon called Tsim Sha Tsui is visible on the right. Morrison Hill and Wanchai are at the middle front while at the back is Central.

Published: Hong Kong Museum of Art 1991, p. 26

此圖為香港海港的地形全圖，在版畫的下方並註明有共約二十個重要陸標的名稱，是香港開埠以來的建設。左前方是銅鑼灣東角，可見渣甸洋行（今怡和公司）的貨倉，海旁建築物並不多。右方九龍半島延伸出來的土地是尖沙咀。中央部分為摩利臣山和灣仔區，後方是中區。

刊載書目：香港藝術館，1991，頁 26。

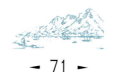
Waterfall at Aberdeen   1817

England, after a watercolour attributed to William Havell (1782 – 1857)

Coloured aquatint, by Thales Fielding

Titled on the stone, "THE WATERFALL at HONG CONG", and "Published by Longman Hurst Rees,

Orme & Brown, London, Oct. 1, 1817".

Acquatint, hand-coloured

Sight: 10.7 x 16.2 cm (4 $^1/_{14}$ x 6 $^1/_4$ in.)

Hong Kong Museum of Art, *AH64.362*

香港仔附近的瀑布   1817

英國·菲爾丁依照威廉·哈維 (1782 – 1857) 的水彩刻印

版畫上附有題識、刻印公司名稱及日期

著色飛塵蝕刻

10.7 x 16.2 厘米 (4 $^1/_{14}$ x 6 $^1/_4$ 吋)

香港藝術館   AH64.362

This view is of the source of fresh water which first attracted the British to Hong Kong Island. Allom and Wright remarked in 1843, that here mariners could procure "... a supply of the purest water, which is seen falling from the cliffs of the Leong-teong, or two summits, in a series of cascades, the last of which glides in one grand graceful lapse into a rocky basin on the beach...." [83]

Havell was the official artist attached to Lord Amherst's Embassy to China which anchored off Hong Kong for three days in July 1816, on its way to Peking. This print served as the frontispiece to Clark Abel's book on the Embassy, *Narrative of a Journey in the Interior of China* (London, 1818). However, Abel stated (p. ix) that he is "answerable" for the illustrations in the book and, as they do not bear the names of professional artists, it may be that Abel created most of the original drawings. In the book, Abel described his experience on July 12, 1816:

> Looking from the deck of the *Alceste* early on the following morning, I found that we were in a sound formed by some small islands, by which it was land-locked in every direction, and of which Hong-kong is the principal. As seen from the ship, this island was chiefly remarkable for its high conical mountains, rising in the centre, and for a beautiful cascade, which rolled over a fine blue rock into the sea. [84]

Related works: Chater 1924, discussed p. 348, illustrated p. 371; the original watercolour attributed to W. Havell and dated c. 1816, is in the collection of the Hong Kong Museum of Art, and is published in Hong Kong Museum of Art 1980, p. 24-25, no. 1.

[83] Allom and Wright 1843, Vol. I, p. 17.

[84] Quoted in Chater 1924, p. 348, no. 2.

此圖描繪的就是香港島最早期吸引英國人到來的主要因素 — 水源。艾林及賴特於1843年曾記述航海者可以在此取得「最純淨的水，在兩個山峰之間飛流下來，化成一段段的瀑布，最後一段則墜落在一片石灘上，形成一個美麗的深潭…」[83]

哈維是阿美士德訪華使節團的隨團畫家，他們於1816年7月在香港海灣補碇三日後，便啟程往北京。克拉克·埃布爾將使節團的經歷寫成一書，名《中國內陸旅遊記》（倫敦，1818），此版畫出現在書中封面內頁。埃布爾在頁IX闡明他可以"解答"有關書中的插圖，那些畫作沒有註明任何職業畫家的姓名，埃布爾也許是大部分畫作的原創者。他在書中提及他於1816年7月12日的見聞：「翌日清晨，我在"阿爾西斯特"號甲板上四處觀望，發現身處由幾個小島組成的海峽，四周都是陸地，其中一個主要的島嶼便是香港。從船上所見，島上佈滿尖角形的山巒，由中央高聳起來，又見一條美麗的瀑布，在一塊藍色的石上流轉，最後奔流入海中。」[84]

相關作品：遮打，1924，詳述於頁348，插圖於頁371；原作水彩畫，相傳是哈維所繪，時約1816年，香港藝術館藏，並刊於其展覽目錄，1980，頁24 – 25，編號1。

[83] 艾林及賴特，1843，第一冊，頁17。

[84] 節錄自遮打，1924，頁348，編號2。

72

View of Victoria Town, Island of Hong Kong   c. 1850

England, drawn by B. Clayton on stone, after Piqua

Lithograph, published by Dean & Co.

Inscribed in the stone, lower left, "Drawn by B. Clayton, from a painting by Piqua."

Sight: 43.5 x 71 cm (17 $\frac{1}{8}$ x 28 in.)

Hong Kong Museum of Art, *AH64.251*

維多利亞城   約 1850

英國，克萊頓依照培呱（譯音）畫作繪製

石版畫，迪安公司印行

下方附有題識

43.5 x 71 厘米 （17 $\frac{1}{8}$ x 28 吋）

香港藝術館   *AH64.251*

The Chinese artist is not known, beyond the inscription by Clayton on this view of Hong Kong. The perspective is very Western in concept and unlike many paintings by the Chinese artist's contemporaries, both known and unknown. If Clayton has copied the original faithfully, then the variations include the depiction of Victoria Peak with a sharper silhouette than usual and the inclusion of numerous Chinese vessels in the foreground with only three Western vessels in the middle ground.

這幅畫原本由中國畫家繪製，但生平不詳。刻版者克萊頓在畫的下方只記有這位原作者的名稱 ― 培呱（譯音）。此圖採用了西方的透視技巧繪畫，風格與同期中國畫家有別。如果克萊頓是忠實地參照原作而刻繪這幅版畫，相信最大不同的地方是他將太平山的剪影刻劃成多角山峰，前方盡是中國船艇，只有三艘外洋船在中央。

73

Flagstaff House   1846

Scotland, after a drawing by Murdoch Bruce (Active 1840 – 1855)

Lithograph, by A. Maclure, hand-coloured,

Sight: 23.3 x 35 cm (9 $^1/_8$ x 13 $^3/_4$ in.)

Hong Kong Museum of Art, *AH 64.389.8*

德己立少將官邸   1846

蘇格蘭，依照默多克‧布魯斯 (活躍於 1840 – 1855) 原畫所刻製

麥克勞爾刻印

著色石版畫

23.3 x 35 厘米 (9 $^1/_8$ x 13 $^3/_4$ 吋)

香港藝術館   *AH64.389.8*

Titled in the stone, "The Residence of Lieut. Governor the Honourable, Major General D'Anguilar/ 28th September 1846". This structure, originally called Headquarter House, was completed just prior to Bruce's drawing of it. Long known as Flagstaff House, because the British flag flew from its staff, it is now the oldest residential structure on Hong Kong Island and is the home, since 1984, of the Flagstaff House Museum of Tea Ware.

Published: Hong Kong Museum of Art 1980, p. 68-69, and 1991, p. 29.

版畫上刻印有標題：「德己立少將官邸，1846年9月28日。」布魯斯於興建工程完竣後不久便繪畫此作。這座建築物早期懸有英國旗，故又名旗桿屋，如今它是香港島歷史最悠久的住宅，自1984年開始便改建為茶具文物館。

刊載書目：香港藝術館，1980，頁68－69及1991，頁29。

74

Spring Gardens, Hong Kong 1846

Scotland, painted by Murdoch Bruce (active 1840 – 1855)

Lithograph, by A. Maclure, hand-coloured,

Sight: 22.8 x 34 cm (9 x 13 3/8 in.)

Hong Kong Museum of Art, *AH64.389.10*

春園景色 1846

蘇格蘭，依照默多克・布魯斯 (活躍於 1840 － 1855) 原畫所刻製

麥克勞爾刻印

著色石版畫

22.8 x 34 厘米 （9 x 13 3/8 吋）

香港藝術館　*AH64.389.10*

The area known as Spring Gardens, now corresponding with Queen's Road East, was developed when fifty plots were auctioned on June 14, 1841. The harbour seen to the left is now the reclaimed district of Wanchai, where a stream, which may have given its name to the area, still flows. In this view, Hospital Hill with the Albany Godowns before it are shown in the background. The second house from the right was once rented as Government House.

Published: Hong Kong Museum of Art 1980, p. 60., no. 19, and 1991 p. 28, no. 13.
Related works: Conner 1986, p. 46, no. 49, the oil painting by Bruce, in a private collection.

圖中的春園是現今皇后大道東一帶。1841年6月14日，該區分成五十幅地段拍賣。左方的海港亦已成為灣仔填海區。附近有一泉水，可能因此而得其名。遠方的背景是醫院山，山前是雅賓利倉庫。圖中右方第二間建築物曾租賃給港督般含爵士作官邸。

刊載書目：香港藝術館，1980，頁60，編號19及1991，頁28，編號13。
相關作品：康納，1986，頁46，編號49，布魯斯的一幅油畫，私人藏品。

75

Spring Gardens, Hong Kong   1846
England, George Chinnery (1774 – 1852)
Watercolour on paper
Sight: 10.7 x 19 cm (4 ⅛ x 7 ½ in.)
Framed: 30.5 x 38.3 cm (12 x 15 in.)
Peabody Essex Museum, Museum purchase, *M3,810-79A*

春園   1846
英國，喬治·錢納利 (1774 － 1852)
水彩紙本
10.7 x 19 厘米 （4 ⅛ x 7 ½ 吋）
原框：30.5 x 38.3 厘米 （12 x 15 吋）
皮博迪艾塞克斯博物館，館方購藏   *M3,810 － 79A*

This watercolour sketch shows the Hong Kong waterfront with Pedder's Hill in the middle ground and the bungalow of Mr. Pedder, first British harbour master, identified by a flag. The premises of Lindsay & Co., Dent & Co., and the Roman Catholic Cathedral are also included. Due to illness, Chinnery spent only six months in Hong Kong during 1846; his brief stay and the illness itself account for the relatively few views produced there.

A nearly identical view by Lieutenant Walford Thomas Bellairs, R.N., is inscribed "Hong Kong, June, 1846."[85] Marciano Baptista painted a watercolour of nearly the same view some years later.[86]

Provenance: Augustine Heard
Related works: Conner 1993, p. 256, pl. 170, a drawing by Chinnery of this view, without the landmass in the foreground, inscribed and dated in shorthand "Drawing of Mr Stanton's house required... correct April 15 [18]46 / correctly filled in April 17 [18]46", in the Toyo Bunko collection, Tokyo.

此一小幅水彩素描繪寫了港島海濱一帶景色。中央是畢打山，崗上有本港首任港務官畢打的辦事處及旗桿。海旁建築包括有林賽洋行、寶順洋行及羅馬天主教堂。1846年，錢納利曾寓居香港，但因患病只逗留了六個月，故此他描繪香港景色的作品並不多。

契爾福德·貝萊爾斯繪有一幅相類景物的作品，附有題識「香港，1846年6月」。[85] 數年後，巴普蒂斯塔亦有一幅相近的水彩畫作。[86]

收藏歷史：奧古斯丁·林德
相關作品：康納，1993，頁256，圖版170，錢納利繪畫了相同景象的素描，但沒有前方的土地，附有速記題識「需要一幅斯坦頓先生屋子的素描…(18) 46年4月15日更正／(18) 46年4月17日補正」，現藏於日本東洋文庫。

---

[85] Hong Kong Museum of Art 1985, pp. 70-71, no. 29.
[86] Ibid., pp. 66-67.

[85] 香港藝術館，1985，頁 70 － 71，編號 29。
[86] 同上，頁 66 － 67。

76

View of Jardine Matheson's Looking North West from Causeway Bay   1846

Scotland, after a drawing by Murdoch Bruce (active 1840 – 1855)

Lithograph, by A. Maclure, hand-coloured,

Sight: 26 x 38 cm (10 ¼ x 15 in.)

Hong Kong Museum of Art, *AH 64.389.4*

從銅鑼灣向西北眺望之渣甸洋行及倉庫   1846

蘇格蘭，依照默多克‧布魯斯 (活躍於 1840 － 1855) 原畫所刻製

麥克勞爾刻印

著色石版畫

26 x 38 厘米 (10¼ x 15 吋)

香港藝術館   *AH64.389.4*

The title is inscribed in the plate and dated September 28, 1846. The view is ostensibly of the great British merchant house of Jardine, Matheson & Co. at East Point, with several Western vessels at anchor, to the left of which are the residences, and to the right of which is Kellet Island and its fort. However, the placid Causeway Bay, with small Chinese vessels at anchor and Chinese residents ambling along the newly cleared road, appears to be of more interest to the artist.[87]

The firm was established by William Jardine and James Matheson in 1828. After taking control of a firm which traced its roots to Canton in 1780, they officially took the name of Jardine, Matheson & Co. in 1832. Among the first to purchase land at the first auction in 1841, they moved the headquarters to Hong Kong where they built the complex of offices, godowns, a slipway and houses on the promontory of East Point.

Published: Hong Kong Museum of Art 1980, pp. 70-71, no. 24.

是畫之標題刻印在畫下方的版面上，並記有作畫日期為1846年9月28日。圖示英商渣甸洋行在東角的公司及倉庫。遠方碼頭旁泊碇有洋船數艘，左方是住宅區，右端是奇力島和島上的堡壘。但吸引畫家注意力的，反而是銅鑼灣港上的中國帆船及在新築的馬路上優悠自在的中國人。[87]

渣甸洋行由威廉‧渣甸和詹姆斯‧馬西森於1828年合力創辦。其實他們早於1780年已在廣州設立公司，1832年才採用渣甸洋行為正式名稱。1841年，他們在香港的首次土地拍賣中競投得東角沿海一帶地方，因此便將公司總部移往該處，並興建貨倉、辦公司、住宅及一通往碼頭的斜滑道。

刊載書目：香港藝術館，1980，頁 70 － 71，編號 24。

---

[87] Hong Kong Museum of Art 1980, p. 70.

[87] 香港藝術館，1980，頁 70。

77

Hong Kong Harbour with Junk and Beached Clipper   1857

Scotland, Dr. Thomas Boswall Watson (1815 – 1860)

Pencil on paper

Sight: 16.5 x 24 cm (6 ½ x 9 ½ in.)

Hong Kong Museum of Art, *AH85.44*

港海上的帆船及快速帆船   1857

蘇格蘭，托馬斯‧屈臣 (1815 － 1860)

鉛筆紙本

16.5 x 24 厘米 (6 ½ x 9 ½ 吋)

香港藝術館   *AH85.44*

Inscribed lower right, "Hong Kong/Oct. 8, 1857", this very fine academic drawing of a ship beached at the base of the hills of Hong Kong, with small houses on the peaks behind, is a rare example of a depiction of the island with an emphasis on its picturesque and romantic setting. The setting may be East Victoria.

Published: Gregory 1985 (40), p. 68, then on loan from a descendant of the artist.

畫中右下方標記有「香港。1857年10月8日」。這幅速寫精確地描繪港島山巒下海灣中的一艘快速帆船，題材罕見。背景山崗上築有小屋，意境優美恬靜。這處地方可能是香港東區的海灣。

刊載書目：格雷戈爾，1985 (40) ，頁 68，由畫家的後人借出作品。

Hong Kong   Oct. 8 1857.

78

The Mint and its Garden 1860s

Unknown artist

Watercolour and gouache on paper

Sight: 47 x 81 cm (18 ¹/₂ x 31 ⁷/₈ in.)

Hong Kong Museum of Art, *AH88.13*

香港造幣廠 1860 年代

畫家佚名

水彩及水粉紙本

47 x 81 厘米 (18 ¹/₂ x 31 ⁷/₈ 吋)

香港藝術館 *AH88.13*

A rendering of the Mint and its formal garden located at the east end of the settlement overlooking, in the background, Causeway Bay. The Mint was erected in May, 1866, and closed in February 1868 because the quality of silver coins was unsatisfactory. The building was later converted into a sugar refinery and was owned by Jardine, Matheson & Co. Sugar Street in the present Causeway Bay took its name from this refinery.

Published: Gregory 1988 (51), no. 82; Hong Kong Museum of Art 1991, p. 42.
Related works: Hong Kong Museum of Art 1980, pp. 106-107, no. 42, and also in Cameron 1978, p. 84, an elevation of the Hong Kong Mint, 1864 by Arthur Kinder (AH64.298).

此圖描繪造幣廠的外貌及其東面的花園，背景是銅鑼灣。香港造幣廠於 1866年5月開業，但因銀圓質素未臻理想，遂於1868年2月結束營業。廠址後來售予怡和公司興建糖廠，銅鑼灣糖街因而得名。

刊載書目：格雷戈爾，1988 (51)，編號82；香港藝術館，1991，頁42。
相關作品：香港藝術館，1980，頁106－107，頁42；金馬倫，1978，頁84，香港造幣廠的正面圖 (AH64.298)，阿瑟·金德繪於1864年。

79

City of Victoria, Hong Kong   early 1860s

China, unknown artist

Gouache on paper

Sight: 48.4 x 113 cm (18 7/8 x 44 1/2 in.)

Framed: 70.5 x 134.6 cm (27 5/8 x 53 in.)

Peabody Essex Museum, Gift of Mr. Lewis A. Lapham, *E81,235*

香港維多利亞城   1860 年代早期

中國，畫家佚名

水粉紙本

48.4 x 113 厘米　(18 7/8 x 44 1/2 吋)

原框：70.5 x 134.6 厘米　(27 5/8 x 53 吋)

皮博迪艾塞克斯博物館，劉易斯・拉帕姆捐贈　*E81,235*

This is a panoramic view of Hong Kong Island from East Point, with the City of Victoria, Victoria Peak, and native and foreign shipping in the harbour. Construction has extended in the city to the mid-levels and the view is sufficiently accurate so that numerous landmarks can be recognized. These include the Cathedral, whose tower can be seen near the waterfront at the exact centre of the painting, and Government House next to this, to the west. Still further to the west is the Clock Tower, erected in 1861.

Provenance: Lewis A. Lapham

Related works: Gregory 1993 (61), no. 95, c. 1870.

此幅香港島海岸圖，繪畫了由東角至維多利亞城一帶及山頂的景色，繁忙的海港上泊碇了多艘中式及西式的帆船。建築物已逐漸由海旁延伸至半山區，景物描寫得也算精確，很多樓房亦能辨認出來。如圖中央的聖約翰教堂，在其西面的督憲府及1861年建成的畢打街鐘樓。

收藏歷史：劉易斯・拉帕姆

相關作品：格雷戈里，1993 (61)，編號 95，一幀約 1870 年的油畫。

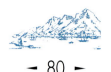

80

Residence of Augustine Heard and Company, Hong Kong c. 1860

China, unknown artist

Oil on canvas

Sight: 44.2 x 58.5 cm (17 ³/₈ x 23 in.)

Framed: 62.8 x 77 cm (24 ⁵/₈ x 30 ¼ in.)

Peabody Essex Museum, Museum purchase, *M17,297*

瓊記洋行大班住宅　約 1860

中國，畫家佚名

油彩布本

44.2 x 58.5 厘米　(17 ³/₈ x 23 吋)

原框：62.8 x 77 厘米　(24 ⁵/₈ x 30 ¼ 吋)

皮博迪艾塞克斯博物館，館方購藏　*M17,297*

In 1840 Augustine Heard, Sr. (1785-1868) of Ipswich, Massachusetts, and Joseph Coolidge of Boston broke away from Russell and Company to found the rival firm of Augustine Heard and Company. Business expanded rapidly in the 1850s to Hong Kong, Shanghai and Fuzhou. In 1856, the head office was moved from Canton to Hong Kong. In this view, the neo-gothic tower of the 1849 St. John's Cathedral can be seen. The tower was erected in 1853.

Provenance: Augustine Heard, Sr.

Related works: Gregory 1993 (61), p. 67, no. 106, a photo c. 1860 which appears to show this building, looking north, and identifies it as one "built as a Record Office by A R. Johnston, the colony's first Deputy Superintendent of Trade; since at that time there was no Government House, it was rented to the first Governor of Hong Kong as their official residence."

1840年，來自麻省易普威治市的奧古斯丁·赫德（1785－1868）及波士頓的約瑟·庫利奇離開旗昌洋行，創辦了瓊記洋行，在商業上互相競爭。到了1850年代，業務發展迅速，擴展至香港、上海及福州等地。總公司更於1856年由廣州遷移至香港。是圖可見聖約翰教堂「新歌德式」設計的塔樓，聖約翰教堂於1849年落成，而高聳的鐘樓則因經費問題而延至1853年才啟用。

收藏歷史：奧古斯丁·赫德

相關作品：格雷戈里，1993 (61) ，頁 67，編號 106，一幀約 1860 年的照片中，其中一座建築物可能就是此間，並說明此是「由這塊殖民地的第一任貿易署副署長莊士敦興建的檔案處；因直至此刻仍然未有督憲府，所以它便租借予第一任港督作為正式的寓所。」

81

View of Hong Kong Harbour   1860 – 1870

Macau, Marciano Antonio Baptista (1826 – 1896)

Watercolour on paper

Sight: 35.6 x 56.5 cm (14 $^1/_8$ x 22 $^1/_4$ in.)

Framed: 56.7 x 76.8 cm (22 $^1/_4$ x 30 $^1/_4$ in.)

Peabody Essex Museum, Museum purchase, *M10,874-A13*

從半山俯瞰香港海港   1860 － 1870

澳門，巴普蒂斯塔 (1826 － 1896)

水彩紙本

35.6 x 56.5 厘米　(14 $^1/_8$ x 22 $^1/_4$ 吋)

原框：56.7 x 76.8 厘米　(22 $^1/_4$ x 30 $^1/_4$ 吋)

皮博迪艾塞克斯博物館，館方購藏　*M10,874 － A13*

This view of Hong Kong harbour, from the hillside overlooking the rooftops of Western residences in Central Victoria, shows Kowloon in the background. The American flag flies from a pole in front of the Factory at the far left.

Published: Brewington 1968, p. 84, no. 367, listed there as an by an unidentified Chinese artist.

此圖前方花木濃蔭，向下眺望，可見港島中區的西式住宅區，左方海旁的洋行門前豎立有美國旗。海港上商船雲集，遠方是九龍半島。

刊載書目：布魯因頓，1968，頁 84，編號 367，說明這是一幀佚名的中國畫家所繪的作品。

藝術家生平

William Alexander (1767-1816)

[England]   Alexander served as draughtsman with Lord Macartney's embassy to China (1792-1794). For ten years following his return to England, he painted scenes of China which he exhibited at the Royal Academy. Many of these were published in George Staunton's *Account of the Embassy* and in Alexander's own books *The Costumes of China* and *The Punishments of China*. The volume and quality of Alexander's work led it to be accepted as the most authentic composite image of China for many years. Alexander was appointed Professor of Drawing at the military college at Great Marlow in 1820, and later was the Keeper of Prints and Drawings at the British Museum.

Marciano Baptista (1826-1896)

[Macau]   A professional artist of Portuguese nationality, he lived in Macau in his early years and it is believed that he worked as an assistant in Chinnery's studio. He is also known to have worked designing stage sets. Baptista moved from Macau to Hong Kong where he concentrated on topographical views.

Auguste Borget (1808-1877)

[France]   Born in Issoudun, south of Paris, Borget started work as a banker. In 1829, at the age of 21 he moved to Paris to become an artist and shared an apartment with Honore de Balzac. He showed at the Salon from 1836 to 1859 and obtained a medal of third class in 1843. In 1836, despite attempts by family and friends to dissuade him, he embarked on a world tour and visited North America, South America (crossing the Andes to Chile and Peru), Hawaii and the Sandwich Islands, the coast of South China (1838-1839), the Philippines and India, returning to France in 1840. It is known that Borget met Chinnery during his stay in Macau and that some of his works reflect the acquaintance. He is today best known for his lithographs published in his *Sketches of China and the Chinese*, Paris and London, 1842. His later years were spent in studying scripture and in charitable work in his native Issoudun and Bourges.

William Bramston (1835-1892)

[England]   Bramston abandoned a career in the clergy to become a painter. He studied in Paris with L. Bonnet from 1875 to 1879. He lived in Lausanne from 1881 to 1887 and showed at the Swiss Society of Fine Arts in 1884.

威廉·亞歷山大（1767—1816）

〔英國〕   亞歷山大以繪圖員身份隨馬戛爾尼使節團（1792－1794）來華。回國後，他用十年時間方才完成其關於中國風貌的畫作，這批作品除曾經於皇家美術學院展出外，更刊載於喬治·斯湯頓所寫的《英使謁見乾隆紀實》及亞歷山大本人所作的《中國的服飾》和《中國的刑罰》等書。亞歷山大的作品在英國流傳甚廣，一向以來是可信性甚高的有關中國的綜合圖説。1820年，他任軍事學院的繪圖教授，其後任職大英博物館，負責管理館內收藏的版畫及素描。

馬西安諾·巴普蒂斯塔（1826—1896）

〔澳門〕   葡藉職業畫家，早年居澳門。相信曾在錢納利畫室中擔任助理，亦曾從事舞台設計工作。巴普蒂斯塔後來從澳門移居香港，專注描繪風景地形畫。

奧古斯特·波塞爾（1808—1877）

〔法國〕   出生於巴黎南部的伊蘇丹。波塞爾原先投身銀行界，1829年逕往巴黎與名作家奧諾雷·巴爾托克同住，並轉業為畫師。在1836至1859年間，他將畫作參加沙龍展，並在1843年獲取第三等獎章。1836年，他不顧親友的反對，進行了一環遊世界的旅程，遊歷了北美、南美（經安地斯山脈到達智利及秘魯）、夏威夷及三文治島、中國華南海岸（1838-1839）、菲律賓及印度，最後於1840年返回法國。在逗留澳門期間，他曾與錢納利相晤，而其畫作中亦反映出他們之間的交往。他的作品曾製成石版畫，刊印在他的《中國及中國人素描集》裡，1842年於巴黎及倫敦出版，流傳廣泛。波塞爾的晚年在其家鄉伊蘇丹及伯吉斯渡過，專注研究聖經及投身慈善工作。

威廉·布蘭斯通（1835—1892）

〔英國〕   布蘭斯通放棄聖職人員的任命而選擇成為畫家。在1875至1879年間，在巴黎跟隨大師邦尼特習畫。1881至1887年間移居瑞士洛桑。作品曾於1884年在瑞士藝術學會展出。

Murdoch Bruce (active 1840-1855)

[Scotland]   One of the most often reproduced artists, Bruce's views of Hong Kong recall the architectural heritage of the settlement. As an architect by training, he was able to capture the colonial architecture, then such an important element of the landscape, and now gone from that landscape. He was also Inspector of Buildings and Overseer of Roads for the Government of Hong Kong. Bruce left for England in the late 1840s and died of illness on the trip.

Theodore de Bry (1528-1598)

[Netherlands]   Draftsman, printmaker and goldsmith, de Bry lived in Frankfurt and also was a publisher there. He worked for a long time in England. His prints, like those of his son, are among the better Dutch prints.

George Chinnery (1774-1852)

[England]   Chinnery left Great Britain in 1802 at the age of 28, spent twenty-three years in India, and twenty-seven on the China coast. He moved again to avoid mounting debts, to Macau in 1825, where he developed a style of drawing much imitated by amateur and professional artists who came into contact with him. It was, however, his painting on canvas which was to have a profound effect on Chinese artists who copied him, especially Lamqua.

Chow Kwa (active 1850-1880)

[China]   This Chinese artist operated a studio in Shanghai from 1855 to 1880 where he painted portraits, port views, miniatures and houses. He signed one canvas in block letters but primarily used a small label with his name attached to the stretchers.

Cutshing (active 1785-1870)

 [China]   A prolific but little-documented silversmith working on Old China Street, Canton, Cutshing appeared to have first marked his wares with a conjoined "CU", and later with "CUT" when his firm moved to No. 8 New China Street from c. 1850 to 1870.

Thomas Daniell (1749-1840)

[England]   Thomas Daniell had been granted permission by the East India Company to "proceed to Bengal to follow his profession of an engraver" on December 1, 1784. He took his young nephew, William, with him as an assistant.

默多克・布魯斯（活躍於1840—1855）

〔蘇格蘭〕   布魯斯的作品產量十分豐富，他本身是一名建築師，因此筆下的香港風景，都清楚地記錄了當時的建築文物，而且刻劃入微。這些甚具殖民地色彩的樓房，現已所餘無幾。他曾獲委任為香港政府的道路監督。1840年代晚期返國時在途中病逝。

狄奧多・德・布里（1528—1598）

〔荷蘭〕   德布里居於法蘭克福，亦曾在英國工作了一段長時間。他身兼數職，是繪圖員、版畫製作師、金匠及出版商。德布里及其子，都是優秀的荷蘭版畫家。

喬治・錢納利（1774—1852）

〔英國〕   錢納利於1802年離開英國，當時他只有廿八歲。後來他在印度居住了廿三年，因逃避債項，於1825年移居澳門，並在此終老，他在中國沿海前後逗留了共廿七年。他的作畫風格，大大影響了與他結交的職業或業餘畫家。尤其是他的油畫，更廣為中國的外銷畫家參照模倣，啉呱是其中一表表者。

周呱（活躍於1850—1880）

〔中國〕   這位中國畫家在1855年至1880年期間於上海開設了一間畫室，專門繪畫人像、海港景色、小型畫像及房舍景物等。他曾在一幅帆布作品上以英文正楷簽署，但通常他會將附有自己名字的標籤貼在畫架上。

吉星（活躍於1785—1870）

〔中國〕   這位銀器匠的店舖設於廣州靖遠街，所製成的銀器用品數量豐富，但有關此工匠的文獻記載甚少。他早期在銀器上刻記有「CU」二相連英文大寫，在1850至1870年期間，他的店舖遷往同文街八號，而他的標記亦改為「CUT」。

托瑪斯・丹尼爾（1749—1840）

〔英國〕   1784年12月1日，東印度公司批准托瑪斯・丹尼爾以雕版師身份前往孟加拉。他並攜同擔任其助理的姪兒威廉一起出發。他們於1785年8月23日抵達黃埔，在中國逗留了數月才前往印度。除了約翰・韋

They reached Whampoa on August 23, 1785 and spent several months in China sketching before going to India. Apart from John Webber, who visited China from 1779 to 1880, they were the first British professional artists to come to South-East Asia. After spending seven years in India, they returned to England in 1793 with Lord Macartney's convoy, via Canton and Macau. Back in England, they produced prints and paintings based on their sketches. Among those were a series of ten known oil paintings of Chinese subjects as well as the collection of acquatints published as *Oriental Scenery*. Six volumes appeared between 1795 and 1815; with the exception of the book entitled *Excavations*, the five others were done by William. Evidence suggests that Thomas Daniell may have painted only three of the Chinese subjects in oil, and it was William who turned most of his uncle's drawings into oil paintings. Thomas was associated with the Royal Academy in 1796 and appointed academician in 1799. The works of William and of Thomas are so intimately linked that they must be considered an indivisible ensemble.

William Daniell, R. A. (1769-1837)

[England]   A landscape painter and printmaker, Daniell showed for the first time at the Royal Academy in 1795, entered the school at the Academy in 1799, was named associate in 1807 and in 1822 became a Royal Academician. He left for India with his uncle Thomas in 1784 and collaborated on the designs and sketches produced by the latter. It was William who printed, for the most part, their *Scenes Orientales*, and who transferred the drawings done by both artists into oil paintings.

Edward Duncan (1803-1882)

[England]   Duncan worked with William Havell and, as son-in-law to William John Huggins, he often prepared aquatint versions of his father-in-law's works. He was a watercolourist and from 1880 to 1882 he frequently showed at the Watercolour Society and at the Royal Academy.

Capt. Robert Elliot, R.N. (? -1849)

[England]   Capt. Elliot was an amateur marine painter of considerable talent who visited India and China from 1822 to 1824. His sketches were re-drawn by Clarkson Stanfield, Samuel Prout, Anthony Van Dyke Copley Fielding and other artists and published as a two volume book in 1833 as *Views in the East; Comprising India, China, and The Shores of the Red Sea*.

伯於1779至1780年訪遊中國外，丹尼爾是首批造訪東南亞的藝術家。他們在印度居住了七年，於1793隨麥夏爾尼勛爵的護航艦返回英國，途中經廣州及澳門兩地，並繪畫了不少速寫。返抵英國後，他們根據速寫繪製了不少油畫及版畫。其中為人所知的是一套十幀的中國景物油畫，至於一些飛塵蝕刻版畫作品則印刊在《東方景貌》的畫冊中。在1795至1815年間，共有六冊面世，除了《發掘》一冊，其餘五冊都是威廉的作品。據資料顯示，托瑪斯·丹尼爾繪畫了約二幀以中國景物為題的油畫，其他的作品主要是由威廉將其叔父的素描作品再繪製成油畫。托瑪斯於1796年加入英國皇家美術學院，並於1799年獲委任為院士。托瑪斯與威廉二人的作品有著緊密的聯繫，他們這對組合可算是完美的配搭。

威廉·丹尼爾（1769—1837）

〔英國〕   威廉是一位風景畫家及版畫家，作品於1795年首次在皇家美術學院展出。他於1799年加入該學院，1809年成為會員，1822年更成為該院院士。在1784年他與叔父托瑪斯一同前往印度作畫，威廉主要根據其叔父的畫稿製作版畫，並刊印在《東方景貌》畫冊中，他並將二人的素描稿件改繪成油畫作品。

愛德華·鄧肯（1803—1882）

〔英國〕   鄧肯與威廉·哈維共事，他亦常常為其岳丈威廉·哈金斯的作品刻製成飛塵蝕刻版畫。他也是一位水彩畫家，其作品曾於1880至1882年期間在皇家藝術學院的水彩學會中展出。

羅伯特·埃利奧特（ ?—1849）

〔英國〕   埃利奧特上校是一位頗有藝術天份的業餘畫家，他在1822至1824年間曾隨軍到訪印度及中國。他的素描作品曾被多位藝術家重繪並輯成畫冊，名為《東方風貌：印度、中國及紅海海岸》，共兩冊，1833年出版。這一羣藝術家包括了克拉克森·斯坦菲爾德、塞繆爾·普勞特及安東尼·菲爾丁等人，他們應未曾踏足中國。

Anthony Van Dyke Copley Fielding (1787-1855)

[England]   Fielding studied with his father, Nathan Theodore Fielding (1775-1818) and then under John Varley. He started exhibiting with the Royal Society of Watercolourists and continued for most of his career, becoming secretary in 1813, and serving as president from 1831 to 1855. He was the best known of the family as a specialist in watercolour painting and a drawing master. He never travelled abroad, unlike his brother Thales.

Thales Fielding (1793-1837)

[England]   A landscape painter, son of T.N. Fielding and brother of Anthony Van Dyke Copley Fielding, Thales Fielding showed at the Old Water-Colour Society, was a member as of February 12, 1829, and exhibited in the Salon of Paris from 1823 to 1824.

William Havell (1782-1857)

[England]   Havell had his debut at the Royal Academy in 1804. As the official draftsman on Lord Amherst's embassy, he reached China in 1816, travelled north to Beijing and then to South China reaching Macau in 1817. He specialized in landscape watercolours and small oil portraits. He was one of the first members of the Watercolour Society and was a beneficiary of the Turner Foundation.

Peter Bernard William Heine (1827-1885)

[Germany/America]   Born in Dresden, Heine came to the United States in 1849. He served from 1852 to 1854 as artist with the Perry expedition to Japan and later made his home in New York City until he returned to Europe in 1859.

William John Huggins (1781-1845)

[England]   As a young man, Huggins was a sailor in the British East India Company and made drawings of ships and landscapes, especially in China. An underrated marine painter who specialized in ships, many of his works, maligned first by John Ruskin, were engraved in aquatint by his son-in-law Edward Duncan. After a voyage to Bombay and China from 1812 to 1814 he settled near the East India House in London and was engaged by the Company to paint its ships. He exhibited at the Royal Academy in 1817 and thereafter until just before his death. In 1834 he was appointed marine painter to King William IV.

Wilson Lowry (1762-1824)

[England]   A printmaker, the son of Strickland Lowry and student of John Browne, Lowry printed landscapes and portraits.

安東尼・菲爾丁（1787—1855）

〔英國〕   菲爾丁早年跟隨其父內森・菲爾丁（1775-1818）習畫，後來師事約翰・瓦利。他的作品最早於皇家水彩學會展出，於1813年他成為該會的秘書，在1831至1855年間，更連任該會會長。菲爾丁是其家族成員中最廣為人知的水彩及素描畫家，但從未到過外地遊歷。

塞勒斯・菲爾丁（1793—1837）

〔英國〕   塞勒斯是一位風景畫家，父親是內森・菲斯丁，其兄是著名水彩畫家安東尼・菲爾丁。塞勒斯的作品曾經在舊水彩學會展出，他於1829年2月12日成為該會會員。而在1823至1824年，他的畫作亦於巴黎畫廊中展覽。

威廉・哈維（1782—1857）

〔英國〕   哈維的作品於1804初次展出於英國皇家美術學院。1816年，哈維以繪圖員身份跟隨阿美士德使節團來華，到過北京，於1817年抵達澳門。哈維擅長水彩風景畫及小型肖像油畫。他是英國水彩學會的首批學員，亦是特納基金的受惠人之一。

彼德・海因（1827—1885）

〔德國／美國〕   海因生於德國德勒斯登，於1849年移居美國。在1852至1854年間他曾以藝術家身份隨佩里訪問團往日本，隨後在紐約居住，直至1859年才返回歐洲。

威廉・哈金斯（1781—1845）

〔英國〕   哈金斯年青時在英國東印度公司擔任水手，繪畫了不少風景及船艦的作品，尤其是中國境內的風物。這位海景畫家的作品往往被人忽略，並曾被約翰・拉斯金誹謗。哈金斯的作品大多由其婿愛德華・鄧肯刻印成飛塵蝕刻版畫。在1812年至1814年往孟買及中國的航旅後，哈金斯便在倫敦東印度公司大樓附近安頓下來，並受委託繪畫該公司旗下之船隻。他的作品自1817年就在英國皇家美術學院展出，直至其逝世為止。在1834年，英皇威廉四世委任他為海景畫家。

威爾遜・勞里（1762—1824）

〔英國〕   勞里是一版畫師，他是斯特里克蘭・勞里的兒子，曾拜約翰・布朗為師，擅刻印風景及人像畫。

Johan Nieuhof (1618-1672)

[Holland]   A draftsman and sailor, Nieuhof travelled to Asia as steward to the ambassadors from the Dutch East India Company to Beijing in 1668, and published *An Embassy to China* (Dutch edition 1655-1657, London edition, 1669). Many of Nieuhof's drawings were engraved and used in the book on his travels and observations with the Embassy. He was assassinated in Madagascar in 1672.

Piqua (19th century)

[China]   This Chinese artist is unknown except for the reference that the print by B. Clayton in this exhibition is after Piqua. He may possibly be Piu Ou Qua (1737-1826), who painted watercolours (ref: Sotheby's New York, October 19-20, 1988); and he may possibly be the PuQua identified only in a series of English prints of street vendors after original Chinese paintings.

John Prendergast (dates unknown)

[England]   Little is known of Prendergast except that he was in China in the 1840s when he made a set of views of Hong Kong and the adjacent areas. A series of views by Prendergast was announced in the Canton Press of 1843 but only two aquatints are now known.

Spoilum (active 1774-1805)

[China]   (Spillem, Spilum) Spoilum is the first Cantonese artist to become known for his Western-style portraits of both Western and Chinese merchants. He painted portraits on glass and canvas, as well as port scenes, landscapes and genre scenes.

Sunqua (active 1830-1870)

[China]   Sunqua was a Cantonese artist known for his oil on canvas ship portraits, port views, landscapes, and watercolour albums. Paintings occasionally bear his signature but more frequently they are labelled on the stretchers or in the albums with the name "Sunqua". Around 1857 he opened a studio in Hong Kong.

Tingqua (active 1840-1870s)

[China]   Assumed to be Guan Lianchang, the younger brother of Lamqua (Guan Zuolin), Tingqua was the leading watercolourist in Canton. He is best known for his views of his own studio, as well as his albums of flowers, birds, insects, trading ports and interiors.

約翰・紐荷芙（1618—1672）

〔荷蘭〕　　紐荷芙是一名繪圖員及水手。他於1668年隨同荷蘭東印度公司委派的使節團到訪中國，充任管事一職，後來出版了《東印度公司使節團訪華紀實》一書（荷文版1655-1657，倫敦版1669）。紐荷芙將他的所見所聞都繪畫下來，並製成版畫刊印在此書中。他於1672年在馬達加斯加被謀殺。

培呱（譯音）（19世紀）

〔中國〕　　這位畫家生平不詳，只在克萊頓的一幅版畫中刻記有「參照培呱一畫作」字句。他可能是一水彩畫師（1737-1826，參考紐約蘇富比拍賣目錄，1988年10月19日至20日）；亦可能是另一位擅繪中國街頭小販的畫家，他的作品被刻製成英國版畫。

約翰・普倫德加斯特（生卒不詳）

〔英國〕　　有關普倫德加斯特的資料並不多，只知道他在華活躍期是1840年代，繪畫了不少香港及其鄰近地區的景貌。他有一系列的作品曾於1843年在《廣州報》上發表，但只有兩幀飛塵蝕刻版畫傳世。

史貝霖（譯音）（活躍於1774—1805）

〔中國〕　　史貝霖是廣州早期以西洋技法繪畫的大師，擅長替中外商人繪畫肖像，作品有油畫及玻璃畫，題材包括海港景色、風景及民生百態等。

新呱（譯音）（活躍於1830—1870）

〔中國〕　　新呱是廣州有名的外銷畫家，擅繪油畫，題材有商港景色、船隻等，也擅畫水彩小品。作品上有英文正楷署名，但更常見是他將英文名"SUNQUA"的標籤貼在畫架或畫冊上。在1857年前後，新呱在香港開設了畫室分店。

關聯昌（活躍於1840—1870年代）

〔中國〕　　舖號「庭呱」，關作霖（啉呱）之胞弟，是譽滿廣州的水彩畫師。他的作品題材繁多，其中有繪畫自己的畫室、花卉、雀鳥、草蟲、商港風貌及家居景物等。

Toonequa (active 1810-1825?)

[China]   This artist is undocumented except for the reference by Robert Burford that his 1838 "Panorama of Canton" is after the work of this artist. This may be the artist who is otherwise identified as Tonqua (and, Tonc Qwa). There was a senior and a junior (also spelled Toonqua), the former mentioned in the Waln list under "Paintings", and the latter as "No. 1 standing; miniature painting".

Dr. Thomas Boswall Watson (1815-1860)

[Scotland]   Trained in Edinburgh, Watson practiced in Scotland and then went to Macau in 1845. He was an amateur draftsman who, under Chinnery's tutorage, improved his style, and in some cases successfully imitated his teacher. As a friend and physician, he attended Chinnery during his final illness. With W. C. Hunter, he organized a sale of drawings and oil paintings found among Chinnery's effects. Watson moved to Hong Kong before returning to Scotland in 1858.

John Webber (c. 1750-1793)

[England]   Webber, the son of a Swiss sculptor, was chosen at the age of 24 to accompany Captain Cook on his third voyage. He visited Macau in 1779 and published his book *Views in the South Seas* after his return to England in 1780. Webber was elected Royal Academician in 1791.

Charles Wirgman (1832-1891)

[England]   The lesser-known brother of B. T. Wirgman, Charles was a landscape painter, caricaturist and figure painter. He worked for the *Illustrated London News* during the Opium War and settled in Yokohama in 1860.

Yeuqua (active 1840-1880s)

[China]   Little is known about the life of this Cantonese painter (also spelled Youqua) except that he set up workshops under the name of "Yeehing" in Canton and Hong Kong. He is known for his port views, landscapes, still-lifes and flowers.

Sources for biographies: Forbes 1975, Benezit 1976, Gregory 1985, Conner 1986, Hong Kong Museum of Art 1987, Crossman 1991.

通呱（譯音）（活躍於1810—1825？）

〔中國〕   生平不詳。只於羅伯特·伯福德於1838年繪畫的廣州全景圖中，標明是參照此畫家的作品而繪。在沃恩的名單中，有一位「老通呱」位列於「繪畫」一欄中，而另一位「小通呱」則屬「第一等畫家；小型肖像畫」。

托瑪斯·屈臣（1815—1860）

〔蘇格蘭〕   早年在愛丁堡學醫，1835年畢業後，在蘇格蘭行醫，1845年東渡濠江，受錢納利的指導後，畫技日進，作品風格亦酷肖乃師。作為摯友及醫生，屈臣在錢納利彌留之際，陪伴在側。後來他與威廉·亨特從錢納利的遺物中，揀出一批油畫及素描作品，並籌劃了一次售賣會。屈臣醫生後來移居香港，1858年返回蘇格蘭。

約翰·韋伯（約1750—1793）

〔英國〕   韋伯的父親是一位瑞士雕塑家。他在廿四歲時受挑選跟隨庫克船長的第三次航旅前往中國。他於1779年造訪澳門，翌年返回英國後，出版了一書名為《南海風貌》。韋伯於1791年成為英國皇家美術學院院士。

查爾斯·沃格曼（1832—1891）

〔英國〕   沃格曼擅長繪畫風景、人物及諷刺畫，曾於鴉片戰爭時期為《倫敦畫報》工作。1860年他移往日本橫濱定居。

煜呱（活躍於1840—1880年代）

〔中國〕   活躍於廣州的十九世紀外銷畫大師，生平不詳。他在廣州及香港都設有畫店，舖號「怡興」。他擅長繪畫商港風光、花卉靜物等。

藝術家生平資料參考書目：福布斯，1975；貝尼澤，1976；格雷戈里，1985；康納，1986；香港藝術館，1987；克羅斯曼，1991。

BIBLIOGRAPHY

Abel 1818: Abel, Clark. *Narrative of a Journey in the Interior of China*. London, 1818

Allom and Wright 1843: Allom, Thomas and Rev. Wright, G. N. *China*. 2 Vols., London, 1843

Avery 1926: Avery, Lillian Drake. *A Geneaology of the Ingersoll Family in America 1619-1925*. New York, 1926

Bard 1993: Bard, Solomon. *Traders of Hong Kong: Some Foreign Merchant Houses, 1841-1899*. Hong Kong, 1993

Benezit 1976: Benezit, Emmanuel. *Dictionnaire des Peintres, Sculpteurs, Dessinateurs et Graveurs*. 10 Vols., Paris, 1976

Berry-Hill 1963: Berry-Hill, Henry and Sidney. *George Chinnery 1774-1852*. Leigh-on-Sea, 1963

Berry-Hill 1970: Berry-Hill, Henry and Sidney. *Chinnery and China Coast Paintings*. Leigh-on-Sea, 1970

Berry-Hill 1979: Berry-Hill, Henry and Sidney. *Merchants, Mandarins and Mariners: 19th Century Paintings of the China Trade*. New York, 1979

Bonsall 1986: Bonsall, Geoffrey. "George Chinnery's Views of Macao", *Arts of Asia*, Vol. 16, No. I, pp. 78-92, Jan-Feb 1986

Borget 1842: Borget, Auguste. *Sketches of China and the Chinese*. London, 1842

Brewington 1968: Brewington, M. V. and Dorothy. *The Marine Paintings and Drawings in the Peabody Museum*. Salem, 1968

Brighton 1981: *William Alexander: An English Artist In Imperial China*. Brighton: The Royal Pavilion, 1981

Choi 1979: Choi, Kee Il. *The China Trade: Romance and Reality*. Lincoln, Massachusetts, 1979

Christman 1984: Christman, Margaret C. S. *Adventurous Pursuits: Americans and the China Trade 1784-1844*. Washington, D.C., 1984

Conner 1986: Conner, Patrick. *The China Trade 1600-1860*. Brighton: The Royal Pavilion, 1986

Conner 1993: Conner, Patrick. *George Chinnery 1774-1852: Artist of India and The China Coast*. Woodbridge, Suffolk, England, 1993

Conner 1996: Conner, Patrick. "The China Coast Collection of Tuyet Nguyet and Stephen Markbreiter", *Arts of Asia*, Volume 26, Number 2, pp. 61-77, March-April 1996

Crawford 1930: Crawford, Mary Caroline. *Famous Families of Massachusetts*. 2 Vols., Boston, 1930

Crossman 1967: Crossman, Carl L. "The Rose Medallion and Mandarin patterns in China Trade porcelain", *Antiques*, 1967; reproduced in Elinor Gordon, *Chinese Export Porcelain*, New York, 1975

Crossman 1984: Crossman, Carl L. "Watercraft of the Pearl River in the Early 19th Century", *The Twelfth Annual Peabody Museum of Salem Antiques Show*, catalogue, 1984

Crossman 1991: Crossman, Carl L. *The Decorative Arts of the China Trade*. London, 1991

Cuthbertson 1986: Cutherbertson, Brian. "Macau Past and Present: Introduction", *Arts of Asia*, Vol. 16, No. 1., pp. 57-65, January-February 1986

Du Halde 1738: Du Halde, Pere J.-B. *Description of China, Korea and Tibet*. 2 Vols., London, 1738

E.I.M.S. Catalogue 1821: *East India Marine Society Catalogue*. Salem, Massachusetts, 1821

Elliott 1833: Elliott, Robert, Capt. *Views in the East: comprising India, Canton, and The Shores of the Red Sea*. 2 Vols., London, 1833

Forbes 1975: Forbes, H. A. Crosby. *Chinese Export Silver 1785 to 1885*. Milton, Massachusetts, 1978

Forbes 1984: Forbes, H. A. Crosby. "A Chinese Export Gold Snuff Box Returns to Salem", *The Twelfth Annual Peabody Museum of Salem Antiques Show,* catalogue, Salem, Massachusetts, 1984

Gregory, with date and catalogue number:
Publications of the Martyn Gregory Gallery, London:
1982 (30), *China Trade Paintings*
1983 (34), *China Trade Pictures*
1984 (38), *China Trade Pictures*
1985 (40), *Dr. Thomas Boswall Watson*
1985 (41), *The China Trade Observed*
1986 (43), *Canton and the China Trade*
1987 (47), *Trade Winds to China*
1989 (53), *In The Western Manner*
1990 (55), *Marciano Baptista 1826-1896*
1990 (56), *Paintings of the China Coast*
1991 (57), *Artists of the China Coast*
1992 (50), *Paintings of the China Coast*
1993 (61), *Genius of the China Coast*
1993 (62), *Alexander Rattray*
1994 (64), *Artists of the China Coast*
1995 (66), *China and the East Indies*

Guillén-Nuñez 1984: Guillén-Nuñez, César. *Macau.* Hong Kong, 1984

Guillén-Nuñez 1990: Guillé-Nuñez, César. *Marciano Baptista e A Sua Arte.* Macau, 1990

Guimet 1992: *Du Tage á la mer de Chine: Une épopée portugaise.* Paris, 1992

Hervouët 1986: Hervouët, François and Nicole, and Yves Bruneau. *La Porcelaine des Compangies des Indes: A Décor Occidental.* Paris, 1986

Hillard 1900: Hillard, Katharine. *My Mother's Journal.* Boston, 1900

Hong Kong Museum of Art, and date: publications of the Hong Kong Museum of Art
1980: *Hong Kong: The Changing Scene: A Record in Art*
1981: *Pearl River in the Nineteenth Century*
1982: *Late Qing China Trade Paintings*
1983: *Scenes of Two Cities*
1985: *George Chinnery, His Pupils and Influence*
1987: *Gateways to China*
1991: *Historical Pictures*

Howard 1974a: Howard, David Sanctuary. *Chinese Armorial Porcelain.* London, 1974

Howard 1974b: Howard, David Sanctuary. *The Pearl River on Porcelain.* Impresna Nacional, Macau, 1974; originally printed in *Boletim do Instituto Luís de Camões,* no. 1, Vol. III

Howard 1984: Howard, David Sanctuary. *New York and the China Trade.* New York, 1984

Howard 1994: Howard, David Sanctuary. *The Choice of the Private Trader.* London, 1994

Howard and Ayers 1978: Howard, David Sanctuary and John Ayers. *China for the West.* New York, 1978

Hunter 1882: Hunter, William C. *The Fan Kwai at Canton.* London, 1882

Hutcheon 1975: Hutcheon, Robin. *Chinnery, the Man and the Legend.* Hong Kong, 1975

Hutcheon 1979: Hutcheon, Robin. *Souvenirs of Auguste Borget.* Hong Kong, 1979

Keswick 1982: Keswick, Maggie. *The Thistle and The Jade: A Celebration of 150 Years of Jardine, Matheson & Co.* London, 1982

Kiernan 1985: Kiernan, John Devereux. *The Chait Collection of Chinese Export Silver.* New York, 1985

King 1980: King, Edward. "Chinnery's Years in Macao", *Orientations,* Vol. II, No. 4, pp. 32-33, April 1980

Lansdown 1787: unpublished manuscript, *Journal of the Ship Marquis of Lansdown,* kept by the Ship's Surgeon, 1787-1788, Peabody Essex Museum, Stephen Phillips Library, Salem, Massachusetts

Leal Senado 1990: *Marciano Baptista e A Sua Arte,* Leal Senado de Macau, Gallerias de Arte, 1990

Le Corbeiller 1974: Le Corbeiller, Clare. *China Trade Porcelain: Patterns of Exchange.* New York, 1974

Lee 1984: Lee, Jean Gordon. *Philadelphians and the China Trade 1784-1844.* Philadelphia, 1984

Lisbon 1983: *XVII Exposiçao Europeia de Arte, Ciência e Cultura: Jeróimos II.* (7 Vols.), Lisbon, 1983

Loines 1953: Loines, Elma. *The China Trade Post-Bag of the Seth Low Family of Salem and New York.* Manchester, Maine, 1953

Lothrop 1967: Lothrop, Francis B. *George Chinnery (1774-1852) & Other Artists of the Chinese Scene.* Salem, Massachusetts, 1967

Low 1829: Low, Harriet. Unpublished manuscript journal, Volume 1, Library of Congress, 1829

Macao 1985: *George Chinnery - Macao.* Macau, 1985

Morse 1926-29: Morse, Hosea Ballou. *The Chronicles of the East India Company trading to China 1635-1834.* 4 Vols., Oxford, 1926-1929

Mudge 1962: Mudge, Jean McLure. *Chinese Export Porcelain for the American Trade 1785-1835.* New York, 1962

Nieuhof 1669: Nieuhof, Johan. *An Embassy from the East-India Company of the United Provinces to the Grand Tartar Cham.* London, 1669

Orange 1922: Orange, James. *Pictures by George Chinnery in the J. Orange Collection.* London, 1922

Orange 1924: Orange, James. *The Chater Collection: Pictures relating to China, Hongkong, Macao, 1655-1860.* London, 1924

Phillips 1956: Phillips, John Goldsmith. *China-Trade Porcelain.* Cambridge, Massachusetts, 1956

Putnam 1924: Putnam, George Granville. *Salem Vessels and Their Voyages.* Salem, Massachusetts, 1924

Ride 1996: Ride, Lindsay and May. *An East India Company Cemetery: Protestant Burials in Macau.* HKUP, Hong Kong 1996

Scheurleer 1974: Scheurleer, D. F. Lunsingh. *Chinese Export Porcelain.* New York, 1974

Setterwall 1974: Setterwall, Ake. *The Chinese Pavilion at Drottningholm.* Malm, 1974

Smith 1979: Smith, Philip Chadwick Foster. *More Marine Paintings and Drawings in the Peabody Museum.* Salem, Massachusetts, 1979

Staunton 1797: Staunton, Sir George. *An Authentic Account of An Embassy From the King of Great Britain to the Emperor of China.* London, 1797

Staunton 1797a: Staunton, Sir George. *An Historical Account of the Embassy to the Emperor of China.* London, 1797

Stoddard 1856: Stoddard, Caroline. Unpublished journal, Phillips Library, Peabody Essex Museum, Salem

Thill 1973: Thill, Joan Kerr Facey. *A Delawarean in the Celestial Empire: John Richardson Latimer and the China Trade.* Master's thesis, The University of Delaware, 1973

Tillotson 1987: Tillotson, G.H.R. *Fan Kwae Pictures: Paintings and Drawings by George Chinnery and Other Artists in the Collection of The Hongkong and Shanghai Banking Corporation.* London, 1987

Warner 1976: Warner, John. *Tingqua: Paintings from his Studio.* Hong Kong, 1976

Warner 1980: Warner, John. "Paintings of the China Trade", *Orientations,* Vol. II, No. 4, pp. 36-42, April 1980

Whitehill 1949: Whitehill, Walter Muir. *The East India Marine Society and the Peabody Museum of Salem: A Sesquicentennial History.* Salem, Massachusetts, 1949

Williams 1976: Williams, C. A. S. *Outline of Chinese Symbolism and Art Motives.* New York, 1976

中文參考書目 （按漢語拼音次序排列）

陳希育：《中國帆船與海外貿易》，廈門大學出版社，1991

范蘭蒂：《澳門的教堂》，澳門文化司署，1993

廣州博物館（編）：《廣州文物與古蹟》，文物出版社，1987

廣東省文史研究館：《廣東文物》，上海書店，1990

亨特（著），沈正邦（編）：《舊中國雜記》，廣東人民出版社，1992

蔣祖緣、方志欽（編）：《簡明廣東史》，廣東人民出版社，1993

梁嘉彬：《廣東十三行考》，私立東海大學，1960

凌雲書房：《中國歷史地名大辭典》，東京，1980

司徒尚紀：《廣東文化地理》，廣東人民出版社，1993

香港藝術館（編），香港市政局出版：
  《香港的蛻變》，1980
  《珠江十九世紀風貌》，1981
  《晚清中國外銷畫》，1982
  《香港及澳門風貌》，1983
  《東土風物 — 錢納利及其流派》，1985
  《十八及十九世紀中國及沿海商埠風貌》，1987
  《歷史繪畫》，1991

中國歷史文化名城叢書編緝部、黃埔區文聯（編）：《黃埔、長洲旅遊縱觀》，廣東省地圖出版社，1991

中外關係史學會（編）：《中外關係史論叢》第二輯，世界知識出版社，北京，1987

HK$ 190

Hong Kong Catalogue sponsored by Asian Cultural Council, Hong Kong

Printed by Fairmount Printing Factory Ltd.

DAS
ALAMANNISCHE GRÄBERFELD
VON BÜLACH

VON

JOACHIM WERNER

VERLAG BIRKHÄUSER BASEL
1953

Druck: Buchdruckerei Gassmann AG., Solothurn
Printed in Switzerland

HELVETIAE HOSPITALI
FORTVNAE REDVCI